$#15.95

D1360066

# CARAMEL
# KNOWLEDGE

# CARAMEL KNOWLEDGE

*Bostess Bupcakes, Peanut-Butter Coffee,
Herring in a Cloud, Wienie Zucchini
and More Food and Culinary Musings
for the Twisted Mind*

EXPANDED EDITION

## Al Sicherman

*1817*

HARPER & ROW, PUBLISHERS, NEW YORK

Cambridge, Philadelphia, San Francisco, Washington
London, Mexico City, São Paulo, Singapore, Sydney

Grateful acknowledgement is made for permission to reprint the following recipes from the following sources:

"Italian Salad Dressing" and "Eggplant Casserole Deluxe" from *Cholesterol Counter*, by Elizabeth S. Weiss and Rita Parsons Wolfson. Copyright 1973 by Elizabeth S. Weiss and Rita Parsons Wolfson. Reprinted by permission of The Berkley Publishing Group.

"Canapes de Pescadito" ("Two-na Appetizer") and brownie portion of "Brownies in a Cloud" from *Best Loved Recipes of the American People* by Ida Bailey Allen. Copyright 1973 by Ruth Allen Castelli. Reprinted by permission of Doubleday, a division of Bantam, Doubleday, Dell Publishing Group, Inc.

"Petit Fours," "Coconut Macaroons," "Dropped Oatmeal Chippies" ("Dropped Chippies") from *The New Doubleday Cookbook* by Jean Anderson and Elaine Hanna. Copyright 1975, 1985 by Bantam, Doubleday, Dell Publishing Group, Inc. Reprinted by permission of Doubleday, a division of Bantam, Doubleday, Dell Publishing Group, Inc.

"Boula Boula Soup" from *The Dione Lucas Book of French Cooking* by Dione Lucas and Marion Gorman. Copyright 1947 by Dione Lucas. Copyright 1973 by Mark Lucas and Marion F. Gorman. Reprinted by permission of Little, Brown and Company.

"Soft Pretzels" ("Big, Soft Pretzels") from *Make Your Own Groceries* by Daphne Metaxas Hartwig. Copyright 1979 by Daphne Metaxas Hartwig. Reprinted by permission of Macmillan Publishing Company.

"Carnelian Carrot Coins" ("Oriental Carrot Appetizer") from *The Modern Art of Chinese Cooking* by Barbara Tropp. Copyright 1982 by Barbara Tropp, illustrations copyright 1982 by Bill Chiaravalle. Reprinted by permission of William Morrow & Company, Inc., Publishers.

Copyeditor: *Margaret Cheney*
Designer: *C. Linda Dingler*

---

Library of Congress Cataloging-in-Publication Data

Sicherman, Al.
  Caramel knowledge.

  Includes index.
  1. Cookery. 2. Cookery—Anecdotes, facetiae, satire, etc. I. Title.
TX715.S574   1988      641.5      87-45667
ISBN 0-06-096232-1 (pbk.)

45, 123

# Contents

# *Acknowledgments*

There are a million cookbooks, most of which I look through every week in my search for recipes to mangle . . . umm . . . to adapt to my very peculiar needs. I've found several cookbooks to be especially good references, and—although they hardly need this from me—I'd like to recommend them: *Mastering the Art of French Cooking* (Julia Child, Louisette Bertholle and Simone Beck), *Best Loved Recipes of the American People* (Ida Bailey Allen), of course *The Joy of Cooking* (Irma Rombauer and Marion R. Becker) and most of all, because of its completeness and its very good index, *The New Doubleday Cookbook* (Jean Anderson and Elaine Hanna).

On a more personal level, my thanks to various folks at the Minneapolis *Star and Tribune* for various reasons: some for encouraging me to put this book together, some for helping me to put this book together, and most for listening to me grouse while I put this book together. Special thanks to friend and colleague Mary Hart for all three.

Special thanks, too, to Becky Toevs, Julie Williams, Susan Peterson, Peg Meier, Terry Wigand, Ingrid Sundstrom, Susan Stan, Roxanne Kroll, Linda James and, of course, Catherine Watson—the "regulars" at my table—who continue to show up every week, no matter how strange the dinner I inflict upon them. (I know they're all women. They know it, too, and they keep asking me why I don't invite men more often. Listen: It's my pâté, and I'll cry if I want to.)

And, finally, thanks to designer Jody Smith, food writer Lee Svitak Dean and copy editor John Addington for able assistance in many moments of need.

"You don't know who your friends really are until you spill a bag of garbage or try to write a book."

—Anonymous

# *Introduction*

Each of these very strange food columns has appeared in the Minneapolis *Star and Tribune*. I have personally prepared every recipe in this volume in my own personal kitchen, and I have sampled each of them with my own personal mouth.

And that's not all. As a bonus to qualifying purchasers, I have included (scattered here and there throughout the book and absolutely free of additional charge) a number of "Little Mysteries"—selections from my attempts in the newspaper to solve some of the nagging food-related questions that might keep you awake some night but that aren't worth asking anybody else.

(Am I a sport, or what?)

# The Mock Food Meal

When I was a lad in Milwaukee, I took violin lessons. I don't know how that developed—I don't remember being wildly crazy about violin music. Maybe my parents heard the line about it being easier to run with a violin than with a piano.

Anyway, however it happened, there I was in grade school with a violin—not loving it, but getting along with it O.K. Until, in what must have been my second year of lessons (I think I was in the fourth grade), the dreaded Recital in the School Auditorium was scheduled.

I was not, as you might imagine, thrilled by the prospect of standing out on the stage, by myself, in front of God and the first through sixth grades, with nothing but my violin to defend me. And when I found out what I was supposed to play, it became worse.

It was "Mockingbird Hill," which you might recall if you are as far up the hill as I am. It has a melody that goes up and down a lot, necessitating frequent moves from one string of the violin to another. At my level of proficiency this was, I knew, going to be a disaster.

As the days of practice wore on, my worst fears were confirmed. I stunk.

Everyone kept telling me I was doing fine. I knew I stunk.

On the big morning I waited nervously in the wings while classmates whose parents had subjected them to the trombone, clarinet and drums strutted and fretted their hour upon the stage and then (except for an occasional whimper) were heard no more.

It was my turn.

My heart was in my mouth, along with my stomach and several other internal organs. My violin teacher and the school principal, beaming, were starting to prod me onto the stage. I knew I was about to humiliate myself.

And then a remarkable thing happened—a thing that hasn't happened again more than three or four times in my life at such a critical juncture.

I refused.

I just would not go out on that stage and become a laughingstock. As memory serves, while the two adults stared at me, I walked out of the wings, down the steps and took a seat in the audience, still holding the violin. If I remember correctly, there was a scattering of grateful applause. I think it was one of the best moments of my life.

It also, you may have noted, appears to have nothing to do with food.

Well, not everything worth remembering has something to do with food. But, as it happens, I have acquired the power to weave the most tenuous filament of association into a cable that allows me to drag in four or five recipes and several columns of type.

Watch:

I remembered the "Mockingbird Hill" incident recently while looking at some old sheet music, and that started me thinking about mock apple pie, a dish made with Ritz crackers instead of apples. I don't know why anybody would feel the need to make apple pie with Ritz crackers, since there is seldom a great apple shortage, but if you want to do it you can.

*That,* and a conversation with some colleagues, started me thinking about other mock foods. A check through recent cookbooks didn't turn up many, so food mockery seems to be an activity no longer much practiced (except by vegetarians, who make lots of mock things with soybeans), but older cookbooks were, comparatively speaking, loaded with them.

I knew that mock foods used to be around, because I remembered mock chicken legs made with veal. It's sure no surprise that folks aren't serving many mock chicken legs anymore, given the price of veal.

Quite a few of the other mock dishes that I turned up also involved veal, but I did find a number that didn't, and that could be made without taking out a second mortgage. Thus, history will record, was born the Mock Food Meal.

This appetizer is the only part of the meal that I made up. I did that for three reasons: I couldn't find any mock appetizers, this one sounded like it could be pretty good and the name is an outrageous spoonerism.

Actually, I figured, if it worked out this might really be a practical mock dish. Making guacamole depends on finding ripe avocados, and it has been my experience that the chance of finding ripe avocados in a supermarket is like the chance of finding the red jelly beans left in a bowl on somebody's coffee table. If there ever were any, somebody else already got them.

You can plan ahead, of course, and buy your avocados long in advance so that they are ripe when you need them, but I don't know anybody who plans *that* far ahead. (You can eliminate this whole problem by buying frozen guacamole already made, of course, but you can buy entire frozen dinners already made, too. If you've read this far in an article about cooking, I assume that is not the kind of solution that appeals to you.)

So let's make guacamole with softened butter instead of mashed avocado.

Opinions were clearly divided on this one. Some folks found it too rich and a little greasy. Others (myself included) thought it was wonderful. You be the judge. Send your opinion to the Judge Avocado General's office.

---

### Mockaguole

2 sticks (½ pound) softened butter
½ to 1 small tomato
1 small onion
1 small clove garlic
2 tablespoons lemon juice (juice of 1 lemon)

1 to 2 teaspoons chili powder
2 drops or more Tabasco
3 to 4 tablespoons flour
5 or 6 drops green food coloring
Corn chips

Cream the softened butter in a mixer or food processor.

Chop the tomato and the onion and put the garlic through a garlic press. Drain off juice, retaining only the solids. Add tomato, onion, garlic, lemon juice, chili powder and Tabasco to the butter and beat or process until well blended.

If liquid has separated out, pour it off. Sift in and blend the flour, as needed to make the mixture hold together. Add food coloring to approximate the amazingly unlikely color of guacamole.

Serve with corn chips. Serves 8 to 10.

---

The next dish also required my intervention, although not as severely. (If you want classic mock dishes from cookbooks, you'll have to be just a little patient. They're coming.)

Mock turtle soup is about the only mock dish that lots of people have heard of. A natural to make, right?

Wrong. Guess what is the principal ingredient in every recipe I found for mock turtle soup.

No. Guess. Come on. Stop cheating by looking ahead.

Oh, all right. The principal ingredient in mock turtle soup is a calf's head.

I don't mind making things like mockaguole. I *like* making things like mockaguole. But I'm *not* cooking a calf's head.

So I improvised.

*Mock Mock Turtle Soup*

1 (10½-ounce) can beef bouillon
1 (10½-ounce) can beef consommé
½ to 1 pound beef stew meat
Dash allspice
Dash thyme
3 cloves
6 peppercorns
1 small onion, sliced

2 tablespoons butter
2 tablespoons flour
½ cup tomato juice
Juice of ½ lemon (about 1 tablespoon lemon juice)
Salt, pepper to taste
¼ cup sherry

Pour the canned bouillon, consommé and 2 soup cans of water into a Dutch oven and bring to the simmer. While the soup is heating, trim all fat from the stew meat and cut the meat into ¼-inch-thick slices. Cut the slices into ¼-inch-wide strips. Add to the soup along with the allspice and thyme.

Tie the cloves, peppercorns and onion in a hunk of cheesecloth and add to the soup, or put them in a metal-mesh colander or strainer and suspend it in the soup. (One way or the other, we'll want to fish them out of the soup easily.) Cover and simmer the soup about 20 minutes.

Melt the butter in a large saucepan. Stir in the flour and cook, stirring, over medium heat about 1 minute. Slowly add a few spoonfuls of the soup, stirring. Continue stirring in soup, a ladleful or so at a time, until the paste is quite thin, then pour the paste into the large soup pot and stir in well.

Add tomato juice, lemon juice, salt and pepper. Simmer 5 minutes. When ready to serve, add the sherry and simmer 2 minutes. Serves 6.

For the main dish, these days you might be tempted to get back at mock chicken legs made with veal by making almost anything that calls for veal (scaloppine, wiener schnitzel, etc.) and substituting sliced turkey breast or deboned and flattened chicken breast for the veal. That's an excellent substitution, and I highly recommend it, but it's time we have some classic mock dishes.

How about "mock duck"? It's one I'd never heard of, frankly, but it cropped up in a number of older books—in two forms.

One involves an entire quarter of lamb, cut to look like a duck. ("Have the butcher prepare a forequarter of lamb for mock duck. . . .") Something tells me that a request like that wouldn't get you a very kind look at the meat counter these days.

Luckily, there's a second version of mock duck, made with a flank steak. That isn't cheap, but I bet you could do it with a round steak, too. The idea is to slit the steak almost all the way in half ("butterfly" it), fill it with a seasoned meat-and-bread mixture, and sew it up, tying off a bit at both ends, to resemble head and tail.

It doesn't *taste* like duck (and it doesn't really *look* like a duck, either). But it looks sort of halfway between a steak and a drawing of a duck. It is kind of fun, and various folks can be rude when they ask for parts of it.

*Mock Duck*

1½ pounds flank or top round steak (about 6 inches wide and 10 to 12 inches long)
1 teaspoon salt
¼ teaspoon pepper
¼ teaspoon ginger
5 tablespoons butter, divided
½ cup bread crumbs

About ¾ pound ground beef
1 small onion, finely chopped
1 or 2 tablespoons chopped parsley
Salt, pepper to taste
Paprika
Coarse thread for sewing
½ cup water
1 (10½-ounce) can beef bouillon

Trim off all fat from steak. Carefully slice it in half edgewise, but leave about an inch unsliced at one edge, so you can open it up like a book or a butterfly. (This isn't nearly as hard as it sounds if you have a sharp knife. If you don't, you're in a heap of trouble.)

Season the open (inside) faces of the steak with the salt, pepper and ginger.

Melt 3 tablespoons of the butter, mix in the bread crumbs, ground beef, onion and parsley, and salt, pepper and paprika to taste.

Pat the mixture evenly over one of the inside surfaces of the steak.

Close the steak up and, making the stitches an inch or so apart, sew up the 3 open sides with coarse thread. (Trust me. Use coarse thread. Ordinary thread tends

to break rather than pull back out of the mock duck when you are getting it ready to serve.)

Tie coarse thread about 2 inches down around each of 2 corners of the rectangle separated by a long side, and tighten to form the "head" and the "tail."

Preheat the oven to 250 degrees. Combine the ½ cup of water and the canned bouillon and heat to boiling.

Meanwhile, melt the remaining 2 tablespoons of butter in a 9-by-13-inch pan on the top of the stove and sear the "duck" in it on all sides.

Pour in the hot bouillon mixture, add the duck and cover with foil. Bake about 1½ hours, until the "duck" is tender. Remove thread and serve. Serves 4.

For the vegetable, I made some broccoli with mock hollandaise sauce.

I have to say something about mock hollandaise sauce. Folks might make some mock foods, like the Ritz cracker pie, I guess, just because they are kind of interesting. They might make others to substitute for an expensive or hard-to-find ingredient. And they might make still others because they offer shortcuts.

My guess is that mock hollandaise sauce, which exists in many, many forms in current cookbooks, is around because people believe that real hollandaise sauce is hard to make. Some of the mock hollandaise sauces *are* easier, but those sounded dreadful (adding some lemon to cream of chicken soup, for example).

Here's one that isn't half bad. It sure isn't hollandaise sauce, either—it has a kind of a flour-gravy quality—and I think it's at least as much work as the real thing, if not more. What it has to recommend it is that it is based on a flour white sauce, so it is not likely to curdle, like real hollandaise, if you get the heat too high.

## Mock Hollandaise Sauce

6 tablespoons butter, divided
2 tablespoons flour
1/4 teaspoon salt
Pepper

1 cup milk
2 egg yolks
1 tablespoon lemon juice

In a saucepan over low heat, melt 2 tablespoons of the butter. Stir in the flour, salt and pepper and heat, stirring, about 1 minute. Add the milk, a little at a time, stirring constantly, until all the milk is in and the sauce is smooth.

Beat the 2 egg yolks lightly, then stir in a few tablespoons of the hot mixture. Stir the diluted egg yolks into the hot white sauce. With the white sauce over very low heat, and stirring constantly, add the lemon juice and the remaining 4 tablespoons of butter—one at a time, waiting for one to be almost fully incorporated before adding the next one. Makes about 1 1/2 cups.

Even a mock meal has to have a dessert, right? But a *mock* dessert. Or two.

First, a mock-pumpkin-pie recipe from a 1929 pamphlet for a popular breakfast cereal. It tastes like pumpkin pie, but so would almost anything if you put in ginger, cloves, nutmeg and cinnamon. The color is more tan than brown, so I would cover the surface with whipped cream. (No, not extruded plastic topping. Real whipped cream. Even for a mock meal, I draw the line there.)

## Grape-Nuts Mock Pumpkin Pie

1/4 cup boiling water
1/2 cup Grape-Nuts
2 cups milk, scalded
1/4 cup sugar
4 tablespoons flour
1/8 teaspoon ginger

1/4 teaspoon cloves
1/4 teaspoon nutmeg
1/2 teaspoon cinnamon
2 eggs, well beaten
1 baked 8- or 9-inch pie shell
1 cup heavy cream, whipped

Pour boiling water over Grape-Nuts. Stir. Let stand 10 minutes, then add milk.

Combine sugar, flour, ginger, cloves, nutmeg and cinnamon. Add to Grape-Nuts mixture and cook in a double boiler, stirring and lifting (the Grape-Nuts tend to settle) until thickened—about 5 minutes.

Stir a little of the hot mixture into the eggs, then pour the diluted eggs into the hot mixture, stirring, and continue to cook and stir 2 to 3 minutes longer.

Cool a few minutes, pour into baked pie shell and chill. Top with whipped cream. Serves 6 to 8.

Now we come to the dish we have spoken about already: Ritz Cracker Mock Apple Pie. The recipe is from the Ritz cracker box. This *looks* like apple pie, which really is kind of amazing. But it doesn't taste at all like it. If you were blindfolded, you'd say it was lemon pie. But unless some troublemaker points that out, folks are so convinced by how much it looks like apple that they tend not to notice that it tastes like lemon.

One guest said it tasted like apple pie to her—because her mother always made Ritz Cracker Mock Apple Pie. She did not know why.

Another guest had never heard of it before, and even through several discussions of it earlier in the meal he had not quite gotten the message about it. He knew there were Ritz crackers in the pie, but I'm not sure where he thought they were. He clearly thought the filling was apples. "No," I said, "it's Ritz crackers." "Yes, but what's the fruit?" "Ritz crackers."

Now do *you* get it?

Here's the point: Even if we someday run out of apples, we can still have apple pie—if we haven't also run out of lemon juice. (And Ritz crackers.)

---

## *Ritz Cracker Mock Apple Pie*

**Pastry for a 2-crust 9-inch pie**
**36 Ritz crackers**
**2 cups water**
**2 cups sugar**
**2 teaspoons cream of tartar**

**Juice of 1 lemon (2 tablespoons lemon juice)**
**Grated rind of 1 lemon**
**1 to 2 tablespoons butter or margarine**
**½ teaspoon cinnamon**

Roll out the bottom crust and fit it into a 9-inch pie pan. Break the Ritz crackers coarsely into the pastry-lined pan. Doesn't look much like apples, does it? Combine the water, sugar and cream of tartar in a saucepan; boil gently for 15 minutes. Add lemon juice and lemon rind. Cool.

Preheat the oven to 425 degrees. Pour the syrup over the crackers, dot with the butter and sprinkle with cinnamon. Now it still doesn't look like apples, but it tastes like lemon.

Cover with the top crust, seal the edges and cut slits in the top crust to let steam escape. Bake for 30 to 35 minutes, until the crust is crisp and golden. Serve warm. Serves 6 to 8.

# *Food That's Good for You*

When I was growing up in Milwaukee, just as when you were growing up in Ashtabula or Punxsutawney or Fort Snelling, my little sweeties, it was customary for members of my family to encourage me to eat various things I didn't want to eat by telling me that they were good for me.

You know the kind of thing I mean. "You'll never grow up to be big and strong like your Aunt Ethel if you don't eat all your broccoli."

I don't know about you, but when I was faced with something like veal breast, I didn't care if it was good for me or rotten for me; I wasn't about to eat any.

My mother once got me to eat mushrooms in a manner I consider truly reprehensible. She cut them into some unrecognizable shape and put them into chop suey, where she didn't normally use them. When I asked what they were, she told me they were Chinese evergreens. I was dumb enough to eat them, and of course I thought they were great. I still hold that against her.

The aunt of one of my childhood friends was a relatively recent immigrant from Eastern Europe. She was clearly inclined to explain the merits of her cuisine but was hampered by limited command of English. She shortened her pleading with him to one rather forceful remark: "Eat! Is good. I made."

The thing about foods that people always insisted were good for you is that they were foods that kids didn't particularly like. I can't remember ever being told that spaghetti and meatballs or chocolate cake or peanut butter and jelly sandwiches were good for me (although they must have been—they made me what I am today), because I was perfectly willing to eat them without any extra advice.

It is a truth, not well recognized by the mothers of kids of my generation, that the more people insist that something is good for you the less you want to eat any of it.

My father, by contrast, never seriously wheedled me to eat things. He apparently felt that it was necessary to say *something,* but it usually turned out to be something like "You'll love the lima beans. They give you curly pimples."

In honor, then, of Father's Day, and in acknowledgment that father did indeed know best (I still dislike veal breast but I'll eat lima beans any time), I modestly present a meal of things that people always say are good for you.

But in recognition that there may be children present and that boiled beets are still boiled beets no matter how much iron or whatever they give you, I have arranged to present those good-for-you foods in one degree or another of disguise.

I don't warrant that any of these recipes (except the dessert) will appeal any more to kids than does the food in its more traditional presentation, but I think adults might find them interesting.

Carrots, you will no doubt remember hearing, are supposed to give you good eyesight. I can attest to the truth of that contention. I was always able to spot carrots being prepared—even at very great distances—and to try not to be home when they were finally served.

I don't remember any more what is wrong with carrots from the kid point of view, but even now unadorned boiled carrots strike me as among the least interesting things you could put on a plate.

I know, however, that carrots can dare to be great. I've eaten great carrots.

So today I offer a highly unusual carrot recipe. I can't say that everyone will like it, but I'll probably make it again, and it got a definite "Hmmmm" from the two other folks on whom I tried it out.

The liquid in which the carrots marinate is usable again for other things (like mushrooms and green beans, and as a sauce for meats), so don't be appalled at how much of it there is.

The recipe is based on one in *The Modern Art of Chinese Cooking,* a nice book by Barbara Tropp.

## Oriental Carrot Appetizer

1 (10¾-ounce) can chicken broth
1 soup can water
1 (10-ounce) bottle (that's right, the whole bottle) soy sauce
⅓ cup Chinese rice wine (or substitute dry sherry)

5 slices of fresh ginger the size of a nickel
1 green onion, cut into 3-inch lengths
1½ star anise, broken into 12 points
¼ cup sugar
½ pound carrots

This recipe requires marinating time.

Prepare the sauce: Put the chicken broth, water, soy sauce and wine in a saucepan. Slap the ginger slices and the onion pieces on a cutting board with the flat side of a heavy knife (to release the juices) and add them to the liquid, along with the broken pieces of star anise and the sugar.

Bring to a boil and simmer, stirring occasionally, for about an hour. Strain the sauce and use it to prepare the carrots.

Trim and peel the carrots. Cut them on a sharp diagonal into slices about ¼ inch thick (try to make them the same thickness, so they all get done at the same time).

Bring the sauce to a simmer and add the carrot slices. Cover and simmer 15 minutes, stirring once or twice. Turn off the heat and let the carrots steep 30 minutes covered and then 1½ hours uncovered.

Strain the used sauce through wet cheesecloth, pour it into a jar and refrigerate or freeze it for use with other vegetables or over meats. (It will keep in the refrigerator for a week.)

Put the carrots in a shallow bowl (careful—they break easily). They can be eaten warm or be refrigerated overnight (covered with plastic wrap) and eaten cold. If you choose the latter alternative, which gives them a more unusual texture, just before serving them invert them into a serving bowl so that the sauce that has settled to the bottom is now prettily on the top.

Serves 2 to 3 as a warm vegetable or 5 to 6 as an appetizer. Afterward you'll be able to read the recipe in the dark.

---

Beets have earned a firm place in the I-don't-want-any parade. (What kid cares what nutrients he gets? In fact, I don't care either.) This recipe beets a lot of others for tanginess—I liked it quite a beet.

---

## Mustardy Beets

4 tablespoons butter
1 tablespoon tarragon vinegar

1 tablespoon Dijon mustard
1 (16-ounce) can diced beets

Melt the butter in a saucepan. Stir in the vinegar and mustard.

Drain the beets. Put them in the saucepan and heat, stirring, until the mixture is warmed through.

Serves 4. If you eat lots and lots and lots of this, it will give you so much iron that your epitaph can say "Rust in Peace."

---

For the main course, of course, an intelligent person has no choice but to serve fish, it being so widely known as a brain food.

Fish was also widely known in my childhood circles as a *disgusting* food, so it would surprise my mother to know that I am actually recommending it to 579,847 of my closest friends.

To be honest, what I'm really recommending is the sauce. Some years back, when I was working ever-so-briefly in France, my colleagues took me to dinner at a hotsy-totsy restaurant, where I ate the best sauce-with-fish it has ever been my pleasure to get outside of. It was described as a beurre rouge (red butter), and I resolved to duplicate it upon my return to these shores.

Alas, most cookbooks did not list such a sauce, and the only one I found that did so described it as another name for lobster butter, whose ingredients include the coral or eggs of various shellfish. My refrigerator has never been deeply stocked with the coral or eggs of various shellfish, so I never made beurre rouge.

Then, quite recently, I found another—and much simpler—recipe for beurre rouge. "Ho, ho," I said to myself (or words to that effect). This new recipe is merely a variation of beurre blanc (white butter), which is a reasonably common sauce and quite simple. Red wine is substituted for the white wine and/or vinegar in the beurre blanc and voilà (or, as we say over here, there you go): Beurre rouge.

That struck me as so simple an idea that I made no advance preparation at all when I intended to serve it.

None.

At the last minute I discovered that I hadn't even bought any red wine.

I had some white wine to serve with the fish (wine for thy stomach's sake, of course—another good-for-you food), but trying to make red butter with white wine didn't seem likely to be very productive.

As a desperate substitution, I used some tawny port that I had on the basement stairs. The result was quite sweet and not red. I would call it beurre khaki, but it actually went rather nicely with the fish (if you like sweet sauces).

On a retest with Burgundy, the beurre rouge turned out to be very nice indeed, and a somewhat better accompaniment to fish than beurre khaki—but not what I remembered. The next time I have a refrigerator full of shellfish coral, I'm going to give that one a try. In the meantime, here's the easy version, which I really do recommend (and the fish is excellent, too).

## Poached Sole with Red Butter

**FISH:**

**4 fillets of sole**
**Lemon juice**
**Salt**
**White pepper**
**3 tablespoons butter**

**1 cup dry vermouth**
**½ cup water**

**SAUCE:**

**1 shallot**
**3 tablespoons red wine**
**¼ pound unsalted butter**

Preheat the oven to 350 degrees.

Wash the fish in water with a little lemon juice in it. Dry it well and sprinkle lightly with salt and white pepper.

Fold the fish fillets in half lengthwise and arrange them in a buttered baking dish. Butter a piece of waxed paper the size of the dish.

In a small saucepan, melt the 3 tablespoons of butter and add to it 1 tablespoon of lemon juice, a dash of salt and pinch of white pepper. Add the vermouth and water and bring to the boil. Spoon the hot liquid over the fish fillets and cover them with the piece of buttered wax paper (buttered side down).

(Continued)

Put the dish in the oven for 10 to 15 minutes or until the fish flakes with a fork, then remove the fish to a warm platter and serve with the sauce.

To prepare the sauce, put ½ tablespoon of water in a small saucepan to see what that much liquid looks like. Discard the water and dry the pan.

Chop the shallot very fine. Put it in the small saucepan with the wine and boil until there is about ½ tablespoon remaining. Reduce the heat to very low. Cut the butter into 8 pieces and stir them in, one at time, adding one just before the previous one is fully gone, to make a smooth, creamy sauce. (If the first pieces of butter become liquid instead of working into a sauce, the burner is too hot. Turn it *very* low, like I said. The sauce should be creamy, not greasy.) Strain out the bits of shallot, if you're fussy, season with salt and white pepper and serve with the fish.

Serves 4. You certainly won't be sorry you tried this one. Not only does it taste good, after you've eaten it you'll be so smart you'll be able to perform astounding feats of brain power—like guessing the number of times the letters s, m, a, r and t appear in this article. (The answer is at the end, for those of you who just won't eat fish for *any* reason.)

---

One more good-for-you vegetable, please. Everybody knows what it's going to be, right? If you're a little slow this morning, I'll give you two hints:

It's green.

It's icky.

No, not okra. I'm not that mean. Spinach.

I must admit that my favorite spinach recipe has already appeared in the newspaper several times.

Ordinarily I would say that it's not my fault if you haven't been attentive. I can't keep printing the same recipes over and over, just waiting for you to notice them and cut them out. But just for you sweeties who've bought this book, you'll find it with the SPAM recipes. Leave out the SPAM if you like; it's great either way.

This substitute is quite good. It is blessed with lots of butter and a very nice covering of béchamel sauce and cheese.

Altogether a grownup version of the food that gives you big muscles, so let's give it a French name.

**SPINACH:**

2 (10-ounce) packages frozen chopped
   spinach
9 tablespoons butter, divided
3 egg yolks
$1/2$ cup heavy cream
Salt and pepper

**SAUCE:**

1 cup milk
$1 1/2$ tablespoons flour
$1/2$ cup coarsely chopped onion
1 clove
1 bay leaf
Pinch of nutmeg
$1/4$ cup grated Parmesan cheese

*La Favorite de
Popoeil*

Preheat the oven to 350 degrees.

Prepare the spinach according to package directions. Rinse, drain and squeeze the spinach until it is dry. In a large frying pan, sauté the spinach in 4 tablespoons of the butter until the spinach has fully absorbed the butter.

Beat the yolks. Blend in the cream, salt and pepper. Stir the mixture slowly into the spinach.

Melt 4 more tablespoons of the butter in a pan, allowing it to cook until it just begins to turn brown. Be careful not to let it burn. Stir the browned butter into the spinach.

Butter a $1 1/2$-quart oven-safe casserole or mold and fill it with the spinach. Put the casserole in a pan of hot water and bake about 30 minutes.

While the casserole is in the oven, prepare the sauce:

Heat the milk in a small saucepan. In another pan melt the remaining 1 tablespoon of butter over low heat, and stir in the flour. Continue to cook, stirring, for 2 minutes, then slowly add the hot milk, stirring. Add the onion, clove, bay leaf and nutmeg. (If you don't have one or two of the seasonings, go ahead anyway; it'll work out just fine.) Simmer the sauce 10 minutes and strain out the solids.

When the casserole is cooked, pour the sauce over it (or unmold it onto an oven-safe platter and then cover with sauce).

Top with grated cheese and run briefly under the broiler to brown.

Serves 6. (Try to keep from smashing furniture with one hand when you've finished eating your helping.)

---

Now we come to dessert. If you've been holding your breath, afraid I'd ruin dessert by adding cod-liver oil, you don't know me very well. There are still a few things in life that are sacred. Outdoor baseball may not be one of them, but *nobody* messes around with dessert in my house.

I did want to do something at least a *little* good for you, though. I remembered getting anguished letters after I made bread pudding with chocolate sauce, wondering why I hadn't simply made chocolate bread pudding. Well, O.K., that's a perfect excuse to make something with bread crusts, which are alleged to give you curly hair or something. Actually, I used the rest of the bread, too.

## *Chocolate Bread Pudding*

3 cups milk
3 (1-ounce) squares unsweetened chocolate
1 (1-ounce) square semisweet chocolate (optional)
½ cup sugar

2 eggs
1 teaspoon vanilla
2 cups (packed) bread crusts and whatever other parts of the bread you care to contribute, cut or torn into 1-inch pieces

Heat the milk and chocolate, including the extra ounce of semisweet if you want it *really* chocolate, in a double boiler until the chocolate is melted. Combine the sugar and eggs and beat until just blended. Slowly add the chocolate mixture to the eggs, stirring constantly. Add the vanilla.

Grease a 1½-quart baking dish and put the bread pieces in it. Pour the chocolate mixture over the bread and let it stand 20 minutes. Preheat the oven to 350 degrees.

Stir the pudding, set the baking dish in a 9-by-13-inch pan and add hot water to the pan until it is about an inch deep. Bake the pudding 45 to 50 minutes (check near the end to make sure there's still water in the pan), until the blade of a knife comes out clean. Eat, and wait for your hair to curl. Serves 6.

---

This article has been subjected to a computer analysis, which revealed that, not counting this sentence, it contains 3,774 occurrences of the letters *s, m, a, r* and *t;* the analysis also revealed that the writer needs professional help.

---

### Little Mystery #1: Pimientos

How does the pimiento get into the olive?

**Solution:** A spokesperson for Lindsay Olive Growers, Lindsay, California, said that until recent years it was mainly done in Spain, by hand. The pimiento was punched into the pitted olive with a little pin.

Now we're in the age of mechanical stuffing, he explained. The pimiento is ground into a paste, a jelling agent is added to the paste and a pimiento ribbon is formed, which hardens into a jelled strip, called a tape. The tape is rolled up and fed into a machine that pits and stuffs the olives.

A coring knife comes in from one end and cores out around the olive pit, producing a large opening. Then a small punch pin comes through from the other end and punches out the pit. The pimiento tape is inserted into the large hole and cut off.

Pimiento *tape?* Isn't that the pits?

# A Dark View
# of the Chocolate Fad

We're a nation of trend followers.

Ten years ago, the only people in America drinking Perrier and eating croissants were effete snobs and Frenchmen held here against their will. Now there are umpteen kinds of sparkling water available at Red Owl, and everybody with an oven is turning out fat crescent rolls.

Taco salad is threatening to replace the restaurant grilled-cheese sandwich.

There are parts of Minneapolis in which you can't go two blocks without stepping on a quiche.

Until now, I watched these trends with indifference or resignation. So what if the croissant, once a hard-to-find treat but always wonderful, is now more common than the cinnamon roll but often lousy?

So what if you can't find a nice bottle of cream soda at the store because of all the imported mineral water?

Indifference or resignation, I repeat, until now.

Now the trendsetters, the despoilers of delight, the waterers-down of wonder, have begun to hit where I live.

They're messing around with chocolate, and I suppose they won't be happy until it's in everything we eat, much more expensive and not very good.

The dilution has already begun. A flood of promotional material for a "chocolate cookbook" arrived in the office recently, gasping and groaning about the wonderful recipes to be found therein. It offered three examples, two of which used cocoa, not chocolate. (That's if memory serves correctly; it might have been all three—I was so put off that I threw the stuff away.)

Yes, cocoa is a perfectly nice ingredient, and plenty of people like it fine. But it's not chocolate. I'm afraid this kind of thing is the harbinger of much more to come. Food technologists have long ago substituted cocoa and inexpensive artificial flavors for chocolate in lots of apparently chocolate items in grocery stores. (A hint is the word "fudge" in the name instead of "chocolate." If it says "chocolate" there's got to be *some* chocolate in there, although the principal flavor ingredient is often cocoa and the chocolate is down with the BHA, BHT, mono- and diglycerides, giving a whole new meaning to the phrase "below the salt.")

How many of the chichi chocolate items that are on their way will be worth eating?

We now have "devil's food" Twinkies (with no chocolate in them) and fancy gold-foil-wrapped chocolate bars that are no better than the cheaper ones they're edging out.

Mark my words: It will get worse. Bill Blass has put out "designer chocolates" (whatever *that* means), and there are outrageously priced confections covered with "white chocolate," which has about as much flavor as wallboard.

It could turn ugly, too. You could waltz into your neighborhood drugstore one day to buy a few Hershey's Special Dark bars and be met by a guy built like a McCormick reaper, who will smile at you through steel teeth and tell you that the free ride is over and that they're gonna cost you five bucks apiece.

That probably won't happen, but even if the gentrification of chocolate remains civilized, I greatly resent it.

I was eating chocolate before it was being advertised in *The New Yorker* or written about in *Time* magazine. Lots of you were, too. But now there are others in the market—people who don't really love the stuff like you and I do but who wait in line to buy fashionable Godiva chocolates at $21 a pound, depriving you and me of the chance to get them for the $8 or $9 they probably would have cost under more-limited demand.

Not everything that rides the crest of the chocolate wave is terrible, of course. Sandra Boynton, the woman who draws the chocolate-consuming hippos that grace (if that is the word) calendars and T-shirts, probably would not have been able to interest publishers in her wonderfully funny little book, *Chocolate—the Consuming Passion,* had chocolate not become such a hot item.

(A sample of Boynton, on carob: "Some consider carob an adequate substitute for chocolate because it has some similar nutrients [calcium, phosphorus], and because it can, when combined with vegetable fat and sugar, be made to approximate the color and consistency of chocolate. Of course, the same arguments can as persuasively be made in favor of dirt.")

If Boynton gets rich on her marvelous book, that's great. But I object to many of the others who are seeking to make a chocolate mint, because I know what's going to happen. See, as those of you who find my words going directly to the heart (or perhaps to the stomach) already know, the world can be divided into two classes of people:

• Those who *really love* chocolate. (People I have seen described as "chocolate-intensive personalities.")

• Those who hate it, don't care for it or like it well enough but would sometimes just as readily eat some strawberries. (Everybody else.)

Because those in the first category are already buying all the chocolate they can carry, it is those in the second category at whom the trendy merchandising is being directed. Those second-category folks don't like chocolate all that well, so the stuff that's coming, however fancy its design or wrapper, is likely to be less-than-satisfying to the real chocolate person.

For those of you in the first category, my brothers and sisters in a dark but delicious bond, I feel the least I can do in these times of trouble is to pass along some recipes to cherish as the world crumbles blandly around us.

Others be warned: These aren't recipes for the faint of taste. My partner, Kate Parry, whose preference in chocolate runs to things the color of package-wrapping paper, would hate every one of them. On the other hand, there is already plenty of "chocolate" stuff for you folks, and more on the way. Have some Fudge Sticks or something.

We should have lost a fair number of cocoa, carob and "white chocolate" fans by now, so I'll assume I'm talking only to hard-core (or should it be soft-center?) chocolate lovers.

This is my opportunity to go for broke—to pass along some really intense chocolate stuff.

That puts me in something of a dilemma. A few of my favorites have been around a while. I don't want to give you second-string recipes just because the better ones have become a little shall-we-say classic. On the other hand, you've paid your money, and you shouldn't be getting recipes you've already seen. This isn't the Ann Landers column, after all. (I'm not being completely selfless in this regard; when my grandchildren compile the posthumous *Compleat Works of Al Sicherman,* I don't want them to think I cheated because I used the same recipe twice.)

Here's a compromise. I'll reproduce an all-time great or two, which will be clearly identified, and I'll try out a few new things, too. O.K.?

Note: Many of these recipes call for semisweet chocolate in one-ounce squares. Those who prefer their chocolate a little sweeter (and a little cheaper) might substitute chocolate chips.

In an article I wrote a while back about dipping things in semisweet chocolate, I tried dipping potato chips. They were truly marvelous. I knew that chocolate and salt combined nicely, but the crispness of the potato chip added another dimension.

Recently a colleague mentioned that his mother-in-law makes chocolate-covered popcorn. I didn't need to hear another word; I know a winning idea when I hear one. It also appealed because, I figured, you could pour the chocolate into a bowl of popcorn and do the coating just by tossing it with a couple of large spoons.

Hand-dipping is messy any time; in the summer it's really dreadful.

If you make chocolate popcorn in the summer you must keep it refrigerated, but that's a small sacrifice. A small warning: Don't grab a handful to eat a little at a time. (It melts in your hand; not in your mouth.)

After I brought the popcorn into the office, the colleague's wife phoned to say that her mother's version isn't messy. But it's made with cocoa and milk. We don't want to hear about that right now, do we?

---

## Chocolate-Covered Popcorn

½ cup or so (your standard batch) unpopped popcorn
Oil for popping
Salt
8 (1-ounce) squares semisweet chocolate

Line a couple of baking sheets with waxed paper.

Pop the popcorn however you normally do that. Salt and pour into a large bowl. As best you can, remove any "OMs." (I'm trying not to be sexist. The Popcorn Institute in Chicago, which calls them what everybody else calls them, also calls them "spinsters"—not much better.) You don't want the unpopped kernels in there because once they're covered with chocolate they're hard to see, and you might hurt a tooth if you bite one.

Melt the chocolate and pour it over the still-warm popcorn. Toss thoroughly, using two very large spoons. Using the spoons, spread the coated popcorn onto the waxed-paper-covered pans and cool in the refrigerator until the chocolate has set. Break apart any big clumps before you pour the chocolate popcorn into a bowl to serve.

---

This is among the best desserts I've ever eaten, and I think it's one of the two or three best I've made. It has been around the block a time or two. So what? It's dense, creamy and very, very rich. It's also rather easy to make, although quite expensive. Lots of folks will find it much too rich and not sweet enough.

The heck with them.

Others, hearing the cholesterol-laden list of ingredients, will want to file a complaint with the American Heart Association.

What can I say?

Note: After this article appeared in the newspaper I improved the recipe, and that modified recipe appeared in a much later article. Because you, dear book reader, deserve only the best, what follows is the improved version.

I made the original recipe approximately a zillion times and I love it, but let's be frank: It had (gasp!) a butter-seepage problem. No matter how much you softened the butter beforehand, some would weep out of the batter while the cake was in the oven and while it was cooling. You could catch the butter with pans and paper towels so it didn't make a mess, but that was a bother, and the loss of butter didn't improve the cake one bit.

This method produces a somewhat creamier cake (the whole thing has always been like incredibly rich fudge anyway) and no mess.

**¾ pound (3 sticks) unsalted butter**
**2⅔ cups (16 ounces) semisweet**
  **chocolate chips**

**1 cup milk**
**7 egg yolks**
**Heavy cream, whipped, for topping**

## Great Chocolate Goo Cake

Melt the butter over low heat and allow it to cool to room temperature.

Preheat the oven to 350 degrees. Cut a round of waxed paper to fit the bottom of a 9-inch springform pan. Butter the sides of the pan and one side of the waxed paper. Place the paper in the pan, buttered side up.

In a saucepan over very low heat, heat the chocolate and milk, stirring constantly, just until the chocolate is melted. You will note that at every step the batter for this cake smells even better than it did at the last one. Pour the mixture into the large bowl of an electric mixer.

Beat on low speed, just to smooth out any bitsy lumps of chocolate. With the mixer running at low speed, add about a seventh of the melted butter (a shy ¼ cup) and beat at low speed only until the butter is fully absorbed. Then add an egg yolk and beat, at low speed, just until the mixture has fully absorbed it. Don't raise the speed of the mixer, because we don't want to beat in any air. It's not supposed to be a fluffy cake; it's supposed to be a fudgy lump of goo.

Continue to alternate additions of butter and egg yolk until all are used up, scraping the bowl with a rubber spatula and beating after each addition only until incorporated. When the mixture is smooth, pour it into the prepared pan.

Set the pan on a cookie sheet (despite my wonderful improvement it might still weep a bit). Put the whole thing in the oven (not near the top).

Bake for 25 minutes. It will be soupy in the middle and look like a mistake, but unless you forgot to turn the oven on, it is done. The cake will not have risen so as you'd notice.

Allow it to cool on a rack, then refrigerate a few hours, until firm. It may be kept refrigerated a day or two.

When ready to serve, cut around the side of the pan with a small, sharp knife and release and remove the side of the pan. Cover the dessert with a flat plate and invert.

Carefully (it takes a bit of doing) pry up and remove the bottom of the pan and the waxed paper.

Decorate with whipped cream. (I like to make a simple lattice pattern that lets the dark, dark chocolate show through.) Serves 12.

---

Some time ago, I got a letter from reader Deborah Weiland recommending this cake, which is quite similar to the preceding one but also contains a significant flavor boost from strong coffee.

Weiland's recommendation, in part: "This is a cake that will bring you to your knees."

Actually, to be perfectly honest, it bounced me off the ceiling. I ate a big piece about 10 P.M. and, between the chocolate and the coffee, I wasn't able to get to sleep until 4:30 the next morning.

It's great, but eat it early.

## Mocha Fudge Cake

1 cup plus 2 tablespoons very strong
   brewed coffee
18 (1-ounce) squares semisweet
   chocolate, chopped
2¼ cups sugar
2¼ cups (4½ sticks) unsalted butter
9 eggs

TOPPING:

1½ cups heavy cream
¼ cup confectioners' sugar
½ teaspoon vanilla

Note: Weiland says about the coffee: "I grind the amount of espresso beans I would use for about two large cups [and make the 1⅛ cups of coffee from that]. This is important. I believe instant anything or ground regular coffee have no place in this cake."

Preheat oven to 250 degrees. Line a 9-inch springform pan with heavy aluminum foil, across the bottom and up the sides, and butter the foil lightly but thoroughly with unsalted butter.

Combine coffee, chocolate, sugar and butter in a large saucepan. ("The feeling of using more than one box of butter in one recipe," Weiland writes, "is indescribably lovely.") Stirring constantly, heat to 130 degrees.

Lower heat and whisk in 9 eggs. (I beat them very lightly first, to make them easier to whisk in.) Pour into the prepared pan and bake 2 to 2½ hours. When it is done the top looks a little crisp and the sides are cracking. Cool, remove the springfrom pan, cover the cake and refrigerate overnight or up to a week.

When it cools, the center of the cake falls a little. Since the cake will be inverted, you might first want to cut away the ridge around the edge. (Anyone who thinks you throw this crispy chocolate stuff away should stop reading right now. Of course you eat it, as your reward for having made the cake.) Several hours before serving, invert the cake onto a platter and remove the foil. Whip the heavy cream with the confectioners' sugar and the vanilla until it is thick enough to spread. Frost the cake with half the whipped cream, then, using a pastry bag with a star tip, pipe rosettes all over the top.

Serves 12 or more.

Here's a nice little item that's reasonably easy to do and rather attractive, too. Unlike half the things being served in restaurants that are called chocolate mousse but are nothing more than chocolate (or maybe even cocoa) pudding, this has beaten egg whites and all the real stuff.

**Chocolate Mousse Parfaits**

3 (1-ounce) squares semisweet
   chocolate
3 eggs, separated

2 to 3 tablespoons rum, brandy,
   orange liqueur, etc.
1 cup heavy cream

Melt the chocolate in a double boiler or in a saucepan over very low heat. Beat the egg yolks until they are thick and creamy. Stir a bit of melted chocolate into the egg yolks, then stir the egg yolks into the rest of the chocolate. Stir in the liqueur.

Whip the egg whites until they are stiff and fold them into the chocolate mixture.

Whip the cream until it is stiff. Spoon thin layers of chocolate and cream into serving glasses, finishing with cream. If the first layer of cream sinks, set the remaining chocolate into the freezer for a few minutes, stirring occasionally, until it gets a bit firmer. It's nice to make the top layer of cream a little fancy, so if you have a pastry bag, you might use that.

Or just fold the whipped cream into the chocolate mixture. The effect is not quite as elegant as layers but is lighter-looking. (Don't be misled—it's just as good.) Serves 4 to 6.

Here's a quickie version of the Great Chocolate Goo Cake, or if you add coffee, Mocha Fudge Cake. It's not as good as either, but it takes only half an hour, start to finish.

**Rich Chocolate Dessert**

6 tablespoons unsalted butter
1 (6-ounce) package (1 cup) semisweet
   chocolate chips
2 tablespoons brown sugar
2 tablespoons granulated sugar

3 tablespoons flour
2 teaspoons instant coffee powder
   (optional)
2 eggs, separated

Preheat the oven to 450 degrees. Butter a 6- to 8-inch oven-safe frying pan or skillet. Melt butter and chocolate together in a saucepan over very low heat. While chocolate is melting, stir in both sugars. When butter, sugar and chocolate are fully combined, stir in flour (and coffee, if you like). Remove from heat.

In a small bowl, beat the egg whites until they stand in soft peaks. In another bowl, beat the egg yolks and rapidly stir the hot chocolate mixture into them, a little at a time to avoid cooking the egg yolks.

Fold in the egg whites and spoon the mixture into the buttered pan. Bake for 10 to 12 minutes. The outer edge is firm; the middle is gooey. Serves 2 or 3.

Next a recipe supplied by a colleague, who got it from a friend, who got it from somebody else, who got it who-knows-where. The first time I made it, each of the four layers developed huge humps, and they looked like bathmats. The cake tasted fine, so I did it again. The result was much improved, and that version of the recipe is reproduced below. The cake is very densely chocolate. So is the frosting.

## *Chocolate Poem*

**CAKE:**

**10 (1-ounce) squares semisweet chocolate**
**1½ cups (3 sticks) butter**
**12 eggs**
**3 cups confectioners' sugar**
**1½ cups cake flour**

**FROSTING:**

**6 (1-ounce) squares unsweetened chocolate**

**½ cup butter (I used unsalted)**
**4 cups confectioners' sugar**
**2 teaspoons vanilla**
**⅔ cup heavy cream**

**DECORATION:**

**Chocolate curls, almonds**

Preheat the oven to 350 degrees. Grease and flour four 8- or 9-inch layer-cake pans. Melt the chocolate and butter together in a large saucepan.

Note: The following mixture gets to be quite voluminous; it comes near the top of the large mixer bowl. You might want to make it in two parts.

Beat the eggs until they are lemon-colored. Sift the confectioners' sugar and add gradually to the eggs. When all the sugar is in, beat the eggs for 10 to 15 minutes. (If your mixer gets very hot, give it a brief rest.)

Sift the flour 3 times. With the mixer on low speed, add the flour to the egg mixture, and beat slowly until it is fully blended. Fold in the chocolate.

Pour into the 4 prepared pans and bake 25 minutes. The cake will test done with a toothpick well before that. Don't be fooled. If you take them out too soon, the layers will be like bathmats. (Trust me.)

While the cake cools, prepare the frosting:

Melt the chocolate. Cool. Cream the butter until it is light and fluffy. Add the confectioners' sugar and the chocolate alternately, a little at a time, beating after each addition. As liquid is needed, add the vanilla and then the cream, a little at a time. Use about a cup of frosting to frost the first, second and third layers, and use the rest for the top and sides. Decorate with semisweet chocolate curls and almonds.

---

The writer has laid in a supply of semisweet chocolate; he is not coming out until Bill Blass goes away.

# A Healthy Meal

I should learn when to say no.

When a friend asked me to help him move his oak roll-top desk into a third-floor walkup, I should have said no.

When I was asked to drive nine kids, all under ten years old, to a movie (in my five-passenger car) I should have said no.

And when it was suggested that I put together a healthy meal as a response to what was sure to be a devastating analysis of my dietary habits (arranged by colleague Kate Parry for an article on three folks' food consumption), I should have categorically refused.

I didn't refuse because it really sounded like a good-enough idea: Take the office glutton (me) and have him demonstrate that a healthy meal can be just as appealing and tasty as the disgustingly rich meal he really wanted to eat.

It didn't work.

As I write this I have not yet seen what the experts had to say about my food preferences, but I know the kind of thing it's likely to be. Nice as they probably are, these are the kind of folks who exist to tell you that you're doing something wrong.

Everybody likes to tell you that you're doing something wrong, of course. My partner Kate has been positively beside herself waiting for the experts' opinion of my intake. And when I asked her what sorts of things she thought I might eat for this experimental healthy meal, it was as though I had opened a floodgate of diet information.

The worst of it is that this information is so depressing. I might not eat the most balanced diet in the world, but I really don't think that, even if I decided to improve it, I need to rip it apart and start from the ground up. I've been staying alive on it quite nicely so far.

But consider the following exchange with Ms. Parry after I had examined some of the books she offered me (I admit I sought her out in the cafeteria, where she was hiding from me):

Me: "Gee, this is miserable. Nothing really works. Even skinless chicken has almost as much cholesterol as beef. And something that's low in cholesterol may still have lots of calories."

Kate: "You're making it too hard. You can *have* some fat. You can *have* some cholesterol. You can *have* two eggs a week."

Two eggs a *week?* I left the room.

What surprised me most in my very brief research was the difficulty I had in finding some just-plain-healthier menus. Our department gets lots of cookbooks and diet books, and I figured it would be but a few minutes' work to page through them until I found a reasonably appealing meal that was low in all the things it should be low in and balanced in all the things that should be balanced.

Well, Kate claimed to have such a book at home, and our boss said she had one, too. And the day after my noble experiment Kate thought of one that we have at work. But the bulk of the "get-healthy" books on our shelves tend to emphasize one aspect or another of diet: lowering calories, lowering cholesterol, lowering salt, lowering carbohydrates, and (it seemed to me) on and on.

Piecing together a meal out of that maze was, to put it mildly, no fun. I'm not a menu planner to begin with. If I were, I might already be planning healthy menus. Instead, I just pick up what I need for whatever appeals to me as a main course, and then I think of things that I might like to eat along with it. My only considerations are flavor, texture, color and maybe temperature, in that order.

When I had to sit there and actually consider the nutritional makeup of every lousy item I planned to cook, I got really irritated, and I began to snap at my colleagues. It was like having to find out who built the bus I was planning to ride to work, or establishing the fiber content of my chair cushion before I sat down.

But, as Horton the Elephant observed, a promise made is a debt unpaid, so I pitched in.

There were, it seemed to me, three ways to approach the business of designing a healthy meal:

• I could take the kind of meal I normally eat (I should point out that I don't normally eat preserved meats as often as I did in the period examined by the nutrition experts, but my father had just sent me a four-foot summer sausage), and attempt to duplicate it in a healthier way. I might try to make hollandaise sauce with soy lecithin and polyunsaturated oil instead of egg yolks and butter, for example. I decided that would be ludicrous. It certainly wouldn't taste as good, and it bordered on (if it didn't cross over into) food faddiness instead of healthy eating.

• I could make a very plain meal that wouldn't appeal to me—broiled fish with a teaspoon of butter, lots of plain vegetables with lemon juice. But that sounded depressing—more like hospital or health-farm food than I wanted to consider.

• I could try to find some appealing-sounding recipes in the healthy cookbooks. That seemed least likely to be a disaster, and I didn't want a disaster. I really wasn't setting out to prove that the only thing I can enjoy eating is deep-fat-fried fat.

I had a brief run-in with Ms. Parry over a promising-looking book that offered French gourmet cooking for good health. She didn't like the authors' credentials—one is a food writer, the other a lawyer; neither is a nutritionist or medical doctor.

That over (I gave up), I picked out some recipes from a low-cholesterol guidebook, checked them against a calorie and carbohydrate table in another book to make sure they weren't too awful, and ran the whole thing past the basic-food-groups chart in still a third book.

Here's what I decided to have:

**Eggplant casserole deluxe,** featuring eggplant, polyunsaturated oil, onion, celery, garlic, spices, tomato sauce and tomato paste, green pepper, mushrooms, a lot of spaghetti and some bread crumbs. It sounded fairly good, although I wondered at the presence of the very large amount of spaghetti—but this was a cholesterol-cutting book and spaghetti has no cholesterol.

**Cold green beans, with a low-cholesterol Italian dressing** consisting of wine vinegar, polyunsaturated oil and spices. The eggplant casserole looked to me pretty much like a complete meal, but I felt it needed a side dish. I'm not a lettuce-and-tomato person, so this would do for salad as well as for an extra vegetable and something tangy. Left to my own devices I would have used a vinaigrette made with olive oil, which, I learned, is monounsaturated, whatever that means, and *real good.*

Between those two items I certainly had enough for a meal. Not a seven-course feast, to be sure, but a perfectly adequate meal—except for dessert.

Now I must explain that, although I like to eat well, as far as I'm concerned it isn't the main course that can make or break a meal; it's the dessert. And I just couldn't bring myself to have any of the highly touted fruit desserts that I kept running across in these books. Fruit is a dessert in the same way a glass of Welch's grape juice is an apéritif.

O.K., I said to myself, you're just not going to have a scrumptious dessert tonight. You'll live. Settle for something tolerable, and then quit.

Raspberry gelatin struck me as a reasonable choice—no cholesterol, relatively few calories, pleasant enough to look at, reasonably sweet and a whole lot better than eating an apple. (If you don't appreciate the vast difference between fruit for dessert and fruit gelatin for dessert, see me later.)

Whipped cream on top would have made it a whole lot better, but that was clearly out of the question, so I decided to see whether yogurt can be whipped—or at least spritzed in curly spirals out of a pastry tube.

Reenter Ms. Parry.

Kate: "You're supposed to make healthy foods that are *appealing.* Does that dessert appeal to you?"

Me: "Not a lot, but . . ."

Kate: "Well, then, why don't you have some fruit?"

Me: "%&@#!"

(The curtain must descend briefly to cover an exchange in which I ranted almost senselessly about fruit.)

Our boss, attracted by the noise, came over and joined Kate in trying to convince me that there were plenty of wonderful, healthy things I could have for dessert. I think she was also trying to keep me from throwing something at Kate. I kept muttering that I'd rather have Jell-O.

Finally somebody found a diet book that appeared to be full of amazingly gooey items.

I smelled a rat.

Pointing to a recipe for a soufflé with chocolate and Grand Marnier, I shouted, "All right, then, I'm making *THIS!*"

I fully expected Kate to find some reason to rule it out. Instead she looked at the recipe and noted with pleasure that a serving of the soufflé had half the calories of a serving of ice cream. I noted back, louder, that it was a serving half as big as a serving of ice cream and that I was beginning to think this whole thing was a lot of hooey.

Thus primed for a healthy meal or a heart attack, whichever came first, I went home to cook.

Thanks to the milk in the soufflé, the meal would contain something from every food group but meat. If I felt the need afterward, I reasoned, I could have a slice or two of summer sausage.

The eggplant casserole turned out O.K., after I simmered down enough to make it, but the flavor was strangely thin—quite possibly there was too much spaghetti, or too little salt, or both. (I almost never salt food beyond what's in the recipe—not a health concern, I'm just not fond of salt and don't keep it on the table.) My best guess, though, is that some butter, or the fat from the meat that I would normally have included, would have spread the flavor more fully to the spaghetti.

The green beans and slim Italian dressing were all right, too, but again just a little underflavored.

I would, nonetheless, make both of those recipes again, unchanged if I had to, or punched up a bit with more flavorful oils and/or fats.

A side note: A spokesperson for the Department of Food Science and Nutrition at the University of Minnesota is quoted in a recent news release from the Institute of Food Technologists as saying that fats in the diet are important sources of nutrients and are responsible for many of the characteristic flavors, aromas and textures. "They are also," she continued, "the most concentrated sources of food energy in the diet. . . ."

Right on! Sounds like a recruiting poster for the Grease Corps.

Oh, all right. Honesty compels me to add the rest of that quote: Fats are also "responsible for some of the dieter's problems." Mutter, mutter.

Anyway, on to the chocolate and Grand Marnier soufflé, which turned out to be a serious mistake.

The recipe called for a choice of egg substitute or egg yolks and for either semisweet chocolate or carob chips. In the interest of science I'm willing to use an egg substitute instead of wonderful egg yolks, but lips that touch carob shall never touch mine, so I stuck with the semisweet chocolate.

It turned out not to make much difference. I make a soufflé very much like this one in every other regard. With roughly the same volume of milk, eggs, cornstarch and liqueur in this recipe, mine uses 3 ounces of unsweetened chocolate and 9 tablespoons of sugar. This one uses 1½ ounces of semisweet chocolate—the equivalent of 1 ounce of unsweetened chocolate and 1½ tablespoons of sugar.

Had I noticed that in advance, I would have picked something else to make. The result, as you might expect, was drastically underflavored. So much so that my boss, to whom I brought a sample, said it had no chocolate flavor at all.

Kate liked the flavor.

The color, given the lack of chocolate, was an unappealing light gray-brown.

The other problem is the use of egg substitute for egg yolks. Commercial egg substitute is 99 percent egg white. The substitute suggested in the cookbook is about 75 percent egg white. In neither case is there enough oil, emulsifier—or whatever is so yolky about egg yolks—to give a soufflé any body. This one shot up out of the bowl like it had been inflated with a service-station air hose, but it collapsed to a puddle when I took it out of the oven. It was fully baked all right, but very, very limp. I suppose it would have behaved more nicely had I used egg yolks instead of the substitute. Given how it tasted, I don't care to find out.

When all is said and done, and even before all is said and done, I'd much rather have a good bowl of Jell-O than a pale imitation of a rich dessert.

An hour after I was done with dinner, I had a chocolate bar.

Sorry.

The recipes for Eggplant Casserole Deluxe and Italian Salad Dressing are from *Cholesterol Counter,* a nice little book by Elizabeth Weiss and Rita Wolfson. The authors do not appear to be nutritionists or medical doctors, but their book contains a cholesterol chart that seemed to satisfy Ms. Parry.

---

### Eggplant Casserole Deluxe

1 eggplant (about 1¼ pounds)
¼ cup polyunsaturated oil
1 onion, chopped
1 rib celery, chopped
1 clove garlic, minced
1 teaspoon salt
¼ teaspoon pepper
½ teaspoon basil
¼ teaspoon oregano
2 tablespoons red wine
2 tablespoons tomato paste
2 (8-ounce) cans tomato sauce
1 pound spaghetti or vermicelli, cooked according to package directions and drained
1 green pepper, seeded and chopped
¼ pound fresh mushrooms, cut in thirds
1 tablespoon minced parsley
2 tablespoons bread crumbs

Wash the eggplant but do not peel it. Cut off the stem end and discard it. Slice the rest into ½-inch cubes (cut into ½-inch slices, then cube the slices).

Heat the oil in a Dutch oven. Add the eggplant cubes, onion, celery and garlic and sauté, until the onion is translucent and the eggplant is lightly browned.

Add the salt, pepper, basil, oregano, wine, tomato paste and tomato sauce. Stir to mix well, bring to a boil, cover and simmer over low heat for 10 minutes.

This is a good time to cook the spaghetti, too, in a separate pot.

Into the eggplant mixture stir the green pepper, mushrooms and parsley and simmer 5 minutes longer.

Preheat the oven to 350 degrees.

Grease a large casserole dish with corn-oil margarine or some more polyunsaturated oil, and layer a third of the cooked spaghetti over the bottom. Top with a third of the eggplant mixture. Repeat twice more, using up all the spaghetti and eggplant mixture. Sprinkle the bread crumbs over all.

Bake uncovered for 20 minutes. Serves 5 or 6 as a main dish, 8 or 10 as a side dish.

## Italian Salad Dressing

2 tablespoons wine vinegar
5 tablespoons polyunsaturated oil
1 clove garlic, peeled

¼ teaspoon oregano
Paprika to taste
Salt, pepper to taste

Shake all ingredients together in a jar with a screw-top lid. Refrigerate for 2 or more hours, to allow flavors to blend. Before serving, remove the whole garlic clove.

Makes a scant ½ cup. Serve over tossed salad, or chilled steamed green beans, cucumber slices or anything else, for that matter.

This chocolate and Grand Marnier soufflé recipe is from a book written by a woman who is described as a registered dietitian. It is a terrible recipe anyway.

## Grand Marnier Chocolate Soufflé

(NOT RECOMMENDED, but maybe you have a friend with no taste)

1 tablespoon cornstarch
¾ cup prepared nonfat milk
¼ cup semisweet chocolate or carob pieces
3 tablespoons Grand Marnier (or other orange liqueur)

½ cup egg substitute, or 3 egg yolks, beaten
4 egg whites, at room temperature
½ teaspoon cream of tartar
½ teaspoon low-calorie margarine

Combine cornstarch and milk in a saucepan and stir until cornstarch is dissolved. Bring to a boil, lower heat and cook, stirring constantly, for 1 minute after it boils.

Add the chocolate and the liqueur, remove from heat and stir until the chocolate melts. Cool slightly and mix in the egg substitute or egg yolks, 1 tablespoon at a time or 1 yolk at a time. Set aside.

Preheat the oven to 350 degrees.

Beat the egg whites at low speed until

they are foamy. Add the cream of tartar and beat at high speed until stiff, glossy peaks form. Stir a fourth of the egg whites into the cooled chocolate mixture to lighten it, then gently fold in the remaining whites.

Grease a 1½-quart soufflé dish with the margarine and turn the mixture into the dish. Bake 35 to 40 minutes, or until set and puffy.

Serve immediately. (Or, better, don't serve at all.)

This is the chocolate soufflé I usually make. I would prefer one bite of this to six barrels of the preceding one. (To be absolutely honest, I would really prefer no dessert at all to any amount of the preceding one.)

## Good Chocolate Soufflé

9 tablespoons sugar, divided
1 tablespoon cornstarch
⅔ cup whole milk
3 (1-ounce) squares unsweetened chocolate

3 tablespoons coffee liqueur (or 3 tablespoons strong, sweet black coffee)
4 eggs, separated

In a saucepan, mix 6 tablespoons of the sugar with the cornstarch. Add a very small amount of the milk and stir to make a paste. Slowly, and stirring to avoid lumps, add the rest of the milk.

Bring to the boil over medium heat, stirring constantly. Reduce heat and cook, stirring, 1 additional minute. Add the chocolate and stir until it is melted. Stir in the coffee liqueur or coffee. Allow the mixture to cool for 5 minutes. Preheat the oven to 350 degrees. Lightly butter a 1½-quart soufflé dish. (You could use a diet margarine, I suppose, as a gesture.)

Beat the egg yolks lightly. Add a few tablespoons of the chocolate mixture to the egg yolks, stirring. Now stir the egg yolk mixture into the chocolate mixture. Set aside.

Beat the egg whites, gradually adding the 3 remaining tablespoons of sugar, until the whites hold peaks and are firm but not dry.

Gently fold the whites into the chocolate mixture and pour into the soufflé dish. Bake 35 to 40 minutes. Yum!

# The 9-by-13 Cookbook

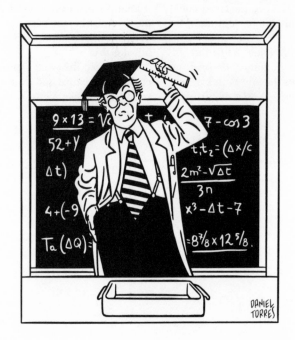

Whenever there's a popular new appliance, there is always a cookbook or two written especially to go with it. There have been mini-deep-fry cookbooks, blender cookbooks, hamburger-cooker cookbooks, food-processor cookbooks, crêpe-pan cookbooks, and on and on. I modestly propose one more specialty cookbook— one that should have been produced some time ago.

Welcome to the wonderful world of 9-by-13-inch pan cookery!

As you get accustomed to using your new pan, you'll wonder how you ever got along without it. There's hardly a category of food—be it appetizer, main course, vegetable or dessert (or even soup, if you are truly desperate)—that cannot be prepared in the versatile 9-by-13-inch pan.

Your 9-by-13-inch pan requires no electric cords, special tools or lessons. Operation is simplicity itself. Just fill it up and watch it work!

Before you use your new 9-by-13-inch pan, you'll want to familiarize yourself with it. Note that it is about 9 inches wide and approximately 13 inches long.*

---

*Note to owners of 8-by-12-inch pans. You'll find that most software for the 8-by-12 is upward-compatible to the 9-by-13. Minor adjustments may be necessary; consult your dealer for details.

Sometimes the pan is referred to as a "9-by-13-by-2." That, you'll soon discover, is because it's about 2 inches deep.

In Europe, this pan is referred to as the "23-by-33-by-5." Can you guess why?

On the following pages are numerous recipes designed to take advantage of the versatility of your new pan. The 9-by-13-by-2-inch pan is so good at so many things that some have called it "the kitchen in a seventh-of-a-cubic-foot." Even Craig Claiborne recommends it.

Wondering what to make first with your new 9-by-13? Just let your imagination run wild! The many uses of the adaptable 9-by-13 will delight your family and make you a big hit at the . . .

Oh, dear reader, I can't keep this up. I take off my hat to Mable Hoffman and all the others who crank out these specialty cookbooks, but keeping up that manic enthusiasm is too much for me.

If the truth were told, there's only one cookbook I ever really wanted to write, one for the slow-cooking pot, and that's just because I wanted to use this title: *The Betty Cooker Crockbook.*

But as long as I got us started on 9-by-13-inch pans, let's go ahead and make some things in them. A couple of quick asides, and then we'll get to the recipes.

Just in case you measured your oblong pan and came away puzzled, you should know that not every "9-by-13-inch pan" is indeed 9 inches wide and 13 inches long. In fact, after a brief but exhausting survey, I conclude that hardly *any* 9-by-13-inch pan is 9 inches wide and 13 inches long. There probably are some; I couldn't find a single one.

A brand-new Ekco pan measures 8⅞ inches by 12¾ inches; others of different ages and manufactures varied, mostly under but some over, by as much as half an inch. A 1974 bakeware brochure produced by Wear-Ever Aluminum says that the American Home Economics Association and the American National Standards Institute set up standard sizes for bakeware, but it notes that "a manufacturing tolerance of plus or minus ¼ inch is allowed." It doesn't even hint at the reason.

Surely in this day of microcomputers and space shuttles, we can produce a 9-by-13-inch pan that is a whole lot less than ¼ inch off. It isn't, after all, like the boxes of crackers whose "contents may settle in shipping." If the pan measured 13 inches long when it left Ekco, it would measure 13 inches long when it reached you (unless it reached you at a velocity approaching the speed of light).

(It isn't often that one gets to invoke the Lorentz-FitzGerald Contraction in a food article, but it isn't often that one's boss is on vacation, either.)

Actually, I suspect that the pan-dimension phenomenon is related to lumber, a field of endeavor in which a 2-by-4 is more like 1½ by 3½.

Incidentally, the area of a nominal 9-by-13-inch pan is 117 square inches and that of two 8-by-8-inch pans is 128 square inches—about the same—so the 9-by-13 holds a double recipe of any bar cookie intended for an 8-by-8. The area of two 9-inch round pans is about 127 square inches, so any cake recipe intended for two of those could as well be made in one 9-by-13.

One other thing, if your 9-by-13 is glass (Pyrex, for example), or glass-ceramic

(CorningWare). A spokesperson for Corning Glass said that "because, in a conventional oven, glass and glass-ceramic dishes absorb heat faster than metal pans, baking temperature should be 25 degrees lower for glass materials." Got that? O.K., let's cook!

You could bake this appetizer on cookie sheets. But the 9-by-13 does a splendid job and isn't as big. (There's no advantage to that, but it is true.)

## Cheese Appetizers

3 tablespoons butter or margarine
1 cup (4 ounces) shredded Cheddar cheese
1 teaspoon steak sauce
½ cup flour

Dash of salt
1 teaspoon paprika
2 tablespoons sesame seeds (optional)
12 smallish pimiento-stuffed olives
12 toasted pecan halves

These can be prepared ahead of time and refrigerated, unbaked. Cream butter, beat in cheese and steak sauce. Combine flour, salt, paprika and sesame seeds. Blend into butter-cheese mixture until there is no dry, uncolored flour remaining.

Put about a teaspoon of dough in the palm of one hand. Drop an olive or pecan half into it and mold the dough around it, adding a bit of dough if necessary to enclose the olive or pecan half sparingly but completely. (You could use all olives or all nuts, but giving guests a choice is always nice). When ready to serve, preheat the oven to 400 degrees. Place dough balls in an ungreased 9-by-13-inch pan. Bake for about 12 minutes, until they are golden brown. Makes 24.

Here's a vegetable that's just made for the roomy interior of a 9-by-13-inch pan. The cookbook in which I found it suggests that it makes a delicious poultry stuffing, too. It *is* the kind of thing that would substitute marvelously for mashed potatoes. ("Which would *you* rather have, Mr. Tompkins? Mashed potatoes . . . or Rice and Sweet-Potato Casserole?" "I'd have to say the Rice and Sweet-Potato Casserole." "How about *that,* Mrs. Tompkins?" "Well, I guess it's Rice and Sweet-Potato Casserole, then. I wish *he'd* make it, though.")

## Rice and Sweet-Potato Casserole

2 ribs celery
2 medium onions
½ cup butter
1 (7-ounce) package uncooked quick-cooking rice (about 2 cups)
2½ cups chicken broth (two 10¾-ounce cans), divided

2 tablespoons brown sugar
1½ teaspoons salt
½ teaspoon pepper
¾ teaspoon rosemary
1 (18-ounce) can vacuum-packed (not syrup-packed) sweet potatoes
2 eggs, lightly beaten

Chop the celery and onion. Melt the butter in a 5-quart Dutch oven. Stir the celery, onion and rice into the hot butter and cook over low heat, stirring occasionally, about 10 minutes, until the rice is pale yellow or until you are sick of stirring. Reserve ½ cup of chicken broth. Stir in the remaining broth (about 2 cups) and the brown sugar, salt, pepper and rosemary. Cover the pot and bring the mixture to boiling.

Lower the heat and simmer, stirring

occasionally, about 15 minutes or until the rice is tender. Uncover, remove from heat and allow to cool briefly. Preheat the oven to 325 degrees.

Cut the sweet potatoes into ½-inch pieces (you can do that fairly well while they're still in the can), add them to the rice and toss gently. Mix the lightly beaten eggs with the remaining ½ cup of chicken broth, and blend into the rice mixture. Grease a 9-by-13-inch pan and turn the rice mixture into it. Bake for about 25 minutes, until the top begins to brown. Serves 8 to 10.

---

When talk turns, as often it does, to the 9-by-13-inch pan, one of the first main-course dishes that comes up is lasagne. Here's a nice, flavorful version.

---

### Lasagne

1 pound Italian sausage
1 medium onion, chopped
1 clove garlic, put through a garlic press
1 tablespoon dried basil
½ teaspoon salt
1 (16-ounce) can whole tomatoes, with liquid
1 (8-ounce) can tomato sauce
1 (6-ounce) can tomato paste

1 (8-ounce) package lasagne noodles
3 cups (24 ounces) creamy cottage cheese
½ cup (3 ounces) grated Parmesan cheese
2 tablespoons parsley flakes
2 beaten eggs
1 teaspoon salt
½ teaspoon pepper
1 pound sliced mozzarella cheese

If sausage was purchased in casings, remove the meat from the casings. Slowly brown the sausage and onion in a skillet until the sausage is broken up and well cooked and the onion is translucent. Drain fat from pan.

Add garlic, basil, salt, tomatoes and liquid, tomato sauce and tomato paste. Stir, cutting the tomatoes into chunks with the edge of the spoon. Simmer uncovered for 30 minutes, stirring occasionally.

Meanwhile cook the lasagne noodles according to package directions. Drain, rinse in cold water and drain again.

Preheat the oven to 375 degrees. Combine the cottage cheese, Parmesan cheese, parsley flakes, eggs, salt and pepper.

Put half the noodles in a 9-by-13-inch pan. Spread with half the cottage-cheese filling. Top with half the mozzarella cheese and half the meat sauce.

Repeat: noodles, cottage cheese, mozzarella and meat sauce.

Bake about 30 minutes. Let stand 10 minutes, to firm and cool slightly.

Makes 12 servings.

---

Here's something straight out of 1950s Sweet-Sixteen parties, but it remains very tasty.

It would make excellent picnic fare if your oven is close enough to the picnic for the dish to arrive hot. (Wrapping in many layers of newspapers helps, and it also helps get rid of newspapers.)

The flavor is pretty tomatoey-mustardy. If you'd like to tone down that Coney Island aura a bit without losing the tang, add some soy sauce. (Taste before topping with the cornbread batter.)

## Cornbread-Topped Bean and Bratwurst Bake

1 pound cooked bratwurst (or frankfurters), cut into ½-inch pieces
2 (1-pound) cans baked beans
½ cup ketchup
½ cup water
1 tablespoon prepared mustard
Soy sauce to taste (optional)

**CORNBREAD:**

¾ cup sifted flour
1 tablespoon sugar
1½ teaspoons baking powder
1 teaspoon salt
⅔ cup cornmeal
1 egg, lightly beaten
⅔ cup milk
¼ cup cooking oil
⅓ cup finely chopped onion (1 small onion)

Preheat oven to 400 degrees. Combine bratwurst, beans, ketchup, water, mustard and soy sauce in 9-by-13-inch pan.

Sift flour, sugar, baking powder and salt into a mixing bowl. Stir in the cornmeal. Add the egg, milk, oil and onion, stirring only after all are added and only enough to fully combine.

Spoon the cornbread mixture over the beans. (It won't cover fully; you want to make dollops over each portion, rather than try to make an even layer. If you prefer a whole, even layer of cornbread, make a double recipe of cornbread batter. That'll give you more than you need.)

Bake for about 40 minutes, until the cornbread is golden brown.

---

Every nationality that ever sent anyone down in the mines seems to claim that pasties are its own. Let's avoid that controversy by attributing these tasty meat turnovers to a group that surely predates most claimants—everybody else got the recipe from them.

---

## Sumerian-Akkadian Pasties

1 pound round steak
1 cup cubed raw potatoes (about 1 medium baking potato)
½ cup chopped onion (1 small onion)
½ cup chopped celery (less than 1 rib)
½ cup chopped carrots (about 1 carrot)
¼ teaspoon pepper
2 teaspoons salt, divided
3 cups sifted flour
1 cup (2 sticks) butter or margarine
About ½ cup cold water
Milk (for wash)

Cut the steak, uncooked, into very small dice (about ¼ inch on a side—they'll be tough if you make them too big). Combine the steak, potatoes, onion, celery, carrots, pepper and half of the salt in a large bowl. Refrigerate.

Prepare the dough: Sift the flour and the remaining 1 teaspoon of salt into a bowl. Using a pastry blender, cut in the butter or margarine until it is the size of peas. You can use two knives to do this too (have your mom show you how). Stir in just enough water to make the dough hold together. If time permits, refrigerate the dough for an hour or two.

Preheat the oven to 450 degrees. Divide the dough into 8 pieces. Roll each out into a circle on a generously floured surface. The circle should be 6 or 7 inches in diameter.

Put around ½ cup of the meat mixture on one side of each circle. Brush the edges of each circle with water, fold and crimp shut with a fork. Punch a few small holes in the top, to let the steam out.

Put the pies into 2 ungreased 9-by-13-inch pans. Brush carefully with milk. (Try not to let the milk spill onto the pan, where it will burn and stick.)

Bake at 450 degrees for 10 minutes, then lower temperature to 350 degrees and bake 40 to 50 additional minutes.

Serve hot or cold. Makes 8.

---

It's when we come to dessert that the 9-by-13-inch pan really shines (figuratively speaking, because unless you're a compulsive cleaner, your new 9-by-13-inch pan won't literally shine all that long). From the host of bar-cookie recipes, I have selected a rich, firm mocha brownie. I topped it with cinnamon-flavored cream-cheese frosting, but you could certainly use a more traditional chocolate frosting (with liquid coffee instead of other liquid, if you like).

---

## Mocha Brownies

4 (1-ounce) squares unsweetened chocolate
2/3 cup butter or margarine
4 eggs
2 cups sugar
2 teaspoons vanilla

1½ cups sifted flour
1 teaspoon baking powder
½ teaspoon salt
¼ cup instant coffee powder
1 cup chopped nuts (optional) (I think they'd be a distraction)

Melt the chocolate and butter together over very low heat, stirring constantly. Set the mixture aside. Beat the eggs. Gradually beat in the sugar until the eggs are light and fluffy. Add the vanilla. Stir in the chocolate mixture and mix well.

Preheat the oven to 350 degrees.

Sift together the flour, baking powder, salt and coffee powder. Stir into the first mixture. Fold in the nuts, if you have the audacity to go ahead and use them. Pour into a greased 9-by-13-inch pan. (What else?) Bake 30 minutes. Cool, frost if you like—and who wouldn't—then cut into squares.

---

The mocha brownies are O.K. just plain, but this frosting is very nice:

---

## Cinnamon Cream-Cheese Frosting

1 cup confectioners' sugar
2 (3-ounce) packages cream cheese
1 tablespoon milk

1 teaspoon vanilla
½ teaspoon cinnamon

Cream together the sugar and cream cheese. Add the milk, vanilla and cinnamon. If too thin, firm up with additional confectioners' sugar. Frost the brownies after they're cool.

---

Here's a nonbaked summery dessert for the 9-by-13-inch pan, distilled from many similar recipes. I really didn't expect much of this one, particularly since it is so much like so many others that are fine but not breathtaking, but it went over *really* well.

## Frozen Chocolate Mint Cheesecake-Mousse Stuff

1/2 cup butter
1 1/2 cups graham-cracker crumbs (12 double crackers)
1 tablespoon sugar
1 (6-ounce) package chocolate chips

1 (8-ounce) package cream cheese
3/4 cup sugar, divided
1 teaspoon mint extract
2 eggs, separated
1 cup heavy cream

Melt the butter. Combine graham-cracker crumbs, melted butter and the tablespoon of sugar. Press onto the bottom of a 9-by-13-inch pan, and up the sides if there's enough.

Melt the chocolate chips over very low heat. Soften the cream cheese in the large bowl of an electric mixer. Add the melted chocolate, 1/2 cup of the sugar and the mint extract. Beat well.

Put the egg whites into the small bowl of the mixer. Set aside. Add the egg yolks to the chocolate mixture and beat.

Clean the beaters with soap and water. Beat the egg whites with the remaining 1/4 cup of sugar until soft, syrupy peaks form. Fold into the chocolate mixture. Scrape the mixer bowl clean of egg whites, but don't bother washing it or the beaters. Whip the cream and fold it into the mixture.

Pour over the crumb crust and freeze. Serves 10 to 12.

# *Popovers (and Bagels)*

I used to think popovers were hard to make. Or tricky. Or something.

When I was growing up in Milwaukee, there was a restaurant that drew people from as far away as Wauwatosa just on the strength of its popovers. Since nobody in possession of his faculties would even drive around the block to get scrambled eggs, mashed potatoes or toast, as far as I was concerned, it followed as the night the day that popovers were not as easily made.

Then there were the few occasions when my grandmother made popovers. She chose to make them only for company meals, people would rave and rave about them (they *were* big and light and golden), and she always gave the impression, without saying so outright, that their success had been a near thing—due only to skill, luck and living right.

So when I made my first batch some years ago and they all popped very nicely, I was extremely surprised.

I was a little less surprised when they worked the next time, and I'm no longer surprised by them at all. In fact, I think it's almost impossible to make a popover that doesn't pop. I'm sorry, Grandma, but your secret's out: Popovers are a snap.

Easy as they are, and good as they are with a big chunk of butter melting down inside them, I hadn't made popovers in quite a while. Then one night a few weeks ago, while I was in the middle of making an unholy number of crêpes, it occurred to me that there was something awfully familiar about the recipe: equal amounts of flour and milk, lots of egg and a little melted butter.

A quick look at a popover recipe confirmed my suspicion: Crêpes and popovers are made from essentially the same batter.

Well, now.

Besides being a source of powerful wonderment (how can the same batter make something both high and puffy and something perfectly—even desperately—flat?) this revelation made me wonder once more about the possible fallibility of popovers. Is there some ghastly mistake one can make with a popover to confuse it into thinking that it's a crêpe?

How, in other words, does a popover turn into a flopover?

Although there are a lot of popover recipes, the batter does not vary much from one to another. What does differ is the *method* of preparing them. So I decided to try as many of those variations as I could.

(As a contrast in texture, I decided to make some bagels, too, which I'd never done before. They rise, all right, but they're firm.)

The differences in popover instructions are many. Older recipes call for lengthy beating of the batter. Newer ones caution not to beat it more than a minute. Some recipes call for putting the greased pans or custard cups into the hot oven to preheat them before adding the batter. Others don't bother with preheating the pans, and some even insist that the pans and batter go into a stone-cold oven.

That brings us to oven temperature.

The start-stone-cold method suggests turning the oven to 400 degrees and baking for 50 minutes. (If popovers were at all tricky I can't imagine how this method would be generally successful, given the differences in ovens and the amount of time it takes one to heat up compared with another.) More conventional techniques are 450 degrees for half an hour then 15 minutes at 350 degrees, or an even 400 degrees for 40 minutes.

I'll cut a long story short. They all work. Every #$%&! popover I made—and I made a lot of them—popped and looked beautiful.

However, there is the matter of greasing the pans. And here there are differences. Sometimes popovers won't come out of the pan (or out of the custard cups). When that happens it doesn't make much difference how great they look, because by the time you rip them out, leaving the bottoms stuck in the pan, they don't look so good anymore.

You can use a little oil, a lot of oil, a little margarine, a lot of margarine, or a little or a lot of vegetable shortening.

I have concluded, after hours of greasing and baking, that the best method, whether for pans or for cups, is to use a great deal of solid vegetable shortening (Crisco, or whatever). A great deal. Enough so that you can't see the bottom through the white. Leave an extra glob of it in the middle of the bottom of each cup, where the sticking problem is worst. For that added measure of protection, as they say in deodorant commercials, spread some on the top of the muffin pan between the cups, and around the rims of individual custard cups. That way the big puffy tops won't stick, either.

But the most significant thing you can do to eliminate sticking, if you're using muffin tins as opposed to individual custard cups, is to use bright, shiny ones. My old muffin tins, which have been around the block and have acquired that well-used, coffee-bean color, gave me much more trouble than one I bought more recently that is still silvery.

Here is a popover recipe, with variations, every one of which works.

**1 cup sifted flour**
**3 eggs**

**1 cup milk**
**2 tablespoons melted butter**

*Popovers*

Put the sifted flour in a large bowl. In a smaller bowl, beat the eggs lightly. Add the milk to the eggs and mix well. Add the liquid gradually to the flour, beating with a mixer or wire whisk to incorporate it. Beat in the melted butter.

You can beat this mixture just long enough to make it smooth (less than 30 seconds) or beat it 4 or 5 minutes. It doesn't make any difference.

You can preheat the oven to 450 degrees, 400 degrees or not preheat it at all. It doesn't make any difference, except for how long you'll wind up baking the popovers.

Grease the pans or custard cups *very* heavily. Pour the batter into 12 cups, or if you prefer bigger, meatier popovers (as does my colleague Mary Hart), pour it into 6 cups.

If you didn't preheat the oven, turn it to 400 degrees and bake the popovers for 50 minutes. If you preheated it to 450, bake the popovers for 30 minutes, reduce the temperature to 350 and bake for another 15 minutes. If you preheated it to 400 degrees, bake the popovers for 40 minutes. If you put the batter into 6 cups instead of 12, bake for an additional 15 to 20 minutes.

Here are some variations that do make a difference:

Fry 4 or 5 slices of bacon until they are crisp, drain and crumble them and add them to the finished popover batter.

Or add to the finished batter 1/2 cup or more of grated cheese, an extra shake of salt and a little pepper or cayenne.

These are both very nice.

---

While whomping up my fifth or sixth batch of popovers, and not looking forward to them very much, it occurred to me to find out whether I could make one big popover instead of 6 or 12 little ones.

So I rubbed a lot of shortening into a soufflé dish (a regular 1½-quart baking dish probably would work as well) and poured in the whole batch of popover batter.

It puffed up beautifully around the sides. After about an hour, I pulled it out of the oven. It wasn't bad, but it was much heavier than a popover. More like Yorkshire pudding (the batter for which, amazingly enough, is much the same as for crêpes and popovers).

I'd serve the giant popover, with gravy available, as an appealing substitute for mashed potatoes.

Recalling a British lunch specialty called toad in the hole (which is like Yorkshire pudding with sausages in it), and never being one to let a good thing alone, I decided to see what would happen if I put some leftover-type stuff in the popover-soufflé-pudding. It worked very well indeed.

Endless variations on this one are clearly possible:

---

**1/4 to 1/2 pound leftover ground beef,**
**fried, crumbled and drained**
**1/2 cup or more leftover mixed**
**vegetables**

**1/2 teaspoon or more Worcestershire**
**sauce**
**1 recipe popover batter**

*Popleftover*

*(Continued)*

Combine the cooked ground beef, the vegetables and the Worcestershire sauce.

Heavily grease a soufflé dish or 1½-quart baking dish. Put the meat-vegetable mixture in the bottom of the dish and gently pour the popover batter over it.

Bake at 400 degrees for about 1 hour. A lovely crust forms, and the meat and vegetables wind up distributed throughout the rather heavy batter.

Leftover or canned gravy, if available, would be nice but not necessary.

I didn't try this with individual popovers (I won't be able to look a popover in the face for months), but I bet it would work.

Bagel dough is *not* the same as crêpe/popover/Yorkshire-pudding batter. As substantial as the Popleftover is, it's still light and airy compared with the bagel.

But, I was surprised to learn when I made my second batch of bagels (the first recipe wasn't very good), bagels do not *have* to be hard as rocks. Fresh from the oven, these bagels were dense, all right, but they yielded pleasantly when chewed, in the manner of a raised doughnut. Not as easily, mind you, but they did yield.

Some folks may actually prefer the cement-doughnut style. I'm sure these bagels would acquire that texture if left out for a day or two.

The bagels, like so many other things that nobody makes at home, are fun to make at home. Kids would like doing it. *I* liked doing it. You even get to pick out toppings, like sesame seeds or poppy seeds or bits of onion. A gentile friend insisted on topping one with red and green sugar. Wrong.

### *Bagels*

3 cups flour
½ tablespoon salt
5 tablespoons sugar, divided
2 (¼-ounce) packages active dry yeast
⅔ cup lukewarm water
3 tablespoons oil
1 egg
4 quarts water

1 egg yolk
1 tablespoon cold water

OPTIONAL TOPPINGS:

Poppy seeds, sesame seeds, caraway seeds, sea salt or coarsely chopped onion; *not* red and green sugar

Sift together into a large bowl the flour, salt and 2 tablespoons of the sugar. Dissolve the yeast in half the lukewarm water and stir well. Add the oil and the rest of the lukewarm water to the yeast.

Beat the egg and add it to the yeast mixture. Make a well in the center of the flour and stir in the yeast mixture, gathering up all the flour. Mix well and knead 3 or 4 minutes, until the dough is smooth and firm. Cover it with a cloth and let it rise in a warm place for 1 hour.

Turn the dough out onto a floured board and knead it well, until it becomes somewhat elastic.

Divide the dough into 12 equal portions and shape each, rolling between your palms, into a smooth roll about 5 inches long and ¾ inch in diameter. Dip one end in water and pinch the two ends together firmly. Place the rings on a floured board, and even them out into circles as perfect as possible.

Let them rest, covered, for 10 to 15 minutes, until they show signs of starting to rise.

Bring the 4 quarts of water to the boil in a 5-quart Dutch oven or wider pan. Add the remaining 3 tablespoons of sugar and wait for the water to return to the boil. Then add 6 bagels, one by one, using a slotted spoon.

*(Continued)*

When all the bagels are in the water and it is once more boiling, reduce the heat to minimize boil-over, wait for the bagels to rise to the surface if they did not do so immediately, and let them boil for 3 minutes.

Turn them over and allow them to boil 3 minutes more.

Meanwhile, preheat the oven to 400 degrees and lightly oil 2 baking sheets.

Remove the bagels from the water with a slotted spoon, drain them briefly on paper toweling (watch out—if you leave them too long they'll stick), and transfer them to one of the baking sheets.

Repeat this process with the other 6 bagels.

Beat the egg yolk with the tablespoon of water and brush onto the tops and sides of the bagels. Sprinkle, if you like, with your choice of topping. (An assortment is always nice.)

Bake for 25 to 30 minutes, until they are crisp and turning golden brown.

---

## Follow-Up

The day after this column first appeared, the person who so foolishly alleged that it is almost impossible to make popovers that don't rise beautifully (he should have remembered that all generalizations are false, including this one) arrived at his desk to find there a bag of things about three-quarters of an inch high and weighing what seemed to be about a quarter of a pound apiece. Attached was this note: "My husband made these with your no-fail popover recipe."

A quick consultation established that the only respect in which the gentleman, Lynn Christine, had departed from the recipe appeared to be that the lightly beaten eggs had instead been whipped in the Cuisinart. The author of the popover article had attempted what he thought to be every possible variation—oven temperature, amount of batter in each cup, etc.—to see what prevents popovers from rising. He hadn't thought of the Cuisinart.

(Oh, I cannot keep up this third-person pretense any longer. That author, dear reader, that author was me.)

I went home and tested Christine's approach to egg beating. It made no difference at all. The popovers were fine. So I made another batch, in which I attempted, viciously, to *make* them flop. I opened the oven door for five minutes just as the popovers were starting to rise. Then I slammed it. They worked, too. I made another batch, in which I added half again as much flour. Those were heavy, and didn't rise nearly as well as they should, but they did rise.

Next morning on my desk was another batch of low, dense flopovers from Christine, along with a detailed description of his approach. It was an eye-opener for me about what the people at General Mills and Pillsbury call "recipe tolerance." Folks substitute and fiddle with recipes, even when they don't think they're doing so, and a good recipe must permit a wide variation in ingredients and cooking techniques.

The popover recipe called for eggs, milk, flour and butter. It didn't say so, but it assumed that standard ingredients would be used—large eggs, whole milk, all-purpose flour and real butter. Christine, it turns out, had used jumbo eggs (about 20 percent larger than large eggs), one-percent milk (which contains one-fourth of the butterfat of whole milk), unbleached spring-wheat flour (I don't know *what* that does) and margarine. The last substitution is probably perfectly safe in most recipes, the question of flavor aside. But I was sure that, between the eggs, milk and flour, Christine had gone too far.

Then I read what he *did* with the ingredients. The recipe called for adding the milk to the eggs, stirring that mixture gradually into the flour and then adding the melted butter. Christine (who is, according to his wife, a good cook and makes tricky things like soufflés without difficulty) beat the eggs in the food processor, added the milk and margarine and spun that mixture around, then added the flour and spun that just until it was mixed.

Well, I can tell you, I was pretty smug. What with substituting for every ingredient and changing the method, I said to myself, no wonder Christine's popovers didn't work. I was going to conclude this follow-up with the standard advice Mary Hart uses on these occasions: "If it didn't work the first time, try following the recipe." I went home and made them his way, except for the spring-wheat flour, which I couldn't find at my neighborhood grocery.

They worked.

So I called around, found some unbleached spring-wheat flour, and made another batch, slamming the oven door viciously as it began to rise.

They came out fine.

Negotiations the next day with Christine's wife, Faith, who is a computer systems coordinator at the paper, produced this suggestion: She would ask Christine to make another batch, using my ingredients and method. He did. It flopped.

Maybe it has something to do with the moon. We'll explore this further, I'm afraid. In the meantime, Christine has volunteered to test any other "no-fail" recipes.

---

### More Follow-Up

Regular readers will recall that we have been dealing, for the past few weeks, with the problem of the short, squat popover. (Irregular readers might consider adding some fiber to their diets.)

In the interest of giving an accurate impression, I should point out that, when the original article appeared, I got many calls and notes from folks who had made the popovers and were successful. I even got a letter from Carolyn and Henry Mar, in Brookings, South Dakota, saying that the Popleftover, the giant popover I had suggested as a way to use up odd bits of food, had succeeded and done wonders for some capon scraps.

But I also got a letter from Debbie Michels, of Columbia Heights, Minnesota, who said that she's been making Betty Crocker's popover recipe successfully for years. She tried mine and it bombed.

And Glenda Wright, of Minneapolis, wrote to say that until six months ago she would have agreed that popovers are foolproof. But last year she made a batch that flopped, and so has every batch she's made since—using the same recipe and the same containers she's always used.

I also got a hint from Renee Burrows, of Loretto, Minnesota, who says that, although popovers do pop with other oven-temperature arrangements, she gets her best results by putting them in a cold oven, setting it for 450 degrees and baking them for 40 minutes. Useful information, but the Christine mystery lingered.

That's where it all stood until a week ago when, muffin tin in hand, I invited myself to the Christines' to make popovers.

Now, Christine is, if I may steal a phrase from P. G. Wodehouse, as pleasant a fellow as ever bit a sandwich. But after our early phone conversations I was beginning to think that his cooking technique might be the problem. After his third failure it developed that he had never sifted the flour. I couldn't believe that so small a thing would cause his problem, but we'd eliminated almost everything else, so I resolved to stand over him with a bludgeon and make sure he used the #$% sifter. I even brought my sifter along.

And I brought my oven thermometer, too, on the theory that if they were cooked at too low a temperature his popovers were perhaps setting before they could rise.

I can't stand much more of this, so I'll cut it short. He and I each made a batch of popovers. We both followed the recipe exactly, sifting and all, and put both batches into a preheated oven at 400 degrees (confirmed by thermometer).

Both batches *worked*.

Could the problem have been the sifting? It seemed very unlikely.

I was quite discouraged, but Faith, Lynn's wife, provided a welcome break by making a very nice free lunch. (Who says there's no such thing?)

After lunch, Lynn and I made one more batch of popovers each, neither of us sifting the flour. Mine went into a cold oven (the method he had been using, and which I had already tested successfully) and his went in after the oven had come up to temperature. Both batches worked too!

I absolutely don't get it. What had happened to make all of his previous efforts flop? And what had changed since then?

We are down, now, to a thin straw indeed. He says that the eggs he used for all three batches that flopped had been in the refrigerator for a few weeks. I have set aside some eggs, and I'll make another batch of popovers with them in three or four weeks, to see if they'll bomb. Stay tuned.

In the meantime, we do have one hint, confirmed in a letter from Mrs. Dennis Kramer, of Elk River, Minnesota. Popovers do *not* rise very well in nonstick pans. Each of the two batches that Christine made under my watchful eye was split between two six-cup pans, one a regular metal muffin pan and one a pan with a nonstick surface. In both batches, the popovers in the nonstick pan were lots lower than their counterparts in the traditional pan.

And even without that information, the evening was not a total loss from the point of view of the popover. Faced with two more batches of popovers after lunch, Faith suggested that we spoon some of her chocolate mousse into them.

They were *wonderful!* Ice cream would be a very nice second choice.

There's a spoilsport in every crowd, though. When I enthused about this discovery later to a friend, predicting that the chocolate-mousse popover would sweep the country and that eight-foot plastic popovers would soon be seen revolving on poles atop franchise restaurants, she gave me a withering glance and said, "You've just invented the cream puff."

---

### Still More Follow-Up

This is the last failed-popover theory for a while:

Esmé Evans, of Minneapolis, wrote to offer what she calls Evans's Theory of Relative Competence: Every time you figure out how to cook something new reasonably well, you cease being able to cook something you thought you had mastered.

She bets that Lynn Christine, who produced some of the worst-looking popovers ever to defile a table, must have "just learned how to make coulibiac or pithiviers or something else wonderful and therefore used up his competence quotient for the month."

"There was a year or two there, a while back," Evans wrote, "when every cake I made fell. I couldn't figure out what was the matter; I was using the same oven, same recipes, same ingredients, same everything, and yet the cakes, which looked fine when I tested them with a broom-straw, would heave great sighs of exhaustion and sink into weary little leatherlike puddles.

"Later on I realized that there was something fishy going on, and it had nothing to do with my abilities in the kitchen. What had happened was that I had just learned how to make baklava, and was impressing friends and coworkers with the results of my new skills. Needless to say, I had overdrawn my competence account, and the cosmic kitchen accountants decided to use my cake-making ability to cover the overdraft.

"The same thing happened when I started to make good pie crust; I suddenly lost all ability to separate eggs. It got so that I was unable to make a lemon meringue pie unless my husband was around to separate the eggs for me.

"I must say, things seem to have settled down lately, and I have no more than an average number of smushed cakes and yolk-flecked, unbeatable egg whites. And I still seem to be able to whomp out a reasonably tasty pie crust. I assume I can still make baklava, although I won't know for sure until next weekend, when I plan to make it after a year's hiatus. If it's awful, I'll let you know."

We'll be waiting.

---

### Final Follow-Up

Special note for readers of this book:

That's as far as I carried the Popover Predicament in the newspaper. By the time we got to Evans's Theory of Relative Competence I had had the course, weariness clouded my mind, and soon I had completely forgotten my promise to try using old eggs.

But for you, as long as you've already spent this much time on it, let me add a last—and possibly useful—bit of information.

When I realized, in looking over this peculiar bit of material, that I had never tried to make popovers with aged eggs, I took a carton of eggs that had been in my refrigerator a while anyway and moved it to the back, to ensure that I wouldn't accidentally use them up. A week after the "use-by" date on the end of the carton had expired, making them more than a month old, I made a batch of popovers. (Sorry I didn't wait longer than that. But I wanted to find out whether popovers can be made with old eggs, not whether popovers can be made with rotten eggs.)

To end a *very* long story, these popovers rose, but not very darn far. They weren't hockey pucks, but they were sort of muffins. The inside texture, while quite yielding, was uniform dough, not the yawning cavity one expects to find in a popover so that he can get more butter into it. They were not popovers.

So. While I don't want to say this is *the* reason that popovers might not work for some people (because I don't want any mail from people who have just made half-inch-high black-hole popovers using eggs just wrung from the chicken), I will tentatively offer the possibility that it is one reason that popovers might not work for some people. After all this work, I don't want to wind up with egg on my face. Even fresh egg.

# Using Up Parsley

Not long ago I was having breakfast at a restaurant counter, musing idly about whether I needed a new left-front tire, why I haven't made a million dollars and where babies come from, when I began to notice that the fellow next to me, who was placing his order, sounded like he was undergoing something like the Minnesota Multiphasic Personality Inventory.

Piecing it back together, the conversation between him and the person behind the counter went something like this:

"I'll have the No. 4 breakfast and coffee."

"How do you want your eggs?"

"Over easy."

"Bacon or sausage?"

"Sausage."

"Links or patties?"

"Links."

"Toast or muffin?"

"Toast."

"White or whole wheat?"

"Whole wheat."

"Regular or decaffeinated coffee?"

"Regular."

"Cream or sugar?"

"Sugar."

It seemed absolutely endless. But as I turned it over in my teeny mind I thought of several further questions that would represent only a logical extension of the process, and that some hapless customer might well encounter one fine day:

"Sugar or sweetener for your coffee?"

"Saccharin sweetener or Nutra-Sweet sweetener?"

"Cream, milk or non-dairy coffee whitener?"

"Butter or margarine on your toast?"

"Jelly or marmalade?"

"Apple jelly or cherry jelly?"

The whole thing could add up to rather an unpleasant experience for somebody who was having difficulty making decisions.

Then I thought of one option that I'd bet *nobody*—not even the most breathlessly eager teenage Burger-King-ette—will *ever* offer. And it's one I'd dearly love to be asked:

"Do you want us to throw sprigs of parsley all over the top of your food for no particular reason?"

No, I don't.

Don't misunderstand. I don't hate parsley (although there are many, I'm sure, who like it more than I do). It's just that, even in this age of varied choice, just about everybody thinks it's a neat idea to throw parsley on a plate of just about anything.

I'm sure, too, that there are some folks who eat the parsley that decorates their plates in restaurants. But I'm even surer that a whole lot of parsley goes right back to the kitchen with the dirty dishes.

What a tremendous saving restaurants could make if they switched to reusable plastic parsley for those who don't care to eat theirs.

("Real parsley or artificial?")

I'm told that parsley is a natural breath-freshener, and perhaps that is the origin of the custom of tossing it onto plates of food.

I dunno.

I do know that if you ate all the parsley that comes your way if you dine out very much, you might be kissing sweet a lot of the time but you'd probably have little green things stuck to your teeth a lot of the time, too.

A better suggestion is to save up all that parsley and use it to make something intentionally parsley-laden, like the recipes that follow.

No, serious-minded readers, I don't really mean that you should collect parsley in your pockets or purses and take it home.

That was just me engaging in one of my wild, zany bits of food humor. The only reason I said that was to end the introductory part of this article with a nod toward the recipe portion that follows.

Maybe, to avoid difficulty and misunderstanding, I should do that with more openness and honesty. I'll try.

That's all I have to say about parsley. Here are some recipes:

(Hmm. Honest, but awfully flat. Let me try something in between.)

Even if you don't frequent restaurants with UPS (unnecessary parsley syndrome), you might occasionally buy a big bunch of parsley at a supermarket, use the little bit that your recipe called for and wind up watching the rest of it wilt—or worse—in your refrigerator's produce compartment. Doctors call it Green Accumulation in Crisper-Keeper (GACK). Here are some recipes to help you use up a bunch of parsley before that can happen.

First, of course, a dip. You can vary the amount of parsley a great deal—to accommodate how much parsley you have.

---

## Variable Parsley Dip

1 cup dairy sour cream
1 bunch parsley, washed and chopped (or any lesser amount, for that matter)
1½ teaspoons or more crumbled dried basil

1 tablespoon oil
1 clove garlic, put through a garlic press
½ teaspoon or more salt
Pepper

Combine all ingredients. Serve with chips, crackers or raw vegetables. Serves 8.

---

That makes getting rid of parsley almost too easy. Let's move up one step in difficulty, or you won't respect parsley in the morning.

---

## Parsley Soup

2 leeks
1 medium onion
2 tablespoons butter

2 bunches parsley
3 (10¾-ounce) cans chicken broth
Salt, pepper

Wash the leeks thoroughly and cut them into 1-inch chunks (use only the white part and the bottom half of the green part). Wash the chunks. (Leeks acquire an amazing amount of grit inside them.) Chop them coarsely. Chop the onion coarsely.

Melt the butter in a Dutch oven and sauté the leeks and onions until the onions are translucent.

Wash and chop the parsley, including a few chopped stems. (Maybe I should have said this before: When chopped parsley is not going to be cooked, don't include the stems. They're twiggy. When the parsley is going to be cooked, it is a fine idea to include a few stems here and there.)

Add the parsley and the chicken broth, plus 2 soup cans of water, to the leeks and onions. Cover and simmer for 10 minutes. Pour through a strainer (into a second pot—we're keeping the broth because we're making soup; pay attention). Put the solids into a food processor or a blender (add a few tablespoons of liquid if necessary) and whomp them around until they're nicely puréed.

Return the purée to the broth by pressing it through the strainer, to remove any unpuréed bits. (If it's going to be mostly smooth it should be fully smooth.)

Add salt and pepper and heat to serving temperature. Serves 6 to 8.

It's true that there's fairly little that parsley *doesn't* go with nicely. That's probably why most folks don't really notice the sprig of parsley on their plates at restaurants—it doesn't actually clash with much.

But there are some things with which it goes especially well, and lamb is one of them.

This leg of lamb is an expensive little item, but it's awfully good, so don't be sheepish about serving it.

---

### Parsleyed Leg of Lamb

1 bunch parsley
2 sticks butter, 1 of them softened
3 tablespoons dried basil, crumbled
1 (4- to 5-pound) leg of lamb
3 medium onions

Salt, pepper
½ cup white wine
½ cup dry vermouth
¼ cup water
2 tablespoons cornstarch

Wash and chop the parsley, including a few stems. Combine the parsley, the softened butter and the crumbled basil. Trim fat from the lamb.

With a sharp knife make 6 or 8 deep cuts into the lamb, some on every surface but all widely separated. Force a large spoonful of the parsley mixture into each cut. Spread the remaining mixture over the top of the lamb.

Melt the other stick of butter and pour it into a roasting pan or a 9-by-13-inch pan. Preheat the oven to 300 degrees.

Peel the onions and slice them. Put the lamb in the pan with the melted butter and surround it with the sliced onions. Season all with salt and pepper and cover tightly. (If using a 9-by-13-inch pan, cover tightly with aluminum foil.)

Bake for 30 minutes, then raise oven temperature to 375 degrees, remove the cover and brown for another 30 minutes.

Pour the wine and vermouth over all, reduce the temperature to 300 degrees again, cover the pan and bake 1 more hour (total, 2 hours). This will leave a 4-pound roast done past pink, and a touch of pink in a 5-pound roast. Adjust time up or down, depending on how you like your lamb.

When the lamb is done, remove it to a serving dish and surround it with the onions. Stir the water into the cornstarch in a cup. Skim the fat from the cooking liquid (if you must, but it's very tasty) and pour the cooking liquid into a medium saucepan. Stir in the dissolved cornstarch and cook briefly, stirring, until the gravy has thickened.

You can make the gravy a few minutes early, if you like, by pouring or spooning off most of the cooking liquid before removing the lamb from the oven. Pour some gravy over the lamb and onions and serve the rest of the gravy separately. (I made the gravy a little early and forgot to serve it altogether. That was really too bad, because it was wonderful! I ate it over bread for days afterward.)

Serves 6 to 8.

---

Parsleyed potatoes is a possibility, but that hardly needs a recipe. So how about some pasta? That gives us a chance to get in some much-needed olive oil and garlic.

## Linguine with Parsley and Garlic

1 pound linguine
½ cup olive oil
2 cloves garlic

1 bunch parsley, washed and chopped
Salt, pepper

Prepare the linguine according to package directions. Drain. Meanwhile, heat the olive oil in a saucepan over medium heat. Put the garlic through a garlic press, add it to the oil and sauté very briefly—just until it begins to color. Don't let it darken or it will get bitter.

In a large bowl, toss the pasta with the oil, garlic, parsley, salt and pepper.

Serves 6 to 8.

---

For dessert . . . no, I didn't make anything with parsley for dessert. But I did make something green, mostly because it sounded good but partly to convince my guests (briefly, but it was fun) that I *had* made a parsley dessert.

What I served were little castles of tiny cream puffs, filled with lime custard and partly coated with thin, crackly-hard caramel.

Nummy!

You could skip the caramel part if you want, but I like it a lot.

---

## Amusing Green Dessert

PUFFS:

¾ cup milk
6 tablespoons butter
¾ cup sifted flour
⅛ teaspoon salt
3 eggs

FILLING:

1 cup sugar
6 tablespoons cornstarch
2 cups water
Pinch of salt

4 egg yolks
3 tablespoons butter
⅓ cup lime juice or juice of 2 limes
1 lime rind, grated
About 3 drops of green food coloring

CARAMEL:

2 cups sugar
⅔ cup water
2 tablespoons corn syrup
Whipped cream, for garnish

Make the puffs: Heat the milk in a medium saucepan. Stir in the butter, cut into chunks. Bring the milk to the boil. Reduce the heat to low-medium. Thoroughly stir in the sifted flour and the salt, and cook, stirring, until the mixture forms a ball and cleans the side of the pan. Remove the pan from the heat.

Stir in the eggs one at a time, being sure each egg is completely absorbed before adding the next one (or it gets really messy).

Preheat the oven to 425 degrees. Grease a cookie sheet.

With spoons or a pastry bag, place small ball-shaped mounds of the dough onto the cookie sheet. They should be something like 1 or 1¼ inches across. You will want to make 40 of them (5 each for 8 people), so judge accordingly as you move through the batter. Wet a fingertip with water and smooth down any very jagged peaks, which would otherwise burn.

Bake 15 minutes at 425 degrees, then turn the pan, lower the temperature to 375 degrees and bake 15 more minutes.

Remove them from the oven and let them cool a minute or two.

If you're going to fill the puffs with a pastry bag, poke a small hole in the bottom of each with a sharp knife and return them to the oven for 5 minutes to dry.

If you don't have a pastry bag, slice the top of each puff open about one-third of the way down—trying, if possible, to leave a hinge of dough still holding the cap to the rest of the puff. If you lose, you lose, but make the effort. Don't discard any caps that came off completely because we need to close those puffs after they're filled. Return the opened puffs to the oven for 5 minutes to dry.

Prepare the filling: In a saucepan over low heat, combine the sugar, cornstarch, water and salt. Cook, stirring, until the mixture thickens and eventually boils. Reduce heat to very low, cover, and cook 10 minutes, stirring occasionally.

Beat the egg yolks, and stir in a few spoonfuls of the hot mixture. Stir the diluted egg yolks into the hot mixture. Cook, stirring, 3 minutes longer.

Remove the mixture from the heat and stir in the butter until it melts. Add the lime juice, lime rind and food coloring.

Cool the mixture and, no more than a few hours before serving, fill the puffs, replacing any loose caps. Refrigerate the filled puffs. (Warning: They may get soggy if you keep them in the refrigerator for an extended period.)

If you like, you can stop here and serve the filled puffs in bowls with whipped cream over them or on the side.

Or you can go the extra mile and make the caramel: Grease a cookie sheet and get the serving plates or bowls ready, too.

Combine the sugar, water and corn syrup in a saucepan. Stir to dissolve the sugar, then cover the pan and bring to a boil over high heat without any further stirring. Once the boiling has gone on for 3 minutes, remove the cover but do not stir. Continue to boil for about 10 more minutes, until the syrup reaches about 300 degrees and has begun to color. (It's hard to see the color when it's boiling, so you might lower the heat when the temperature is about 300. Don't let the color get at all dark, or the syrup will taste burnt.)

As soon as the light color is reached, remove the pan from the heat, and, working rapidly—but carefully to avoid burning fingers in hot syrup—dip the top of each puff into the syrup and set it, dipped side down, on the greased cookie sheet.

After all 40 puffs are dipped, put 4 in a square, with the flat syrup "cap" up, on each serving dish. For each dish, lightly dip the bottom of one of the remaining puffs in the syrup and immediately position it on top of the four that are already in place. Serve with whipped cream on the side. Serves 8.

---

During dinner, one guest kept ducking into the bathroom to make sure she didn't have parsley in her teeth.

It occurred to me later that the appetizer dip should have contained parsley, sage, rosemary and thyme, so I tried it. (One cup dairy sour cream; one bunch parsley, chopped; and half a teaspoon each of sage, rosemary [crumbled] and thyme. I also tossed in a clove of garlic, pressed, and salt and pepper.) I thought it tasted like turkey dressing but a friend liked it, so I decided to include it but not prominently. Anybody who finds it here will know that I wasn't crazy about it. I don't want anybody turning green.

# A Digital Dinner

Well, it's almost April. I don't like being the person to tell you this, but you've got less than three weeks to finish up your income-tax returns.

So why are you sitting there on a Sunday morning wasting time with the food section when you've got work to do?

You just don't want to do it right now, do you?

That's understandable if you owe money—putting it off until the last minute makes sense in that case.

But even lots of people who have a refund coming still haven't gotten out the bottle of aspirin and last year's mound of miscellaneous scraps of paper and *done* it.

Maybe it's because chasing numbers around the dining-room table simply isn't your idea of a fun way to spend the afternoon. Perhaps you need something to put you in the mood.

Precisely why I am here.

In the same way that lots of people like to crack their knuckles before they begin to type or play the piano, some of us may need a little special warmup to get the old 1040 flowing.

I suggest cooking with numbers.

(What did you *think* I'd suggest in the food section? Playing tennis?)

There are quite a lot of numerical foods, so this won't be a difficult exercise. Here, for example, is a small selection of numerical goodies that I didn't use:

*A.1. Sauce*
*Nine-Grain Bread*
*Fourtune Cookies*
*Seven-Layer Salad*
*Three-Minute Eggs*
*Thousand Island Dressing*
*7-Up*
*Octopus*
*Nine Lives (if your cat dines with you)*
*Doughnuts, Bagels or Cheerios*

There's also Mont Blanc, but even I will grant that that's a little obscure. Only people who read headlines in the sports pages think of blank as a number. They think of it as a verb, too.

To hold our investigation to a reasonable list, I decided to restrict myself to foods named with single numerals (or digits, if you like)—the integers from 0 to 9. That way we won't have to deal with thousand-year eggs, millefeuille ("thousand leaves"—the French name for what we call the Napoleon) or millet.

For lack of a better term, I'm calling my choices digital foods. That way we can sound stylishly computerized. If you want to carry that electronic idea further, you could throw some chips—chocolate, butterscotch or peanut butter—into one of the recipes, but I don't think that's necessary.

Because I've been kind of busy lately, I didn't try recipes representing all ten digits.

Here's what we eight:

*Two-na Appetizer*
*Three-Bean Salad*
*Six-Legume Soup*
*Fettuccine with Five Cheeses*
*Petits Fours*

Having already chosen to make the Fettuccine with Five Cheeses, I came across something else nice while shopping, so I decided to toss it in. *Quince jelly* (on toast points).

Fourgive me if you can.

So. As they say in the analyst business, let's begin at the beginning.

This appetizer is slightly adapted from one in *Best Loved Recipes of the American People,* by Ida Bailey Allen. I picked it because it looked nice, but it deserves better billing than that. The little canapes were very good indeed—and when folks had gone home and I was cleaning up, I ate several of the leftovers cold. They weren't bad that way, either.

So the extras didn't go for (ahem) naught.

---

### Two-na Appetizer

3 tablespoons butter
3 tablespoons flour
½ teaspoon salt
Pepper
1 cup milk
½ cup finely chopped Brazil nuts
2 tablespoons chopped green pepper
2 tablespoons chopped onion
½ teaspoon Worcestershire sauce
1 (6½- to 7-ounce) can tuna
8 slices bread
Pimiento strips (optional)
Slices of Brazil nuts

Melt the butter in a saucepan, blend in the flour, salt and pepper. Let cook a minute or so over low heat, then gradually stir in the milk. Continue cooking and stirring until the sauce is thickened and smooth.

Add the chopped nuts, green pepper, onion, Worcestershire sauce and tuna. Set aside.

Toast the bread and cut into wedges, strips, triangles, diamonds or whatever pleases your little heart.

Just before you plan to serve them, spread the tuna mixture on the toast shapes, place them on a cookie sheet and run them under the broiler a minute or two (or more, until they are heated through).

Garnish each with a strip of pimiento, if you like, and a slice of Brazil nut.

Makes 24 or so, depending on how small you cut the toast shapes.

---

Next comes the salad, a traditional American favorite that needs no introduction. The only reason I'm introducing it is to mention that tastes in this matter do vary.

Some found the salad just what the arithmetic teacher ordered; others would have preferred it with a bit more vinegar. I won't try to make that decision for you (that's just not my number).

---

### Three-Bean Salad

1 (16-ounce) can cut green beans
1 (16-ounce) can wax beans
1 (15-ounce) can kidney beans
1 medium green pepper
1 medium onion
3 tablespoons sugar
1 teaspoon salt
⅛ teaspoon pepper
½ cup olive oil
6 tablespoons vinegar (or more, he noted acidly)

Drain all three cans of beans well. Use a sieve. An awful lot of liquid remains in the beans if you just tip the can to drain them, and it dilutes the flavor of the dressing.

Chop the green pepper. Cut off about 3 slices of onion, break them into rings and chop the rest of the onion finely (or finally).

Combine beans, green pepper, onion, sugar, salt, pepper, oil and vinegar. Stir well, cover and refrigerate several hours for flavors to blend.

Serves 6.

---

Now to the nice, thick soup. The recipe on which this one is based was called Seven-Bean Soup. It included kidney beans. Since we just *had* kidney beans, I decided to leave them out.

And since, on subjecting the recipe to the minute scrutiny that prudence demands (and patience tolerates) it became apparent that two of the remaining beans were peas, I felt justified in renaming it altogether.

Besides, I was already back from the grocery store before I realized that both salad and soup were based on beans. I figured that, with the soup renamed, the combination wouldn't seem quite so much like I was on some kind of bean toot.

This is an ideal recipe for using up the little half-bags of dried beans and peas that are collecting in your cupboard. If you don't have such a collection, this is an ideal recipe for starting one.

---

### Six-Legume Soup

¼ **cup dried yellow split peas**
¼ **cup dried green split peas**
¼ **cup dried Great Northern beans**
¼ **cup dried lima beans**
¼ **cup dried pinto beans**
¼ **cup dried garbanzo beans**
1 **large onion**
1 **medium green pepper**
1 **rib celery**
1 **carrot**
1 **clove garlic**

2 **tablespoons butter**
2 **bay leaves**
¼ **teaspoon marjoram**
¼ **teaspoon basil**
1 **teaspoon salt**
**Pepper**
4 **beef bouillon cubes (or 4 teaspoons beef bouillon granules)**
1 **cup chopped ripe tomato (or 1 8-ounce can tomato sauce)**
¼ **cup ketchup**

Thoroughly wash and pick over the peas and beans, discarding anything that doesn't look like a pea or a bean. Put them in 6 cups of water in a Dutch oven and bring to the boil. Continue to boil 2 minutes, then remove from the heat, cover and let stand 1 hour. Skim the surface.

Return the beans to low-medium heat and cook about 1½ hours, until they are tender.

Chop the onion, green pepper, celery and carrot and put them in a large saucepan. Put the garlic through a garlic press and add it and the butter. Add 5 cups of water and bring the whole thing to the boil. Continue cooking 20 to 25 minutes until the vegetables are tender.

Drain off and retain the bean cooking liquid. Add the vegetables and their cooking liquid to the beans, and add the bay leaves, marjoram, basil, salt and pepper. Crush the bouillon cubes and add them (or use bouillon granules), and stir in the tomatoes (or tomato sauce) and the ketchup.

Simmer for half an hour or so, adding bean liquid as needed to achieve the kind of consistency you like.

Fish out the bay leaves if you're any kind of person at all, and serve. Makes about 8 servings.

---

Fettuccine has a way of cropping up (and getting misspelled) in lots of recipes these days. Here's another one. This one's pretty good.

This recipe, too, calls for an assortment of things you probably don't have sitting around, but they have the advantage of being cheeses and subject to being used easily in other dishes (or just being eaten, as the produce folks say, "out of hand").

## Fettuccine with Five Cheeses

1 pound fettuccine
3 tablespoons unsalted butter
1 cup grated fontina cheese
1 cup grated Parmesan cheese
3/4 cup ricotta cheese
1/4 cup crumbled gorgonzola cheese

1/4 cup grated Romano cheese
2 tablespoons milk
1/2 cup heavy cream
1 tablespoon brandy (optional)
Salt, pepper

Cook the fettuccine according to package directions.

Meanwhile, melt the butter in a saucepan over low heat. Add the cheeses and heat, stirring, until they are just melted. Stir in the milk and the cream (stop short of the 1/2 cup if the sauce is getting thin). Add the brandy, if you like, and salt and pepper to taste.

Drain the fettuccine, put in a large bowl or several individual bowls and pour the sauce over it. Serves 4 to 6.

Now comes dessert, and none too soon.

What with two-na, three-bean salad, six-legume soup and five-cheese fettuccine, I've been waiting for it for a total of sixteen.

I've always loved petits fours. When I was growing up in Milwaukee and would, like other kids, occasionally get a quarter or fifty cents to spend, while other kids would get squirt guns or jacks or barrettes, I would go to the bakery a few blocks away and buy a petit four or two. (That would be a petit eight.)

They are so *pretty* and so *good!*

The name is really a generic for all kinds of little oven goodies, but one kind has come to corner the market, as it were. The standard petit four—imagine such a phrase!—is little pieces of rich cake (typically genoise, the French sponge cake), dipped in a fruit glaze and then coated with a firm, shiny icing and decorated (with a flower of frosting, perhaps, or a candied violet or some such). Sometimes the cake is cut apart and a gooey filling inserted before the glaze and frosting are applied.

These were surprisingly easy to make.

Not easy, mind you, but not as dreadfully difficult as I had thought they might be.

**CAKE:**

3½ tablespoons butter
4 eggs
¾ cup sugar, sifted
1 teaspoon vanilla
1 teaspoon grated lemon rind
¾ cup sifted cake flour

**OPTIONAL FILLING (ENOUGH FOR ABOUT HALF THE PETITS FOURS):**

1½ tablespoons unsalted butter
½ cup heavy cream
4 ounces semisweet chocolate

**GLAZE:**

1½ cups (1 18-ounce jar) apricot
  preserves
⅜ cup water

**ICING:**

7½ cups confectioners' sugar (about 2
  pounds)
7½ tablespoons light corn syrup
7½ tablespoons water

**OPTIONAL DECORATIONS:**

**Candied violets**
**Chocolate jimmies**
**etc.**
**or:**

**FROSTING FOR DECORATING:**

1 tablespoon water
1 cup confectioners' sugar
Food colorings

Prepare the cake: Preheat the oven to 350 degrees. Grease a 9-by-13-inch pan, line the bottom, sides and ends of the pan with waxed paper and grease the waxed paper. Set aside.

Melt the 3½ tablespoons of butter in a small pan over very low heat. Allow the foam to subside and gently pour the clear part of the butter into a teacup or something else handy, leaving the milky residue in the pan. What you have in the cup is about 3 tablespoons of clarified butter.

Bring an inch or two of water just to the simmer in a saucepan. Turn the heat to low to keep it from boiling. Put the eggs, sugar, vanilla and lemon rind in a large mixer bowl and set it on top of the pan of simmering water, so that it does not rest in the water. Beat the mixture with an electric mixer at low to medium speed, or, if you're a glutton for punishment (and authenticity), use a wire whisk. In any case, beat until it foams and volume is almost doubled.

Take the mixer bowl off the heat and beat with a mixer at high speed several minutes until the batter becomes very thick. (It should flow off the beaters in a single wide ribbon that stays on the

surface briefly before it dissolves.) Add a third of the flour and fold gently. Fold in a third of the clarified butter. Repeat until all the flour and butter are folded in.

Pour and spread the batter into the prepared pan. Bake 20 to 25 minutes until the cake tests done with a toothpick and springs back when touched.

While the cake is in the oven, prepare the optional filling if you're going to use it: Put the butter and the cream in a saucepan and bring the mixture to the boil over low to medium heat. Add the chocolate, stirring until it is melted. Pour the mixture into the small bowl of the mixer and cool it in the refrigerator until it is like honey.

When the cake is done, cool it in its pan on a wire rack 10 minutes, then loosen the edges, invert the cake and re-move the pan. Gently peel off the waxed paper, then turn the cake right side up on the rack and allow it to cool completely.

When it is cool, trim away the dry, hard edges (and eat them as your reward for getting this far; they're pretty good). Cut the cake into small diamonds, rectangles, parallelograms, circles or whatever. A variety of shapes makes a more attractive presentation. Don't make them large. A couple of dainty bites is all they ought to be good for. One inch by two or so is a fine size for the rectangles and parallelograms, for example. A few especially tiny circles (use the center of a doughnut cutter) are nice, too.

If you're going to be filling some petits fours, slice those in half crosswise now. Check on the filling mixture in the refrigerator, and when it is thickened, whip it with the electric mixer until it is light and spreadable. Spread it on the bottom halves of the petit fours that are to be filled and put the tops back on them. Lick the bowl. (Nice, huh?)

Prepare the glaze: Heat the apricot preserves and water in a saucepan over low heat, stirring, until the mixture begins to bubble. Keep going 2 or 3 more minutes, then remove it from the heat and push it through a wire sieve. Discard or eat the stuff that remains in the sieve. Let the strained preserves cool slightly.

The next step sounds harder than it is. We're going to dip the petits fours in the apricot glaze so that the glaze covers the tops and all 4 sides. Set some wire racks over cookie sheets. Spear one of the cakes from the bottom with a large 2-tined meat fork (start with the unfilled ones, to get the hang of it, and to keep chocolate filling out of the glaze that goes on the unfilled ones). The petits fours stay on the fork better if you insert it at an angle.

Dip each cake almost all the way in, so top and sides are covered, and then ease it off the fork, onto a wire rack, undipped side down and an inch or more away from other dipped cakes. (The cookie sheet is to catch the drips.) Let the cakes stand about an hour, uncovered, to allow the glaze to set.

When ready to ice the petits fours, put clean cookie sheets under them. Prepare the icing: Bring some water to the simmer in the bottom of a double boiler. Turn the heat down to keep it at a simmer. Sift the $7\frac{1}{2}$ cups of confectioners' sugar, and put it and the corn syrup and the $7\frac{1}{2}$ tablespoons of water into the top of the double boiler. Heat, stirring, until the sugar dissolves and the icing is quite smooth. Take the double boiler off the heat, but keep the icing over the hot water to keep it liquid.

Now comes another part that sounds tricky but isn't: Using a large spoon or ladle, pour enough icing over the top of a petit four so that it covers the top and runs down and covers all 4 sides. (Move the ladle around to get sides that aren't getting enough on their own.) Don't figure on coming back to give them a second coat to cover missed spots; that would look patchy. Don't worry if it looks like there might not be enough icing; the stuff that runs or drips off onto the cookie sheets can be scraped up and gently reheated in the double boiler to cover the remaining petits fours.

Let the petits fours dry 1 hour, then decorate them and transfer them to a serving plate (or transfer them first and then decorate them). To decorate, use candied violets, chocolate jimmies or whatever, and/or prepare decorative frosting:

Blend the tablespoon of water into the cup of confectioners' sugar (adjust so frosting is thick but not dry). Divide into small bowls and color some green, some yellow, etc., for making simple flowers. Load the frosting into a pastry tube and have your way with it. Or use a bunch of envelopes, cutting off a tiny tip of the corner to pipe thin lines, a wider slit (pinched almost shut) to shape leaves, and so forth.

Store in a cool, dry place where you can't get at them until you are ready to serve them. They're wonderful.

When the writer polished off the last of the petits fours, he had a Three Musketeers bar.

# *Binkies and Bostess Bupcakes*

I was thinking the other day, while eating a Twinkie, about the recent Hostess advertising campaign that featured the slogan "Freshness never tasted so good." Lest I give the wrong impression, I should point out immediately that I *like* Hostess Cupcakes, Twinkies, Ding Dongs, Ho Hos and the rest. I eat a lot of them.

But, I reflected, I've never thought of them as fresh. I've thought of them as great-tasting, wonderful junk.

It is true that unlike, say, Cool Whip, which you keep in your freezer but which is claimed to "taste fresh as homemade," the Hostess products really are made relatively soon before you eat them. According to a Hostess spokesperson, the "sell before" date stamped on the package should be no more than four or five days from the date the product comes out of the oven.

Nonetheless, I wouldn't normally call a cupcake baked on Monday "fresh" on Friday. If you really wanted a *fresh* Twinkie, I've said to myself almost every time I heard that "freshness never tasted so good" commercial, you'd have to make it yourself.

So I decided to try to do just that. You can't make Twinkies, of course, or Ding Dongs, Ho Hos or Hostess Cupcakes, because those are product names owned by ITT Continental Baking Company, Rye, New York. (Actually, ITT Continental Baking Company, Rye, New York, has subsequently become Continental Baking Company, Checkerboard Square, St. Louis, Missouri. Did you really care?) But you could make something rather like them—say Binkies, Bing Bongs, Bo Bos and Bostess Bupcakes.

Although the items I'm suggesting are imitations, they aren't mock products like the mock apple pie made with Ritz crackers instead of apples. If you can make your own, you can not only make them fresh, you can make them realer than the things they're imitating—with lots of real chocolate instead of so much cocoa, and with whipped cream instead of sweetened whipped shortening.

That way, freshness would taste very good indeed.

Note: Don't use aerosol whipped cream to fill any of these items. It contains *much* more gas than home-whipped heavy cream, and it deflates very quickly. (Eight ounces of cream whips into a pint at home; seven ounces of aerosol cream produces a quart.)

I decided to tackle what seemed to me to be the most difficult item, the Binkie, first. Making the sponge cake batter wouldn't be hard. But the Binkie, to be successful, has to look like a Twinkie, and I'm not aware of any pans with that shape.

So I made some Binkie molds. That turned out not to be very difficult after all, and the Binkies, if I say so myself (and I do), were stunning.

Real whipped cream tastes *lots* better than the standard filling, and, in addition, the filled Binkie is very, very light.

After I ate my first Binkie, I ate a Twinkie (which, I repeat, I have always enjoyed) and there was absolutely no comparison.

---

### Binkies

**(Requires a pastry bag)**
**Lots of aluminum foil**
**3 eggs**
**1 cup sugar**
**¼ cup boiling water**
**1 cup sifted cake flour**

**1½ teaspoons baking powder**
**1½ teaspoons vanilla, divided**
**¼ teaspoon salt**
**1½ cups heavy cream (you might not use it all)**
**2 teaspoons confectioners' sugar**

Prepare 9 Binkie molds as follows (it sounds hard, but it's not):

For each mold, tear off about a 9-inch piece of 12-inch-wide aluminum foil. Fold it in half first one way and then the other. You wind up with a piece of foil about 4½ inches by 6.

Grease one side with solid shortening or margarine. Bend up the longer sides to form the folded foil into a U-shaped trough (6 inches long, about 1½ inches across the rounded bottom and maybe 1½ inches high). Lift one end of the bottom up and in, then turn the sides together at that end, overlapping slightly. Repeat with the other end, forming something like a little bathtub.

Mash the bottoms of the bathtub ends smooth, then fasten the tops of the ends (the head and the foot of the bathtub rim) together by firmly folding the overlapped edge down a little. Making 9 of these won't take you 10 minutes.

The Binkie recipe makes about 18, so you'll use the molds twice. Rather than

trying to regrease the crumb-laden molds after the first use, flatten them out, grease what had been the outside and use that as the inside for the second batch.

O.K.? Molds in place, panel? Then let's go ahead and make Binkies!

Preheat the oven to 325 degrees.

Separate the eggs, putting the yolks in a large mixing bowl and the whites in a small one. Beat the yolks until they are very light. Into the beaten egg yolks, gradually beat the sugar, then the boiling water.

Resift the sifted cake flour with the baking powder, and gradually add the combination to the yolk mixture, beating until the mixture is well blended. Beat in 1 teaspoon of the vanilla. Set aside.

Wash the beaters carefully—there must be no egg yolk on them. Add the salt to the egg whites and beat them until they are stiff but still glossy. Stir a spatulaful of the egg whites into the yolk-flour mixture to lighten it, then lightly fold in the remainder of the whites, incorporating them well but gently.

Pour about 2 heaped tablespoons of the batter into a Binkie mold. The batter will flow, perhaps slowly, into the corners. When it has evened out it should be about half an inch deep (it rises rather a lot during baking).

Because getting the size just right is important, you might try filling and baking one mold first to see whether you are using the right amount of batter. Too little produces a Binkie too short to have enough space inside for filling; too much produces a Binkie that's perfectly fine for eating but looks kind of like a bus.

To bake, arrange 4 or 5 Binkie molds snugly in a loaf pan and bake in the 325-degree oven about 15 to 20 minutes, until 1 or 2 minutes *after* they test done with a toothpick. The top probably will not look very brown.

Allow the Binkies to cool for a few minutes. Using a sharp knife and flexing the molds, gently free the sides of the Binkies and invert them onto a cooling rack. If they don't drop out easily, gently peel the foil away from the Binkies (not vice versa).

Before the Binkies have cooled, use a toothpick as follows to make the holes in the light sponge cake that will hold the whipped cream:

Pierce the flat bottom of each Binkie (the side that was up while it was baking) 3 times—in the middle and halfway toward each end. Wiggle the toothpick around in a circular fashion to enlarge (and perhaps connect) the cavities (but keep the entrance holes as small as you can). Don't go in so far that the toothpick is in any danger of coming out the other side.

Pour the heavy cream into a small bowl, stir in the confectioners' sugar and the last half teaspoon of vanilla, and beat until very stiff. (You might wind up having some of it left, but there are worse things than having leftover whipped cream.)

Fit a pastry bag with your smallest nozzle and fill the bag with the whipped cream. Inserting the nozzle fairly deep, force the cream into each of the holes in the Binkies until it just begins to come back out.

Eat, smacking lips.

Makes about 18 Binkies.

As with all treats containing whipped cream, any Binkies not eaten immediately should be refrigerated. But if they have been refrigerated, they are best if they are allowed to warm for half an hour or so before serving.

If left uncovered long, even in the refrigerator, the outsides of the Binkies get rather crunchy—an undesirable trait in a Binkie—so they should be kept in plastic bags.

They'll get moist in the bags after a few days, so that's about as long as you can keep them.

---

Next, on to the easiest of the things I attempted, the Bostess Bupcakes. That they were relatively easy does not, however, mean that they were less than wonderful.

In fact, they were fantastic.

In addition to the whipped cream, they contain chocolate. To my mind, this gives them a real edge over the Binkies.

It isn't difficult to make a cream-filled cupcake. You can start with any cupcake recipe you want, including one made with cake mix.

But I wanted to make one that would be at least as good as the Hostess version (which is really pretty good).

In my search for the proper Bupcake batter, I was guided by several concerns:

- It must be dark, like the original.
- It must be moist, like the original.
- And it must use only real chocolate (unlike the original).

I think I found the recipe.

---

### Bostess Bupcakes

4 (1-ounce) squares unsweetened chocolate
1 cup milk, divided
1 cup brown sugar
2 eggs plus 1 egg yolk
1/2 cup butter
1 cup white sugar
1/4 cup water
1 teaspoon vanilla
2 cups sifted cake flour
1 teaspoon soda
1/2 teaspoon salt

FILLING:

Raspberry jelly (optional)
2 teaspoons confectioners' sugar

1/2 teaspoon vanilla
1 1/2 cups heavy cream (you might not use all of it)

FROSTING:

2 (1-ounce) squares unsweetened chocolate
1 tablespoon butter
1/4 cup hot water
1/8 teaspoon salt
1 3/4 to 2 cups confectioners' sugar
1 teaspoon vanilla

DECORATIVE ICING:

3/4 cup confectioners' sugar
2 to 3 teaspoons milk

Preheat the oven to 325 degrees. Put the chocolate, 1/2 cup of the milk, the brown sugar and 1 egg yolk into a small saucepan.

Cook over very low heat, stirring constantly, until it has thickened. If it begins to boil, get it off the heat—it has cooked enough. Set the mixture aside to cool.

In a large mixing bowl, beat the butter until it has softened. Sift in the white sugar gradually, continuing to beat until the butter-sugar mixture is light and creamy.

Separate the 2 whole eggs, putting the whites into a small mixing bowl. Beat the yolks, one at a time, into the butter-sugar mixture. In a cup, combine the water, the remaining 1/2 cup of milk and the vanilla.

Resift the sifted cake flour with the soda and salt and add to the butter mixture in thirds, alternating with thirds of the milk mixture. Beat the batter after each

addition until it is smooth. Stir in the chocolate mixture and mix until well blended.

Clean the beaters thoroughly. Beat the egg whites until they are stiff but still glossy. Stir a spatulaful of the whites into the chocolate batter to lighten it. Then lightly fold in the remaining whites, incorporating them well but gently.

Fill well-greased cupcake or muffin tins just a little more than half full. Bake between 12 and 15 minutes, turning the tins once for even baking, and remove them when a toothpick tests absolutely clean. If in doubt, give them an extra minute. They'll tear if they're not fully done. Allow them to cool in the pans for 5 minutes, run a knife around each Bupcake, invert the tins and stand Bupcakes right side up to cool.

When they are cool, use a sharp knife to slice off a bit of each top—a sliver about the size of a 25-cent piece. (Some cooks would take off the whole top, but this would show later, and is most un-Hostess-like.) Save the slivers; we'll be using them.

Using a teaspoon, carefully scoop out a nice chunk of the inside of each Bupcake, but leave plenty of bottom and sides intact—both for strength and because it makes the Bupcake taste good. This stuff is so good, in fact, that you should save the scooped-out parts. (Put some in a bowl with milk or cream sometime. Great.)

Let the scooped-out Bupcakes cool completely. If you like, you can depart from the standard Bostess Bupcake by putting a dab of raspberry jelly into each of the Bupcake cavities before filling them with whipped cream. It's not authentic, but it's delicious.

In any case, stir the confectioners' sugar and the $1/2$ teaspoon of vanilla into the heavy cream and beat it until it is very stiff. With a spoon or spatula, press the cream into the cooled Bupcakes and more or less level off the tops.

Reposition a removed sliver of Bupcake top back onto each Bupcake. (Without it the cream would make the frosting hard to spread.)

Put the Bupcakes into the refrigerator while you make the frosting: Melt the chocolate and butter together over very low heat. Add the hot water and salt. Sift in half the confectioners' sugar, stirring. Add the vanilla and then, while stirring, sift in as much of the rest of the confectioners' sugar as is needed to make a reasonably thick frosting.

Frost the Bupcakes rapidly, before the frosting hardens. Return them to the refrigerator while you make the decorative icing.

You can, of course, buy the icing for the decoration in little plastic tubes at the grocery store, but it's not any work to make it yourself: Stir the milk into the confectioners' sugar. Put the icing into a pastry bag with a tiny tip, or roll a narrow cornucopia with a tiny point out of a piece of good-quality (heavy) letter paper. (Pin the cornucopia together on the side.)

You can make the decoration any way you want it, of course, or you could even skip it. The Hostess Cupcake is decorated with a line of loops. I used a wavy line for my Bupcakes, just in case Hostess has a trademark on the line of loops.

Eat, sighing and groaning.

Makes 20 to 24 Bupcakes. Like Binkies, they must be kept refrigerated and are best if allowed to warm up for half an hour or so before serving.

---

Now to Bing Bongs. These are really just short Bostess Bupcakes, but instead of being frosted on top they are fully covered—top, bottom and sides—with semi-sweet chocolate. (The Hostess versions, of course, are coated with a less costly—and less tasty—product). The finished items look like hockey pucks.

Because it takes a fair amount of expensive chocolate to encase a batch of Bing Bongs, and because the work is fairly messy and can be rather frustrating, I wouldn't advise making Bing Bongs except to serve to people who *really* love chocolate. If you're not sure, stick to Bupcakes.

*Bing Bongs*  1 recipe Bostess Bupcake batter (see preceding recipe)
1 recipe filling for Bostess Bupcakes

(see preceding recipe)
12 ounces semisweet chocolate
4 tablespoons butter or margarine

Prepare the batter as for Bostess Bupcakes, but fill the muffin tins a bit less than half full (producing maybe 30 Bing Bongs). Bake and fill as for Bostess Bupcakes, being careful to flake off any easily removed crumbs on the bottom and sides. Line a baking sheet with waxed paper and put the filled Bing Bongs on it upside-down.

Making Binkies sounds hard but is easy. Coating Bing Bongs sounds easy but is hard. I'm sure that wonderful machines, closely guarded by the Continental Baking Company, Checkerboard Square, St. Louis, have been developed for this process. I don't have one. Neither, I suspect, do you. So we'll have to do it the hard way:

Over very low heat, melt the 12 ounces of semisweet chocolate (or probably more, depending on how good you are at this), along with the butter or margarine.

When all the chocolate is fully melted, use a metal spatula or putty knife to spread some chocolate (as little as possible) evenly across the bottom of each Bing Bong; invert them on the waxed paper and coat the tops and sides. Refrigerate.

(That paragraph condenses into a few seconds' reading what can seem like a lifetime of messy agony if you're trying to do it. But if you're not compulsive about making them extra-neat, it needn't be too difficult. And they'll taste *wonderful.*)

Like Binkies and Bostess Bupcakes, Bing Bongs must be kept refrigerated, and they also benefit from being allowed to warm up for half an hour or so before they are served. Depending on the temperature of the room you're serving them in, though, the chocolate might get sticky.

I had planned to describe here how to make Bo Bos, miniature cake rolls consisting of chocolate cake and whipped cream, covered, like Bing Bongs, with semisweet chocolate. I must instead report total failure.

I tried four separate times, using three different recipes, to make a chocolate cake roll that could be thin enough, and rolled tightly enough, to make a roll an inch or so in diameter. Every single one broke. Some broke many times. It made me appreciate Hostess all the more.

A last note: Since I began to work on the Binkies, etc., the "freshness never tasted so good" advertising campaign seems to have disappeared. In its stead is one that begins with a guy in a hard hat biting into a Hostess Fruit Pie and saying something like, "Mmmmm. Real apples!" That one made me wonder, too. Where has this guy been getting desserts made with un-real apples? Then I figured it out. Somebody had been stuffing his pie with Ritz crackers.

# Classified Ads for Recipes

**MONEY-SAVING OFFER: Send me $10 for the amazing secret of those classified ads for recipes that appear in the backs of magazines.**

You've probably wondered about them. You know which ads I mean. They offer things like "My Fantastic Chili" for only $2.

I've wondered, too.

When I first noticed them, several years ago, I dismissed them out of hand. Who needs to buy recipes blind like that, I thought, when you can examine cookbooks and buy what appeals to you? This phenomenon was bound to disappear soon. A flash, in other words, in the pan.

But they're still showing up, and I decided that it was time to look into them.

**SEND ME $5 and you'll learn what happened.**

There are really two basic questions: How good are these recipes—that is, do you get your money's worth if you send for them? And could you make a killing selling the family recipe for cod-liver soup?

My survey was not exhaustive. I picked up a copy of the *Atlantic* and selected five recipe ads from the twenty-five that appeared there. They were for "Danish Dumplings—rave-producing-melt-in-your-mouth"; "Prize-Winning Italian Dessert"; "First time offered. Three outstanding award-winning cakes"; "Sauerkraut Fudge Cake—bewilderingly delicious. No description suffices"; and "Icy Tea-Based Refresher perfect for summer."

Not a balanced list, perhaps, but I like dessert. And some of the others didn't exactly sweep me off my feet: "Easy, 4 noodle puddings"; "Kosher Stuffed Peppers"; "Family secrets revealed. Fast, easy, economical recipes"; and "Artichoke heart spread/Cranberry Sunset. Hors d'oeuvre and drink—let's [sic] time stand still."

Actually, these ads are kind of fun to read. One in a *Harper's* magazine offered five chicken soup recipes. It began "Surprise ailing friends with exotic home remedy." And in a *Saturday Review* I came across "Elegant brownie recipe, entertaining or family." Kind of hard to picture that one.

### HOW ABOUT sending me $3.50 and I'll throw in the recipes?

I sent off the total of $10 that the five ads in the *Atlantic* required. All the addresses were either post-office boxes or street addresses without names, so I had to send checks without names filled in. That's a very peculiar sensation: it felt as if I were begging to be ripped off.

Actually, because I had to put 18 cents postage each on both my requests and the self-addressed, stamped envelopes that all the ads required, the total outlay for the five recipes was $11.80. (Yes, I did this research in the pre-Cambrian era, when postage was a mere 18 cents, but I think my findings will stand the test of time.)

If $11.80 doesn't already sound outrageous, consider that at that rate a copy of *Joy of Cooking* would cost you more than $6,000. And it would come in lots and lots of little pieces.

### SO SURELY knowing how this all came out is worth a measly $2.50 to you.

Well, O.K., I'll tell you a little more for free.

The first recipe to arrive was Danish dumplings. The sender had written "Danish Dumplings" in the return-address spot on the stamped envelope I'd sent, and I'm sure that the mailman figured it was pornography.

Anyway, what I got for my $2.36 was a badly cut quarter of a sheet of paper containing a recipe, crudely duplicated, for dumplings. The paper cutting was clearly an effort on the part of the sender to reduce costs—from maybe 10 cents to maybe 2½ cents. I resented it. The recipe produced dumplings that were, well, dumplings. Maybe a little fluffier than most. On the other hand, maybe not.

Then came Icy Tea-Based Refresher. This recipe was mimeographed, on a third of a sheet of paper (more cost-cutting).

As written it produced seven quarts. "That's a lot of Icy Tea-Based Refresher," I said to myself, and I cut it in half. I'm glad I did. Three guests and I drank one glass each. Nobody wanted seconds. The consensus was that if there were a tea-flavor Kool-Aid, it would probably taste lots better than Icy Tea-Based Refresher, which was watery, sweet and flat. I poured the other 2½ quarts down the sink. To keep it sweet-smelling.

The next recipe to arrive was the only one worth the trouble of sending away for, although I'm still not sure that any recipe is worth $2.36. This was the recipe for Sauerkraut Fudge Cake. It was nicely typed on a full sheet of paper, cleanly duplicated, and was accompanied by a bonus recipe, on another sheet—this one for Prune-Spice Cake. There was also a note suggesting that I might want to send for some additional cake recipes, and the note was signed (albeit illegibly). It felt like I was doing business with somebody instead of throwing money away.

And the recipe was pretty good. It contained much more chocolate (both cocoa and semisweet chocolate pieces) than the standard sauerkraut chocolate cake, and it also contained a half-pint of sour cream that isn't in the more traditional recipe. And the frosting went with it very well. The folks who ate it liked it a lot.

Then came "Prize-Winning Italian Dessert." Any feelings I had about being ripped off by the first two recipes were nothing compared with this one. It was photocopied directly from a cookbook! So much for copyright laws. Besides that, it's a fairly standard recipe that must appear in darn-near half of the general-purpose cookbooks on the shelves.

It's for Sabayon (or Zabaglione or Zabaione or three or four other spellings)—a French or Italian dessert that might have won a prize in the nineteenth century but has hardly been unusual enough to do so since. (Is the hot dog a prize-winning American delicacy?)

Anyway, I made it and it tasted more or less like it was supposed to. Actually, it was kind of heavy on the wine.

The last thing I ordered (the three outstanding, award-winning cakes for $3) never arrived. Somehow, although I could feel stung on that one, I don't mind it as much as the photocopied page out of the cookbook.

**FOR $1.25, I'll tell you the end of the story.**

**No? Frankly, I'm puzzled. Here I am, willing to part with more than $8.44 worth of recipes and a whole lot more insightful stuff for a mere $1.25 (licensed drivers only, please; you must be over eighteen to enter; offer void where prohibited) and you're not interested. What do I have to do?**

Well, let me tell you just a little more, then.

How about if I give you the recipes I got—just the way I got them?

I might have felt bad about giving away other people's recipes like that (except, of course, for the Sabayon). But I don't, because of what I learned later. I won't tell you *that* for nothing.

---

### Sabayon (or Zabaglione)

6 egg yolks
⅔ cup sugar
Grated rind of half an orange

1 cup [or less] white wine or marsala
1 tablespoon rum or kirsch (optional)

Put cold water in the bottom of a double boiler. Put egg yolks and sugar in the top of the double boiler but do not place over the heat.

Whip the yolks and sugar. Add the orange rind and the wine [you might like to cut the wine in half] and beat constantly [for a minute or so].

Put the pan [the whole double boiler] on the heat and beat constantly until the sauce is thick and creamy. Remove from heat. Add the rum or kirsch if you like.

Serve hot. (Serves 6 as a hot pudding or drink.)

---

That saved you $2.36.

---

**Danish Dumplings**

1 cup water
½ cup butter
1 cup flour
¼ teaspoon salt
2 teaspoons baking powder

4 eggs
3 tablespoons chopped parsley
1 (10¾-ounce) can condensed chicken broth (or stew or other accompaniment to dumplings)

Bring water and butter to a boil. Add flour, salt and baking powder. Mix and cook one minute until mixture holds together in a solid mass. Remove from heat. Cool slightly and beat in eggs one at a time, mixing thoroughly after each addition.

If using chicken broth, dilute according to instructions and bring to simmer.

Add parsley to dumpling batter, then drop by tablespoons into simmering broth or stew. Cover and simmer for 20 minutes.

(The dumplings puff up while simmering and fall after they are uncovered.)

---

That saved you another $2.36. Total savings so far: $4.72.

---

**Icy Tea-Based Refresher**

(Makes 7 quarts)
[But none of them is any good]

3 tea bags
1 cup orange juice or 2 heaping tablespoons powdered orange drink mix

1 cup grape juice
½ cup lemon juice
1½ cups sugar

Bring a tea kettle full of water to boiling. In a very large pot, pour the boiling water over the tea bags. Let it steep until it is strong. While it is still warm, add remaining ingredients and enough water and ice to total seven quarts. Stir.

Serve thoroughly chilled. Taste is different when not cold.

[That last is the recipe seller's own note. We found that the taste when cold was nonexistent.]

---

That saved you $1.36, or more if you take my advice and don't make it. Total savings so far: at least $6.08.

(Recipe requires 10-inch tube pan)
(You can make it in a Bundt pan, but it might stick)

*Sauerkraut*
*Fudge Cake*

⅔ **cup sauerkraut**
2¼ **cups flour**
1 **teaspoon baking powder**
1 **teaspoon baking soda**
¼ **teaspoon salt**
½ **cup unsweetened cocoa powder**
⅔ **cup butter or margarine**
1½ **cups sugar**
2 **eggs**
8 **ounces dairy sour cream**

1 **teaspoon vanilla**
1 **cup water**
1 **cup semisweet chocolate chips**

PENUCHE GLAZE:

¼ **cup butter**
½ **cup brown sugar**
2 **tablespoons hot milk**
¾ **cup sifted confectioners' sugar**

Thoroughly grease a 10-inch tube pan. Cut a ring of brown paper to fit the bottom of the pan and grease that, too.

Drain and rinse the sauerkraut and snip it into very small pieces.

Sift together the flour, baking powder, soda, salt and cocoa. Set aside.

Cream butter and sugar until fluffy, and add eggs one at a time, beating well after each. Beat in the sour cream and vanilla.

Alternately add dry ingredients and water to the butter mixture, stirring after each addition and beginning and ending with the dry ingredients. Fold in sauerkraut and chocolate chips.

Turn into prepared pan and bake at 350 degrees 55 minutes to an hour, or until cake is springy. (Toothpick test won't work.)

Remove from oven, cool 10 minutes, loosen cake from sides of pan with knife and invert on serving plate. Peel paper from top.

Prepare glaze: Melt butter and brown sugar together. Boil one minute or until slightly thickened. Cool 10 minutes, then beat in hot milk. Add sifted confectioners' sugar, stirring, until of glaze consistency. Drizzle over slightly warm cake.

That saved you $2.36. Grand total savings, at least $8.44. How can you pass this up?

**O.K., YOU DRIVE a hard bargain. For 50 cents, I'll tell you how well this recipe business is succeeding for the people who place the ads.**

I must admit I was tempted several years ago to try it out myself. What deterred me from doing that was a full-page advertisement that I saw in the *Saturday Review.* The ad was for a $9.95 book on how to make a lot of money by selling brochures and recipes in classified ads. It went on and on with examples of people who had money pouring out of post-office boxes at them, and in a little box in the middle of the page was a test you could do to verify that it really works.

Long ago, on some early trip to a state fair, my father pointed out to me that when a pitchman says, "You don't have to take my word for it," he wants you to take his word for it. And that the more he explains how you can verify what he's saying, the more people will take his word for it.

(I think my father's life study has been pitchmen. He loves them. Whenever we'd go to the fair, we'd spend most of our time watching guys selling pen-and-pencil sets and blenders. And every time he goes, my father buys some pitchman's cabbage slicer, with which he eventually cuts his thumb.)

The test in the advertisement for the book suggested that you examine a couple of issues of one of these magazines at the library and compare the classified ads. The issues should be ten or twelve months apart, and what you'll find, the book ad said, is that many of the same classified ads appear in both issues. Nobody keeps an ad running if it doesn't make money, the book ad claimed, so they must work.

After I'd sent for these five recipes, I went to the library and performed the test. I compared the July 1980 *Atlantic* (24 recipe ads) with the May 1981 *Atlantic* (31 recipe ads); there were no duplications. Nor were there any duplications between the May 1980 *Saturday Review* recipe ads and those appearing in March 1981.

Thanks for the lesson, Dad.

**LOOK, YOU'VE hung on here this long, it's GOT to be worth 25 cents to you to know how it all comes out.**

By sending second letters to the same addresses and begging the folks who had placed the ads to call me collect, I got one response (from Cynthia Habegger, in Bloomington, Indiana, the woman with the businesslike approach and the Sauerkraut Fudge Cake).

Preliminaries out of the way, I asked her how she had decided to place one of these ads. Had she bought the $9.95 book? No, she said, she just saw the ads and thought it looked like a good way to make some money.

How long had the ad been running? Just one month, she said.

And how was it doing?

**WE'RE DOWN to the wire here. I won't beg. If you're prepared to take $8.44 worth of recipes and aren't willing to give me even the time of day for the Ultimate Secret of the ads in the backs of magazines, I'm not going to try to drag another penny out of you.**

So here it is, free, gratis and for nothing:

How many responses did Cynthia Habegger's ad get?

Counting mine, three.

*Three?* At $2 each, Habegger pulled in $6, minus her duplicating costs—and the cost of the ad. At $1.50 a word, her 16-word ad cost $24. So her net loss was more than $18. At least she hadn't bought the $9.95 book, too.

If that ad pulled in all of three responses from the entire United States, I don't feel too bad about subtracting you folks from the remaining likely buyers of the recipes reproduced here.

Well, actually, Habegger said, there were more than three responses. She got some chain letters. You send your recipe to a bunch of other people, and soon you'll be getting thousands of recipes in the mail. Habegger didn't sound like she believes in chain letters.

Neither does my father.

# Where Snack Foods Come From

When I was a kid in Milwaukee, my Cub Scout troop went through the factory where Mrs. Howe's potato chips were made.

I have only the vaguest memories of what the factory was like. All I recall with certainty is lots of very big machines (I was very little), the last of which spewed potato chips into boxes, and that we got some potato chips to eat.

But that tour established quite firmly in my mind what many other people know too—even people who never heard of Mrs. Howe: potato chips come from factories.

As I grew up and encountered other crunchy things that came in boxes or bags, my powerful mind established these related conclusions: corn chips come from factories; pretzels come from factories; cheese curls come from factories; and, more recently, sesame chips come from factories.

In the past few years, however, I have prepared in my kitchen a fair number of things that ordinarily come from factories (including marshmallows, English muffins and rather excellent home-brewed versions of Grape-Nuts and Twinkies), and it occurred to me recently that I might do the same thing with crunchy snack foods.

This attempt ought not to be quite so hard to understand as why I would make my own marshmallows, for example. Although already-popped popcorn has long been available in bags, most people prefer to pop their own. Why not, then, homemade potato chips, corn chips, pretzels, cheese curls and sesame chips?

Some of you are probably huffing indignantly that you've been making your own potato chips for years. Some, but not many.

It's true that lots of cookbooks indicate that potato chips are still within our grasp. It was a lot harder to find recipes for the other items.

In some cases I made up my own. In some cases I failed miserably.

This, then, is a story of triumph and tragedy, of victory and defeat, and a long day's journey into deep fat.

First, potato chips, the most obvious and the least difficult of today's exercises.

I must say that I was quite surprised at how good homemade potato chips turned out to be. They are very good indeed.

---

*Potato Chips*   **1 or 2 large baking potatoes**          **Salt**
**Oil and/or shortening for deep frying**

One large potato makes a medium bowlful of potato chips. Two would make a very large batch. (Really. A big potato weighs 8 or 9 ounces; a bag of potato chips, including a bit of oil, weighs about the same.)

The trick in making good potato chips is obtaining nice, thin uniform slices. A food processor, unless yours is very different from mine, produces slices that are uniform but much too thick. You might be able to do it with a very sharp knife, but it would be dicey (or maybe, in this case, slicey) and awfully tedious.

Happily, a simple solution exists: use a vegetable peeler.

Wash and peel the potatoes and use the peeler to cut them into paper-thin slices. (It's best to cut in one direction only—widthwise or lengthwise, so that all the slices are about the same size.) Put the slices in a bowl, fill it with cold water and swish things around gently to get rid of surface starch. Dry the slices on paper towels.

In a deep pot, heat the oil (some folks recommend using half oil and half vegetable shortening) to 375 degrees. When the oil is hot, put in a handful of the slices (about a third of a potato)—too many at once would cool the oil and make the chips greasy. Stir the oil to separate any slices that cling together, and fry until they look like potato chips—light golden and crisp—between 3 and 4 minutes.

Drain the chips on paper towels, salt them and repeat with the remaining slices.

---

Next come corn chips. Obviously you don't make them by deep-frying sliced corn. Neither, I established in several frustrating hours, do you make them by deep-frying any kind of rolled-out cornmeal batter. Most of the chips dissolve in the oil, and the cornmeal grains in the survivors are large and gritty. Not right at all. Phooey.

Then in a sudden, blinding flash, it became clear. What you need to do is to make corn tortillas, cut them into chip size and deep-fry them. (Yes, you could *buy* the corn tortillas instead of making them. But that would be wrong.) The chips fried beautifully, and the first one, tried hesitantly—tremblingly—tasted just like a corn chip to me.

What a breakthrough that was! I felt like stout Cortez when, as you may recall, with eagle eyes he stared at the Pacific and all his men looked at each other with a wild surmise, silent upon a peak in Darien. I was silent, too, having hit my peak in Minneapolis.

Where is Keats when you need him?

To make these, you'll need fine corn flour, which is available in many supermarkets under its Spanish name—masa harina.

---

## Corn Chips

**2 cups masa harina**
**1⅛ cups warm water**

**Oil and/or shortening for deep frying**
**Salt**

Stir the water into the masa harina in a bowl. It should make a firm mass, a bit moist but not at all wet.

Now we're going to flatten it out. Expert tortilla makers use their hands; some folks own tortilla presses; Frito-Lay certainly uses machines. We'll adopt a sensible compromise and roll them out between sheets of plastic wrap.

Heat a deep pot of oil to 375 degrees.

Divide the dough into 10 or 12 roughly equal pieces. Place one on a sheet of plastic wrap and cover it with a second sheet. Using a rolling pin, roll the dough out into a rough square about 5½ inches or so on a side. (A 6-inch circle will do, too; you'll just have more scraps to add to the next batch of dough.) Make sure the dough is quite flat; thick spots will make thick, tough chips.

Carefully peel back the top sheet of wrap. (If a little dough sticks to it, don't worry about it; there's plenty left.) Flip the dough down onto a clean countertop and carefully peel off the other sheet. Now cut the dough into rectangles about ½ inch by 1 inch. Ease a spatula under them and drop them into the hot oil.

(That business with all the plastic wrap sounds a bit complicated, but it's not really. And if you roll the tortillas out directly on the counter they'll stick like glue.)

Fry the chips for 3 to 4 minutes, until they are light golden brown. (Meanwhile you can be rolling out the next rectangle, incorporating any odd scraps from the last one.) Drain on paper towels and salt very well. Repeat with the remaining dough.

Some chips develop a sort of double layer, with a bubble between—I think those are from slightly thicker areas of dough. These may be a bit tough at first, but if you let them air-dry a day or so they'll be fine.

---

Buoyed by that experience (and by my ability to spell buoyed), I moved immediately to what I knew would be my biggest challenge: cheese curls. I was unable to find even a scrap of information about cheese curls in any cookbook, so I decided to try the direct approach: Read the ingredients off a commercial label, mix up lots of batches in different proportions and hope. It's not sure-fire, but it often works.

The ingredients varied a bit from brand to brand, but basically they were corn, oil and cheese. Early experience proved that, all other problems aside, if the cheese went into the batter before the batter was fried, it boiled out into the oil and became very unpleasant. Carefully licking the outside of some commercial cheese curls and then eating them verified my conclusion: these are corn curls, dipped in powdered cheese.

So the problem became how one makes corn curls. I'll spare you hours (in fact, days) of agony. Nothing I tried worked. They either fell apart in the oil or were chewy and tough. Clearly they needed to have lots of air whipped into them to make them light and crunchy, but there was nothing like egg white involved to sustain the air.

(I even tried putting egg white in some of them. They were light, chewy and tough.)

Finally, suspecting the worst—that some sort of special machine is intrinsic to their manufacture—I decided to ask somebody in the business. There are a lot of outfits making cheese curls, so I knew that the process is no industrial secret, but I suspected that I wouldn't make much headway if I tried to ask somebody at a giant concern like Frito-Lay. So I called Pate Foods in Hopkins, Minnesota, who turn out a fine cheese curl, among other things.

Tom Vucicevic, with whom I spoke, was very pleasant about it, although he acknowledged that he wasn't on very close terms with the process. The clear upshot, however, was what I feared: a pressurized machine poots the curls of aerated batter out into the hot oil.

Unless somebody out there knows something else, so much for homemade cheese curls.

Some things really *do* come from factories.

Pretzels don't, though. They come from your oven—or so I thought.

Shape aside, there are two basic kinds of pretzels. Big soft ones, sold warm from carts, and the little crunchy ones that come in bags.

First the big soft ones, a recipe adapted from a nice book called *Make Your Own Groceries,* by Daphne Hartwig.

---

### Big Soft Pretzels

1 (¼-ounce) envelope active dry yeast
1 cup warm water
¼ cup sugar
1 teaspoon salt
2 tablespoons softened shortening

1 egg, separated
1 tablespoon water
3½ cups flour, approximately
Coarse salt

Soften the yeast in the warm water in a large mixing bowl. After a few minutes, stir in the sugar, salt and shortening.

Put half of the egg yolk (approximately; it's no big deal) and the tablespoon of

water in a cup, mix and set aside, tightly covered, in the refrigerator.

Add the rest of the egg yolk and the egg white to the yeast mixture and beat in 2 cups of flour until the dough is smooth.

*(Continued)*

Beat in more flour until the dough is stiff. Cover the bowl tightly and refrigerate overnight.

Lightly flour a countertop and cut the dough into 32 equal pieces. Roll each piece into a rope about 12 to 14 inches long, and shape into a pretzel:

Form a U. Fold the left arm of the U down to the right, so it just crosses the the bottom of the right arm. Fold the right arm down so that it just crosses the bottom of where the left arm used to start. Lift the two arm-tips and twist them together half a turn. (This only *sounds* complicated. You know how pretzels are supposed to look.) Press the tips firmly into what was the bottom of the U (work the dough in until it won't separate— "gluing" it in place with water doesn't work all that well).

The dough can be made into 16 pretzels instead of 32, but don't make them so fat they are hard to shape.

Put the pretzels on lightly greased cookie sheets, brush with the yolk-water mixture and sprinkle lightly with coarse salt. (Careful: If you overdo the salt, the pretzels will look wonderful and be almost inedible.)

Cover the pretzels loosely with waxed paper and let them rise in a warm place for about 30 minutes, until they have doubled in bulk. Meanwhile, preheat the oven to 400 degrees.

Bake for about 15 minutes, until they are dark—pretzel-colored, in fact. Serve warm.

---

Recipes for little crunchy pretzels were not so easy to find, but I finally unearthed two, and they were very similar. They read rather surprisingly like the recipes for bagels—after the dough is shaped, the pretzels are dropped into boiling liquid until they float, then they're brushed with beaten egg and salt and baked.

Both recipes called for the boiling liquid to contain both baking soda and carbonate of ammonia, which I picked up at a pharmacy as ammonium carbonate. It smelled very strongly of ammonia, but I checked it out and established that, dreadful as it smells, it is indeed a leavening agent, that it decomposes on heating and that it's the principal ingredient in "smelling salts" (when was the last time you heard of *them?)*, so I guessed that a bit of it in a lot of water wasn't necessarily harmful. (It's also used in some Christmas cookies.) Nonetheless I tried the recipes in two pots—one with and one without the ammonium carbonate.

Both recipes also called for ground caraway seeds to be mixed with the flour and for ground cumin to be sprinkled on the finished pretzels before baking. Intrigued, I tried one batch of dough with white flour and another with rye flour. I wanted to see if you could taste the cumin through the rye.

If you'll stop groaning, I'll wrap this up: None of the pretzels worked—with ammonium carbonate or without; with white flour or rye. They all *looked* fine, they even tasted right, although the rye ones had a bit of a health-food flavor. But they were all tough and chewy. When I baked them longer, they were tooth-breakingly hard. And rolling and shaping lots of small pretzels was an impractical amount of work, too, even had they been good.

I remain convinced, though, that they can be made successfully (if tediously) at home. Having just said that they're too much work, I'm bound to hear from someone who has made them once a week for the last fifty years. When I do, I'll pass along his or her recipe.

Let's finish on a positive note. Sesame chips worked wonderfully well. Here, too, I had nothing to go on but the ingredients listed on labels, and I had to improvise on those (I don't have any soy protein isolate), but they were delicious.

---

**Sesame Chips**

1 1/4 cups flour
1 1/2 teaspoons soy sauce
1/2 cup water

3 1/2 tablespoons sesame seeds
1 teaspoon salt
Oil and/or shortening for deep frying

Combine all ingredients except oil. The dough should be firm and moist, not wet (add flour or water as needed).

Roll the dough out *very* thin on an unfloured surface. Heat the oil to 375 degrees. Cut the dough into rectangles 1/2

inch by 1 inch. Ease a spatula under 20 or so of them, drop them into the oil and fry 3 to 4 minutes, until they are dark golden brown. Drain on paper towels and salt if desired. Eat while frying the rest. They're *good!*

---

After all this deep frying, the writer has considered having his circulatory system purged with 409.

---

### Follow-Up

After the preceding failure to achieve corn curls appeared in the newspaper, I got a call from Al Heigl, of Eagan, Minnesota, who told me that his father, Cyrus Heigl, helped develop the corn curl and the cheese curl in the late thirties and early forties for an outfit in Beloit, Wisconsin, called Adams Corporation (later acquired by Beatrice Foods).

The younger Heigl describes his father's job in ensuing years as "bringing corn curls to the benighted of the world." Should you be, for example, in Iran and want a corn curl, there are machines there to make them.

I called the corn-curl Heigl in Beloit, and he described both the manufacturing process and the discovery. It's interesting, but it's not as important as the transistor, so let's keep it short. Corn or cornmeal is heated by friction. Steam produced from the moisture in the corn is trapped, and as the mash is extruded, the steam sprongs it out—sort of like puffed wheat.

Then the pieces are fried, salted and cheesed.

Now to the important question. Can you make them in your kitchen?

Well, the elder Heigl chuckled, not really. Running a corn-curl machine with two six-inch disks requires about forty horsepower. "And you'd only get a couple hundred pounds an hour."

# Two by Two

Have you ever noticed that many expressive terms in our language that should by all logic be one word are instead pairs of words?

That wasn't very clear, I'm sure, so let's go to the videotape.

Here we see a collection of what might be called junk or debris. Whatever it is, it isn't two things. But listen now as somebody calls it "flotsam and jetsam."

(Don't be a jerk and ask that person which is the flotsam and which is the jetsam. The combination, once two words with distinct meanings, is just part and parcel of the language—woven inextricably into the very warp and woof of our speech.)

Our next clip shows a person who is remarkably active for his advanced age. He is described as having plenty of "vim and vigor." I'd settle for some of either one.

There's a whole kit and caboodle of such paired terms floating around, giving form and substance to our thoughts.

Don't raise a hue and cry—this is a nuts-and-bolts food article, and we are getting to the food.

See, there are lots of food pairs, too—alliances so natural that we don't even think about them. (I have to get to the food eventually—I can bob and weave only so long.)

When peanut butter was invented, for example, it is probable that the inventor's very next words (after "tastes more like fresh-roasted peanuts") were "Does anybody have some jelly?"

And, whichever came first, once somebody got one of the eggs away from one of the chickens he probably served it with ham—or maybe with bacon.

I could huff and puff and produce a list of such natural food pairs, but it would be quite long indeed.

And it is constantly growing, as one year's new-and-different combination becomes next year's tried-and-true standby. That happened to peanut butter and bananas in my lifetime.

There are also, of course, food combinations that *don't* catch on. It didn't happen, for example, to cottage cheese and ketchup, said to be a lunchtime favorite of Richard Nixon. The fans of that combination are few and far between.

(Each will now write an indignant letter, so in a few weeks I will be able to tell you exactly how many there are.)

I was musing about food the other day, on and off, now and again, when I thought of a potentially interesting combination. As I jotted it down I realized that there were several other combination ideas echoing through the canyons of my mind, just waiting for me to give them a try.

As long as they were coming fast and furious, I decided to put my heart and soul into it and have a whole dinner of things that might go together (or might not).

Enough of this and that. If we don't cook soon, you'll be skin and bones instead of fat and sassy.

Come and get it.

The appetizer for this dinner of possibly great combinations is hardly a combination at all—and I'm cheating a bit by presenting it here as something that just occurred to me. I have fairly often used up leftover hollandaise sauce by dipping crackers in it, but I did it only in the privacy of my own kitchen.

It only occurred to me to *serve* the sauce that way when I got a letter from a reader suggesting it. It's very rich but surprisingly good.

I have since misplaced the letter, or I would supply all 579,847 of you with the reader's name. (Who was that masked reader? I wanted to thank him.)

If I still had the name, those of you who prefer bulgur or tofu to hollandaise sauce as chip dip could have written directly to the source of the problem. As it is, I will bear the slings and arrows. But that's O.K., because I'm all wool and a yard wide.

## Hollandaise and Crackers

4 egg yolks
Juice of 1 large lemon
2 teaspoons water
½ pound (2 sticks) salted butter, each stick divided into 8 pieces

Pinch of pepper
Salt
Crackers, chips, etc.

In the top of a double boiler over cold water, or in a light saucepan, beat together the egg yolks, lemon juice and water. Turn on the heat (very low if using a saucepan) and add 2 pieces (about 2 tablespoons) of the butter, stirring constantly with a wooden spoon until the butter is absorbed and the mixture is the consistency of a paste.

(Normally, hollandaise sauce should be made with unsalted butter, for a creamier taste, but as a dip it benefits from some salt.)

Incorporate the remainder of the butter, 2 pieces at a time, in the same fashion,

adding butter just as the last of the previous pieces have almost disappeared. If the mixture starts to separate at all, remove from the heat immediately and stir like crazy until the melted butter is reincorporated.

You may have to take the pan on and off the heat several times.

Stir in the pepper, pour into a dish, allow to cool a few minutes if the idea of a hot cracker dip bothers you, adjust the amount of salt (adjusting upward is much easier than adjusting downward), and serve.

Serves 8 to 10.

Those of you who pay good money every week to read this stuff already know that I'm not overfond of salads.

In fact, I'm barely tolerant of salads. The kind of understanding I've always had with salads runs to mutual nonaggression: if I agree not to eat them, they agree not to spoil my appetite for better stuff.

But I do like salad dressings, and they seem to go best on salads—although, now that I think about it, I haven't tried them as chip dips. Anyway, for several months I've been aware that in the back of my head I have wanted to make a salad dressing with bacon, honey and mustard. Now I've done it, and I'm glad. (It's very good.)

Let there be no wailing and gnashing of teeth by salad lovers. Part of the goodness of the dressing was the spinach and lettuce it went on.

### Bacon-Honey-Mustard Salad

6 slices bacon
2 teaspoons Dijon mustard
Salt and pepper
6 tablespoons olive or vegetable oil

1 tablespoon honey
1½ teaspoons white wine vinegar
1 (12-ounce) bag fresh spinach
½ head lettuce

Cut the bacon into 1-inch pieces and fry until crisp. Drain. Set aside.

Meanwhile, combine mustard, salt and pepper. Stir in the oil, a little at a time, until all is absorbed. Stir in the honey and the vinegar.

Wash the spinach and remove the tough stems. Tear the spinach and the lettuce and put in the serving bowl.

Add the drained bacon to the dressing and warm it gently, stirring. Pour over the greens and toss.

Serves 6 to 8.

For the main dish I decided to see whether olive oil would go well with chicken. It would, indeed.

I substituted it for butter in a sautéed-chicken-and-sauce dish that has long been one of my favorites. Not only did the sauce—a not-very-distant relative of hollandaise—pick up a little extra tang from the olive oil, but the chicken browned much more prettily.

Now I wonder whether the old economics cliché about guns and butter wouldn't work better as guns and olive oil.

### Olive-Oil Chicken

⅓ cup olive oil
6 chicken breast halves (3 whole breasts)
1 teaspoon basil
½ teaspoon tarragon
Salt and pepper

4 cloves garlic, unpeeled
½ cup plus 1 tablespoon dry white wine, divided
2 egg yolks
1 tablespoon lemon juice

Heat the olive oil over medium heat in a large pan (an electric frypan is nice), add the chicken, skin side down, and sauté, turning several times, for 5 or 6 minutes.

Sprinkle with the basil, tarragon, salt and pepper, and drop the garlic cloves into the oil.

Cover the pan and cook about 10

minutes. Uncover, turn the chicken and baste it with the oil. Continue to cook, basting and turning, until it is done—20 to 30 more minutes, depending on how you like your chicken. Check by piercing with a fork. Any juices should be pale. Remove the chicken from the pan to a warm oven.

Crush the garlic cloves in the pan with the back of a wooden spoon, removing and discarding the peel.

Turn up the heat under the oil, pour in the 1/2 cup of wine and boil down the wine-oil mixture, scraping at the pan with the wooden spoon to get up all the nice little bits of chicken and garlic, until the volume is about half what it was after you added the wine.

In the top of a double boiler or in a light saucepan, but not over the heat, beat the egg yolks and the lemon juice and the remaining tablespoon of wine.

Then beat in the cooking liquid—a spoonful at a time at first, a little more rapidly as you near the end. When all the liquid is in, heat the sauce a few minutes over boiling water (or over very low direct heat), stirring until it thickens. Don't overdo it or it will separate.

Pour the sauce over the chicken or into a gravy dish. Serves 6. (The sauce goes very well over any long-grain-and-wild-rice mix, too.)

---

A vegetable marriage didn't occur to me until I was just about ready to cook. I knew that onions go well with almost everything, but I couldn't think of anything that they weren't already well associated with.

Then I got it. You don't very often hear of *corn* and onions. Judging by this experiment (in which, of course, I also threw in some butter and cream), you should hear of that combination every five minutes. It was delicious. The rank and file will love it.

---

### Onion Corn

2 (10-ounce) packages frozen corn
3 medium onions, coarsely chopped
5 1/2 tablespoons butter, divided

2 to 3 tablespoons cream
1/2 teaspoon or more salt
Pepper

Cook corn according to package directions. Drain very well (put it in a colander or sieve and let it drain, then press gently to get out a little more water).

Sauté the onions slowly in 4 tablespoons of the butter until they are barely golden. Stir in the corn and the cream, salt and pepper and heat through. When almost ready to serve, stir in the remaining 1 1/2 tablespoons of butter, just until it is melted.

Serves 6 to 8.

---

If I must be honest (and why not—I'm among friends), it was the surfacing of the following chocolate combination from somewhere deep in my soul that made me come up with this entire combination-recipes theme, just so I could have some excuse for making the dessert.

It combines two of my favorite kitchen aromas, and I wanted an excuse to try it out. It sounded great to me—and it was.

But you must trust me. It might not sound good to you. Take a deep breath. Ready?

It's chocolate . . . and . . . vermouth. Dry white vermouth.

Now, now. Hold on. There are lots of recipes in which chocolate is combined with rum, with brandy, with kirsch, with Grand Marnier. So why not with dry vermouth? In fact, what happens is not that the chocolate acquires a vermouth overtone, which might be kind of odd. It seems to just enhance the winy quality of the chocolate. And it's gooood.

If you're not comfortable with that, make this same little treat without the vermouth, or substituting one of the other boozes mentioned above. It'll be fine any way at all.

It is a simple little goodie, since what I wanted to do was just try out the flavor, and I didn't feel like going to elaborate lengths.

Oh, a lie! And I had decided no more than seven paragraphs ago to be honest. O.K.; enough to and fro. Let's be open and above-board. *Before* I made the simple little treat, I tried making some chocolate-vermouth *truffles.* They bombed. We'll work that out another time.

---

## Glop-Topped Cookies

1½ cups heavy cream
4 tablespoons (½ stick) unsalted butter
1 (12-ounce) package semisweet chocolate chips
3 tablespoons sugar

3 tablespoons dry white vermouth (or, if you must fiddle, some other booze or no booze at all)
1 (7- to 12-ounce) box vanilla wafers (you'll have some left in any case)

Put the cream and butter in a medium saucepan and bring to the boil over medium heat. Remove from the heat, add the chocolate and sugar and stir until the chocolate is fully melted in. Cool and stir in the vermouth.

Cool the pan in the refrigerator (or freezer, but be much more attentive), stirring it occasionally, until it is the consistency of very thick cream or honey. If you inadvertently let it get fully hard, let it warm until you can stir it.

Whip as you would cream, until it is stiff.

Top vanilla wafers with very big blobs of it. (Blade a big peak of it on a cookie with a metal spatula or, for a prettier effect, pipe a big peak of it on with a pastry bag.)

Makes enough wonderful glop to top about 3 dozen cookies (or more if you hold back—unwisely—on the size of the blob on each cookie).

---

Had enough combinations? Then hail and farewell.

# The Batter-Up Dinner

Those who cleave unto the words of Joe Garagiola know that baseball's exhibition season has begun.

Those who are not sports fans may not care, but it is a fact nonetheless and it must be reckoned with, along with the Super Bowl, the Stanley Cup and the Indianapolis 500.

One season following another, laden with happiness and beers.

I myself am not a sports fan. I confess, for example, that I only pay enough attention to the Olympics to know when I can get away with singing "Born to Luge."

And I have not paid much attention to baseball since the Milwaukee Braves traded Bobby Thomson about 1957. My grandmother, a pretty ardent fan, survived that one but was laid low by the similar fate of Billy Bruton.

Until those chilling events, I did follow events in the National League in some detail.

I was pretty young at the time, and I think I can be forgiven what might now seem to be shallowness of commitment.

In fact, the year I took a girl to the opening Braves game I was so young that when she said that she was cold I bought her a cup of hot chocolate.

And she didn't even like the hot chocolate.

Well, enough of my early sex life, such as it wasn't. How, you are probably muttering, can anything even remotely like this be related to food?

I thought you'd never mutter.

It is my pleasure today to bring together ever so briefly the world of the 90-foot diamond with that of the 9-by-13-inch pan; the arena of the horsehide sphere with that of the beefsteak, and the field of the 36-ounce bat with that of the stainless-steel whisk.

Ladeez and gentlemen: Presenting a meal in which every dish is based on the same batter—the Batter-Up Dinner!

Now just a minute. Don't start filing out of the stadium. Give me a chance to explain!

See, the dishes that are all based on this one batter are somewhat different from each other, and many of them are very normal dishes enjoyed by millions of standard Americans.

Not *everything* I make is weird.

For today's dinner, we're going to have popovers, soup with eggdrop-like noodles, steak and Yorkshire pudding, crêpes, and a puffy banana sort-of pancake with chocolate sauce.

Yes, you read that correctly. Big, puffy popovers and ever-so-flat crêpes can be made from the same batter. Just one of the wonders of modern science.

But enough infield chatter. Time to put one over the plate.

After a short stop:

All of these recipes really use absolutely identical batter. So if you're going to make more than one, just make one bigger batch of batter.

If you're going to make them all, you might want to divide the resulting very large batch in two.

We want Batter-Up, not Batter All Over.

O.K. Right off the bat, let's make popovers. I know we've already made them in a previous incarnation, but there is a rounded, Aristotelian wholeness to this article that the artist in me feels would be destroyed were I to omit the popover recipe. Besides, it's already been typed. So we're going to do it all again.

---

### Popovers

**1 cup sifted flour**
**3 eggs**

**1 cup milk**
**2 tablespoons melted butter**

Put the sifted flour in a large bowl. In a smaller bowl, beat the eggs lightly. Add the milk to the eggs and mix well. Add the liquid gradually to the flour, beating with a mixer or a wire whisk. Beat in the melted butter, just long enough to smooth out the batter (30 seconds or so).

I don't know how to continue with these directions without making the same mistake I made the last time: I really found that almost any method produced popovers. And I tried it lots of ways. I even slammed the oven door on them. But I won't say that you can't make them fail. I will say that it isn't *easy* to make

them fail.

Maybe it will be better if I don't give you any choices.

Preheat the oven to 400 degrees.

Heavily grease 9 to 12 (I'll give you *that* much choice, anyway) custard cups or a muffin tin with 9 to 12 cups. Grease all across the top of the tin, too. Pour the batter into the cups (and put a little water in any unused cups in the muffin tin).

Bake for 40 to 45 minutes if you're making 12 popovers, or 50 to 55 minutes if the same amount of batter is used to make 9 popovers, which will be somewhat larger and need longer to bake.

---

Since the popovers are the appetizer for the Batter-Up Dinner, I offer here a nice dip to spread on them should you want (for some unfathomable reason) not to follow the dictates of common sense by eating them with large amounts of butter.

### Dill Dip for Popovers
(or for anything else, for that matter)

3/4 cup mayonnaise
3/4 cup dairy sour cream
1 to 1 1/2 tablespoons dill weed
1/2 teaspoon seasoned salt

2 or 3 drops Tabasco
1/2 teaspoon Worcestershire sauce
1 1/2 tablespoons finely chopped onion

Combine all ingredients.
That's it. Not everything I make is complicated, either.

Oh, yes. If you're making this dip in the summer, you ought to keep it covered—just in case of infield flies.

---

To demonstrate the incredible versatility of this batter, let's take an intentional walk over to the soup pot and make some little drop dumplings.

And, since we're going to have to drop them into something, let's make this very nice and *very* easy soup.

---

### Chicken-Beef Consommé with Little Drop Dumplings

SOUP:

1 (10 3/4-ounce) can chicken broth
1 (10 3/4-ounce) can beef consommé
1 1/2 soup cans water
1 tablespoon tomato paste
1/4 cup dry white vermouth
3 tablespoons dry sherry

TINY DROP DUMPLINGS:

1/3 cup sifted flour
1 egg
1/3 cup milk
2 teaspoons melted butter

Prepare the soup:
In a Dutch oven, combine the broth, consommé, water, tomato paste, vermouth and sherry. Bring to a boil and reduce to a simmer.
Meanwhile, prepare the dumpling batter:
Put the sifted flour in a large bowl. In a smaller bowl, beat the egg lightly. Add the milk to the egg and mix well. Add the liquid gradually to the flour, beating with a mixer or a wire whisk. Beat in the

melted butter, just long enough to smooth out the batter (30 seconds or so).
Those of you who have been paying close attention will have noticed that the dumpling recipe is just one-third of the popover recipe. Goodness, you're sharp!
Drop the batter, part of a teaspoonful at a time, into the lightly boiling soup and continue to cook for 3 to 4 minutes. The batter forms blobs that are sort of like irregular pieces of egg noodle.
Serves 4 to 6.

---

For the main course of the Batter-Up Dinner, I suppose fowl might have been appropriate, but I decided to strike out on my own and make steaks to serve over Yorkshire pudding.

PUDDING:

1 cup sifted flour
3 eggs
1 cup milk
2 tablespoons melted butter

SAUCE:

4 tablespoons butter, divided
2 tablespoons finely chopped onion

2 tablespoons finely chopped shallots
1 cup dry white vermouth
1 (10¾-ounce) can chicken broth
Salt, pepper
1 tablespoon tomato paste
1 teaspoon Worcestershire sauce
2 tablespoons flour
4 (6-ounce) steaks
1 teaspoon chopped parsley

*Steak and Yorkshire Pudding*

Prepare the Yorkshire pudding batter. By this time you must know how:

Put the sifted flour in a large bowl. In a smaller bowl, beat the eggs lightly. Add the milk to the eggs and mix well. Add the liquid gradually to the flour, beating with a mixer or a wire whisk. Beat in the melted butter, just long enough to smooth out the batter (30 seconds or so).

Preheat the oven to 375 degrees.

Heavily grease a 9-by-9-inch pan. Pour in the batter and bake about 35 to 40 minutes, until it is puffy and golden brown.

Meanwhile, prepare the sauce for the steaks:

Melt 2 tablespoons of the butter in a saucepan. Add the onions and shallots and cook over low heat until they are wilted. Add vermouth and chicken broth, salt and pepper to taste and the tomato paste and Worcestershire sauce. Cook about 5 minutes.

While the liquid cooks, work the flour into the remaining 2 tablespoons of butter. Drop this handled butter into the liquid bit by bit, stirring constantly. When all the flour and butter have been added and the mixture is smooth, let it simmer over low heat for 15 minutes.

Prepare the steaks as you normally would (broil or pan-fry).

Stir the parsley into the sauce. Serve each steak with a section of the pudding and pour sauce over all. Serves 4.

Time for a seventh-inning starch. And a vegetable. Let's try something rolled up in that early French invasion, the crêpe.

For reasons not clear—at least not clear to me—while the quiche, a later arrival, has become as common as the hot dog (there are probably no young things around who are sweet sixteen and never been quiched), crêpes have remained the least bit foreign and fancy. But they aren't hard to make.

I chose to wrap the crêpes around some asparagus in lemon butter. You would do well not to make the mistake I made—I cooked the asparagus and then let it marinate several hours in the lemon butter. It tasted fine, but it was pretty soggy.

## *Asparagus Crêpes*

1 cup sifted flour
3 eggs
1 cup milk
2 tablespoons melted butter

ASPARAGUS:

2 (10-ounce) packages frozen
   asparagus spears
6 tablespoons butter

2 tablespoons lemon juice
Salt, pepper

SAUCE:

2½ tablespoons butter
2½ tablespoons flour
1⅔ cups milk
2½ tablespoons lemon juice
Salt
½ teaspoon pepper

Guess how to make the crêpe batter. That's right:

Put the sifted flour in a large bowl. In a smaller bowl, beat the eggs lightly. Add the milk to the eggs and mix well. Add the liquid gradually to the flour, beating with a mixer or a wire whisk. Beat in the melted butter, just long enough to smooth out the batter (30 seconds or so).

To make the batter into crêpes, heat a small skillet over low-medium heat and butter it lightly. Add about 2 tablespoons of the batter, tilting the pan rapidly to cover it with the batter. Cook each crêpe for about a minute, until the bottom is lightly browned. (If it takes more than a minute, raise the heat slightly for the remaining crêpes or they will be dry. If the pan is too hot, on the other hand, the crêpe will start to bake before you can get the batter to cover the bottom of the pan.)

Cook the other side of the crêpe briefly.

Cool the crêpes, overlapping them slightly, on waxed paper. You'll have about 12 to 15.

Cook the asparagus according to package directions.

Melt the 6 tablespoons of butter, add the 2 tablespoons of lemon juice and salt and pepper to taste. Pour into a shallow bowl or pan, and add the asparagus spears. Allow to rest while you prepare the sauce:

In a small saucepan, melt the 2½ tablespoons of butter and stir in the flour. Cook over low heat, stirring, about 1 minute. Very slowly stir in the milk, then the lemon juice, salt and pepper.

Preheat the oven to 350 degrees. Wrap 3 or 4 spears of asparagus in each crêpe and put the rolled-up crêpes in a 9-by-13-inch pan. Pour the sauce over all and bake about 15 minutes, until heated through.

Makes 12 to 15 crêpes.

Almost time to head for the showers. But first dessert. And for that most pleasant of all courses, let's have a puffy banana pancake with chocolate sauce, and let's name it after one of the most famous and most self-effacing baseball players of all time. After all, dessert has been very, very good to me.

1 cup sifted flour
3 eggs
1 cup milk
2 tablespoons melted butter
2 bananas

CHOCOLATE SAUCE:

4 (1-ounce) squares semisweet
  chocolate

6 tablespoons water
¼ cup sugar
2 tablespoons butter
1 egg yolk
1 tablespoon kirsch (optional)
1 cup heavy cream, whipped

*Bananas Esquela*

Come on. If you haven't got the batter part down by now, go sit in the dugout. Oh, all right:

Put the sifted flour in a large bowl. In a smaller bowl, beat the eggs lightly. Add the milk to the eggs and mix well. Add the liquid gradually to the flour, beating with a mixer or a wire whisk. Beat in the melted butter, just long enough to smooth out the batter (30 seconds or so).

Preheat the oven to 375 degrees. Heavily grease a 1½-quart baking dish. Slice one of the bananas onto the bottom of the dish, pour in half the batter, then slice in the other banana and pour on the rest of the batter.

Bake for 40 to 50 minutes. It puffs up nicely and turns prettily golden, and the banana slices distribute themselves all over.

While the whatsit is baking, prepare the chocolate sauce:

Put the chocolate and water in a saucepan over very low heat and stir until the chocolate is melted and the mixture is smooth. Add the sugar, stirring until it is dissolved, then boil gently, stirring, for 4 minutes.

Remove the sauce from the heat and stir in the butter until it is melted. Cool a minute or two. Lightly beat the egg yolk, then stir in a spoonful of the hot chocolate mixture. Pour the diluted egg into the hot chocolate mixture, stirring immediately. Stir in the kirsch.

Serve the hot chocolate sauce over the banana whatsit and top with whipped cream. (If you're staying with the baseball theme, serve the sauce in a pitcher.) Serves 6 to 8.

The writer is terribly sorry, but he didn't feel like making Ty Cobb Salad.

# A Rainbow Dinner

Well, the moving finger writes, as the fellow said. (Nor all your tears, nor many beers, can cancel half a line.)

So, ready or not, we find ourselves once more contemplating the annual rebirth of the planet and, for those who truly abhor winter, the spirit.

It is the season of Easter and Passover, with their messages of renewal and deliverance. It is the season of the reemergence of growing things. And it is the season of puddles.

(At least it is nominally the season of puddles. I didn't stay up late last night writing this while newspaper delivery trucks honked impatiently, so I don't actually know what it's like today. It is entirely possible that we're knee-deep in snow or suffering through a 90-degree drought.)

But if there's anything left in this world that you can depend on, and you can still believe Buddy DeSylva and Al Jolson, not only do April showers come our way but they bring the flowers that bloom in May. So the rain isn't so bad.

And if you can still believe Paul Williams and Kermit T. Frog, there's a rainbow connection in there somewhere, too.

Thank goodness for that, because, as you can tell by the headline, I have to get to rainbows somehow, and all the bluebirds and daffodils in "April Showers" aren't going to do me a bit of good.

Rainbows, as any reasonably aware child can tell you, are the result of the combined diffraction and reflection of sunlight in water droplets. That doesn't make much sense to most adults, but neither do Michael Jackson and punk haircuts. On the other hand, *we* have Frank Sinatra and Grecian Formula 16. And then there's Leon Redbone, whom *nobody* understands.

But I digress.

On the other hand, if I didn't digress, all you'd have to read between the headline and the recipes would be "Here are some recipes," and you'd have to start reading about the presidential election that much sooner. And you don't want that to happen, do you?

O.K. then. Stop shaking your head and muttering about my irrelevant blathering or *I'll* start writing about the presidential election. How would you like *that?*

A rainbow dinner, the subject of this morning's discourse, is not a dinner in which each course resembles a rainbow. (That dinner would be too difficult.) Nor is it a dinner in which each dish is made from rainbow trout. (That dinner would be too weird, even for me.) No, it is a dinner in which each course represents a different color of the rainbow, in order. (That dinner was just right, so Goldilocks ate the whole . . . )

Sorry. Wrong story.

Where was I? Yes. Rainbow dinner.

Before we get too deeply into rainbow-colored food, I thought it might be nice to start with a dish that is a color not found in the spectrum.

You're imagining exotic colors like sky-blue pink or come-and-get-me copper, or colors not possible even to imagine, aren't you, you romantic? I must point out that tan is a color not in the spectrum. Sorry.

Granted that this appetizer is not an exciting color, it is, I think, rather tasty.

## Chicken Spread

1 whole chicken breast, cut in two
3 to 4 tablespoons additional chicken
    fat or butter
2 teaspoons crumbled basil
2 teaspoons crumbled tarragon
Salt to taste
3 cloves garlic
¼ cup dry white vermouth
Crackers

Remove the chicken skin and any fat, and cut the skin into pieces about an inch on a side.

Heat skin and fat in a frying pan until the fat is rendered and the chicken skin is golden brown. Leaving the fat in the pan, drain the skin pieces on paper toweling.

Add the extra chicken fat or butter and the halved chicken breast. Sprinkle with basil, tarragon and salt and put the garlic, unpeeled, in the pan, too. Sauté the chicken as you normally would, turning occasionally, until it is done (about 20 to 30 minutes).

Remove the chicken and allow it to cool a bit. Mash the cooked garlic (still in the pan) with a wooden spoon, which will push the soft insides out of the peel. Discard the peel. Increase the heat under the pan, add the vermouth and cook down for a minute, scraping the pan with a wooden spoon to break up the garlic and to free up any crispy bits of chicken that stuck to the pan.

Tear the cooled chicken into small pieces and put them and the seasoned cooking liquid into a food processor and whomp until the mixture is reasonably smooth. Season to taste.

Just before serving, add the bits of crisp chicken skin. (If you add them early, they'll just get soggy.)

Serve with crackers. Serves 6.

---

Now the rainbow begins, with red. A tomato salad is the obvious choice, even if, like me, you don't care for salad.

You could do something with red lettuce if you must, but since that really isn't very red, I stuck to just a few nicely arranged slices of tomato and a few rings of red onion, topped with a pinkish vinaigrette. Watchers of television commercials know what kind of oil to use if they want to make sure that the tomato sinks all the way through the vinaigrette. Not all of us care.

---

## Pink Vinaigrette for Red Salad

1 teaspoon Dijon mustard
1 large clove garlic, put through a
    garlic press
Salt, pepper to taste
6 tablespoons oil
2 tablespoons red wine vinegar

Combine the mustard, garlic, salt and pepper and slowly stir in the oil. Stir in the vinegar. Shake in covered container. Enough for light dressing on salad for 6.

---

The main course, which is the orange course, of course, could have been duck à l'orange.

But how too predictable that would have been!

Instead we'll have turkey breast fillets à l'orange. (And awfully good ones, too.)

## Orange You Glad We Have Turkey?

Approximately 2 pounds uncooked
  turkey breast
1 orange
1/2 cup butter
3/4 cup orange juice

4 tablespoons orange marmalade
1/2 cup flour
Salt, pepper
1/2 cup white wine

Skin and debone the turkey breast. Slice the meat into 12 pieces of roughly similar size. One at a time, put the slices between sheets of plastic wrap or waxed paper and roll out lightly with a rolling pin. (Enlarge the slices slightly and easily. Don't push so hard that you tear the meat.) Set aside in the refrigerator.

Peel and section the orange. If you like, for a garnish, remove the white pith from a large piece of the peel and cut that peel into 10 or 12 long, thin strips. Tie a knot in the middle of each. Set aside orange sections and peel decorations.

In a large frying pan, melt the butter, add the orange juice and marmalade and cook about 5 minutes over medium heat.

Combine flour, salt and pepper. Dredge the turkey scallops in the mixture. Stir the wine into the orange-butter mixture and add the turkey.

Cook the turkey scallops about 1 1/2 minutes per side.

Just before serving, add the orange sections and stir gently a minute or so to heat them through.

Transfer turkey and sauce to serving platter. Decorate here and there with orange knots.

Serves 6 to 8.

---

Sure, you've got your squashes and your wax beans, but when it comes to downright yellowness, there's really no vegetable that can hold a candle to corn.

This version is so tasty it inspires great warmth of emotion.

## Yellow Fervor

4 slices bacon
2 (10-ounce) packages frozen corn
3 tablespoons butter

1 1/2 tablespoons flour
2/3 cup milk or half-and-half
Salt, pepper

Fry and crumble the bacon.

Prepare the corn according to package directions. Drain.

In a small saucepan, melt the butter, stir in the flour and cook, stirring, 1 minute.

Slowly stir in the milk or half-and-half. Season to taste.

Stir sauce and crumbled bacon into corn. Serves 4 to 6.

---

It might not be very easy to *be* green (Kermit T. Frog again), but *cooking* green is another matter. The choice of green vegetables is . . . ZZZzzzz.

No, really. There are lots of green vegetables. Too many, in fact. So I made a dish with *two* green things, just to get rid of an extra one.

If peas and lettuce strike you as a weird combination, it might ease your mind to know that they are often combined in French cooking. If they do not strike you as a weird combination, how about baked beans and cottage cheese?

## Green, Green French-Style Peas

2 tablespoons dry white vermouth
1 ½ cups shredded lettuce
¼ cup chopped green onions (just the green part)

1 (16-ounce) can tiny peas, drained
1 teaspoon sugar
Salt, pepper
2 tablespoons butter

Put the vermouth in the bottom of a small saucepan. Add half the lettuce. Without stirring, add the onions and peas. Sprinkle on the sugar, salt and pepper.

Dot with bits of the butter and top with the remaining lettuce.

Cover and cook over medium heat for about 5 minutes. Stir gently and serve. Serves 4.

---

Since all the trendy restaurants serve water (or fizz water) with a slice of lime, I thought I'd go them one or two better for the rainbow dinner, and serve slices of orange, lemon and lime in each glass.

I thought it was rather a nice touch. But then what do I know?

In the blue portion of the spectrum, things are a little thin.

There are blueberries, but we're not ready for dessert yet.

There is the blue plate special (this week it's a hot beef sandwich, mashed potatoes and gravy, and canned green beans—beverage and dessert extra), but that's a bit heavy for so late in the meal.

That leaves blue cheese, and a tiny wedge of it for each diner turned out to go quite nicely at this juncture.

Those who learned that the colors of the rainbow have first letters that spell out Roy G. Biv are now waiting for indigo. They can forget it. As far as I'm concerned, we move from blue to purple. If you must, a glass of milk with bluish-purplish food coloring could be served here, and it could be alleged that it came from a cow that mooed indigo.

Now it's dessert time, and there is an obvious choice. Grape something, right? Here's a recipe straight from Welch's, the grape folks, that produces the purplest, and possibly soupiest, apple dessert you ever saw. But it tasted pretty good. I renamed it, of course.

4 medium apples (Rome Beauty, if you
care to preserve the pun)
1 (6-ounce) can frozen grape drink
concentrate
2 tablespoons quick-cooking tapioca
1½ cups unsifted flour
2 teaspoons baking powder

½ teaspoon salt
½ cup sugar
1 egg, well beaten
½ cup milk
½ cup (1 stick) butter, melted
Vanilla ice cream

*Grape Caesar's*
*Ghost Cobbler*

Peel, core and slice the apples and put them in a buttered 9-inch square pan.

Combine the grape concentrate and the tapioca and pour over the apple slices. Yes, it looks odd, but be patient. It tastes fine.

Preheat the oven to 425 degrees.

Sift together the flour, baking powder and salt. Add the sugar. Combine the egg, milk and melted butter and stir gently into the flour mixture. Spread over the apples. Bake for 30 minutes.

Serve with ice cream. Serves 8.

I had intended to wind things up by serving a really peculiar liqueur called Parfait Amour, which is bright purple and rather florid. It turns out that Bols, the Kentucky liqueur folks who used to make it, haven't done so for some time, and I couldn't find any of the imported versions either, so my guests were spared that experience.

As I recall, though, it was kind of expensive, so maybe it's just as well I couldn't find it. I didn't want to spend a whole pot of gold just to end the rainbow meal.

I don't normally discuss anything that takes place at dinner except the eating, but I cannot end this article in honesty without describing what happened after dessert and coffee.

Maybe it had something to do with the springtime feeling imparted by the meal. I don't know. Anyway, while my guests sat around the table talking, I went down to the basement to look for my collection of amusing typographical errors. (When I have a party, boy, it gets wild!) When I returned, I found that the entire group of guests—five regular attendees and two perfect strangers (oh, nobody's perfect; two very nice strangers)—had left the table and were hiding in my bathroom.

I was never offered an explanation. It couldn't have been my company.

All I can think of is that they were looking for the April shower.

### Little Mystery #2: Cheese

Have you noticed that if you open your mouth lately somebody is stuffing Monterey Jack cheese into it? Why are we suddenly eating so much of a cheese that nobody ever heard of ten years ago? Where did it come from, anyhow?

**Solution:** According to the National Cheese Institute in Chicago, Monterey Jack cheese has been around a long time.

They say it was invented by some fellow named Jack in Monterey County, California, and that it was made a great deal on farms in that county starting in about 1892.

The cheeseperson said that in many locales the name Monterey Jack has been replaced by just plain Monterey. In some places it is also just "jack."

As to why it appeared so suddenly on the sandwiches of every fern restaurant in town, the Cheese Institute was not particularly helpful. (A little mystery remains.)

# Things That Go Bump
# in the Oven

Did you ever wonder, when you were eating a piece of bread, how in the world anybody figured out that yeast would do what it does in there?

Or have you wondered what caveman reasoned that smashing a chicken egg into some other stuff would be anything but peculiar? (Or how many times he did it before it occurred to him to remove the shell?)

Probably nobody figured these things out, wise persons answer whenever I wonder them out loud; these were serendipitous discoveries—long-ago accidents that worked out so well that they were repeated. The transistor was born in such circumstances, these wise persons point out; why not the soufflé?

O.K. Fair enough. But in these modern times, when we know darn well how cake is made and nobody thinks it's made any other way, what explains the development of recipes that behave in ways that no reasonably knowledgeable person would expect?

What was in the mind of the person who first made Tunnel of Fudge Cake, for example? Was he or she intent on making a cake with a chocolate-brownie center? Or did a kid track mud across the floor at a critical moment, causing a momentary loss of attention that resulted in tossing the frosting mix into the cake batter?

Surely Pillsbury, which has trademarked the name of the cake and makes both the frosting mix called for in the recipe and the complete-in-one-box Tunnel of Fudge Cake mix, had something to do with it.

Similarly one suspects that General Mills, which produces Bisquick, had a hand in the development of various "Impossible" pies—pie fillings that contain Bisquick and that produce their own crust, sort of, while they bake.

But even if there were an economic interest in the production of these peculiar recipes, what would that mean? Are there people at Pillsbury and General Mills who are paid to sit around dropping iron filings into cake batter in hopes of producing a cake that bakes its own pan?

Or do they add miscellaneous things like aftershave lotion, chicken wings and bubble gum, just to see whether anything good happens?

There are enough of these shall-we-say "odd" recipes around that it seemed worthwhile to find out a little about them.

I called Pillsbury, and consumer relations manager Catherine Hanley told me that the company didn't invent the Tunnel of Fudge Cake—it was a $5,000 winner in the 1966 Pillsbury Bake-Off.

O.K., Pillsbury didn't dream it up. What possessed the woman who did?

Hanley said she was interested in that question herself a few years ago and called Ella Helfrich in Houston, Texas, and asked her. Helfrich told Hanley that she added the frosting mix on purpose, because it was one of the products emphasized in that year's bake-off. She was hoping to get a very moist, brownie-like pound cake. The first time she made it, she said, she took it out fairly early, and the middle was so runny it had to be eaten with a spoon. But she knew she was onto something, and she kept trying until it worked.

"I still don't know," Hanley said, "whether she's a great cook or hasn't the vaguest idea how you put a cake together."

I decided to call Helfrich and find out. "I do this kind of thing all the time," said Helfrich, who clearly knows darn well how to bake a cake. "I always try all the contests," she explained, and, since the idea in so many recipe contests is to use a specific ingredient, Helfrich said she has developed lots of very peculiar recipes.

"I got a small prize from Kraft for some rolls with Marshmallow Creme in them, and I've made a macaroni cake, and a Coca-Cola cake (that was before the one that got so popular) and I've put mashed potato flakes in different things."

Well, that's as good an explanation as anyone is likely to get: You throw lipstick into a cake in the hope of winning money from Max Factor.

But even if Pillsbury didn't actually invent Tunnel of Fudge Cake, aren't there any people over there trying to outdo the Ella Helfriches of our land?

Sure there are, Hanley said. For example, they've developed new recipes to make a high-quality loaf of bread in less time. "They'll take an idea like that," Hanley said, "and keep at it until it works or is abandoned." But that apparently isn't anyone's regular job. "On the whole," she said, "they're doing specific projects that aren't as creative." Like more-normal recipes for the backs of packages.

So hang in there, Ella, we need you!

Meanwhile, here's the Tunnel of Fudge Cake recipe, as it appeared on the backs of some Pillsbury frosting mix packages. Hanley noted that even though the recipe has been adapted to make it as "tolerant" (of errors and mismeasurement) as possible, it is still a very tricky cake because it's nearly impossible to tell when it is done enough to come out of the oven.

My own experience is that you just have to have faith and let it stay in as long as the recipe says it is supposed to, ignoring the rather done-looking brownie crust that develops earlier. After all, if you can't trust Pillsbury, who can you trust?

## Tunnel of Fudge Cake

(A Pillsbury recipe)

1½ cups margarine or butter, softened
6 eggs
1½ cups sugar
1 (13.9-ounce) package Rich 'n Easy

Fudge or Double Dutch frosting mix*
2 cups flour
2 cups chopped walnuts or pecans*
2 teaspoons water

Preheat oven to 350 degrees. Using solid shortening, generously grease a 12-cup fluted tube pan or 10-inch angel-food tube pan.

In a large bowl, cream the margarine. Add the eggs, one at a time, beating well after each addition. Gradually add the sugar, creaming the mixture until it is light and fluffy.

Reserve ½ cup of the frosting mix. By hand—use a spoon—stir in the remaining frosting mix, the flour and the nuts. Stir until well blended. Pour batter into prepared pan and bake at 350 degrees for 60 to 65 minutes. [You can't test this cake with a knife or a toothpick because it's *supposed* to be gooey inside. Let it go the full 60 to 65 minutes; it should develop a shiny, brownie-like crust well before then.]

Cool the cake 1 hour *not* inverted, then remove it from the pan. Cool completely before glazing.

Prepare the glaze by blending the reserved frosting mix with the 2 teaspoons of water. Spoon over the cooled cake.

Store tightly covered. Makes 16 servings.

---

If you just hate the idea of making cake from scratch (even if it includes frosting mix), Pillsbury makes a complete Tunnel of Fudge Cake mix. But it's not the same. You prepare the cake batter and the batter for the gooey part from packets. Then you pour the cake batter into a Bundt pan and add the gooey part on top, being careful to keep it away from the sides of the pan. Apparently it sinks further into the cake during baking. There isn't very much magic in that.

Let's move on, then, to the "Impossible" pies, which rely on the addition of Bisquick to provide something between a self-forming crust and a filling thick enough to eliminate the need for a crust.

There have been a number of such pies over the years, starting with Impossible Coconut Pie, and including recently Impossible Chicken Pie (which won $10,000 in the National Chicken Cooking Contest), Impossible Garden Pie and, for a Halloween theme, Impossible Pumpkin Pie.

In the never-ending battle for truth, justice and peculiar food articles, I called General Mills, the maker of Bisquick, and tried to get to the bottom, as it were, of the crustless pie.

Marcia Copeland, director of Betty Crocker food services, was as helpful as she could be, which wasn't very.

---

*According to the original recipe, both this particular frosting mix and the nuts are essential for the success of the cake. Unfortunately, Pillsbury recently stopped making these frosting mixes. I made the cake using a Red Owl frosting mix and it worked fine. Despite my deep and abiding faith in Pillsbury, I guess I wasn't too surprised at that. Pillsbury has reissued the recipe in a new form with no frosting mix at all, but that's no fun.

General Mills, it seems, didn't invent the Impossible Pie any more than Pillsbury did the Tunnel of Fudge Cake. And, in this case, the real inventor is unknown so we can't ask what drove him or her to the extreme of dumping Bisquick into a pie filling. At least it wasn't a Bisquick contest.

"We can't pin down exactly how it started," Copeland said. *"American Home* magazine ran an article about it four or five years ago, and it began circulating as a grass-roots thing." Newspaper food sections around the country would reproduce the Impossible Coconut Pie recipe now and then, but "in the beginning we didn't see much potential in it," she said, "because it doesn't use much [Bisquick]."

But as the number of variations grew (and it become apparent that the Impossible was within their grasp), the General Mills folks began working up their own Impossible recipes. "We've done both dessert and main-course variations," Copeland said, "including an Impossible Cheeseburger and an Impossible Fudge Pie."

Although the Impossible pie wasn't their own idea, General Mills, too, has people trying to develop original recipes. "We continually look for the new idea, the new breakthrough," Copeland said. "And we constantly look for the new idea that would be a new product or a new way to use an older product."

I wonder whether they've tried iron filings yet.

---

*Impossible Pumpkin Pie*

(A General Mills recipe)

¾ cup sugar
½ cup Bisquick baking mix
2 tablespoons margarine or butter,
   softened
1 (12-ounce) can evaporated milk

2 eggs
1 (15- or 16-ounce) can pumpkin
2½ teaspoons pumpkin pie spice
2 teaspoons vanilla

Preheat the oven to 350 degrees. Grease a 9- or 10-inch pie plate. Beat all the ingredients together until the mixture is smooth. Pour it into the pie plate [but do not fill quite to the rim—the pie rises during baking]. Bake 50 to 55 minutes, until a knife inserted in the center comes out clean.

If you're expecting that an actual pie crust will somehow form under the pumpkin, you're expecting a bit much even from something called Impossible Pie. It is, nonetheless, a pumpkin pie, and it manages to hold itself together as though it had a crust. Close enough.

---

There are three other items that I thought of when my mind, such as it is, turned to recipes that don't behave normally. All of them have been showing up in church cookbooks for years, and even attempting to find the person truly responsible for one of them is a task I decided not to undertake.

The first is sometimes called Fudge Upside-Down Cake, or other names to that effect, but it is most often referred to as Pudding Cake. It's a batter that's put into a pan and topped with dry ingredients and boiling water. The result, after all of this undergoes half an hour in the oven, is a cake on the top and chocolate sauce underneath. It's pretty good, too.

## Chocolate Pudding Cake

1¼ cups sugar, divided
1 tablespoon butter
½ cup milk
1 cup flour
1 teaspoon baking powder

¼ teaspoon salt
5½ tablespoons cocoa, divided
½ cup chopped walnuts
½ cup brown sugar
1¼ cups boiling water

Preheat the oven to 350 degrees. Cream together ¾ cup of the sugar and the butter. Add the milk, mixing well. Combine the flour, baking powder, salt and 1½ tablespoons of the cocoa, and add to the butter mixture, mixing well. Pour into a buttered 9-inch square pan.

Sprinkle the batter with the walnuts. Combine the remaining ½ cup of sugar, the ½ cup of brown sugar and the remaining 4 tablespoons of cocoa. Spread over the top of the batter. Pour the boiling water over all.

Bake at 350 degrees for 30 minutes. If you're doubtful that it's done, don't plunge the toothpick or knife all the way in, because the bottom is gooey even when the cake is finished.

Next comes Crazy Cake (or, more often, Krazy Kake). This one is in a class by itself. Tunnel of Fudge Cake and Pudding Cake produce a gooey portion along with the cake. Impossible pies eliminate the need for buying or making a crust. Krazy Kake has absolutely nothing to recommend it; it simply is put together weirdly.

If that turns you on, you ought to see my car.

## Krazy Kake

3 cups flour
2 cups sugar
6 tablespoons cocoa
2 teaspoons salt
2 teaspoons soda

1 teaspoon vanilla
1½ tablespoons vinegar
10 tablespoons vegetable oil
2 cups water

Preheat the oven to 350 degrees. Pour all the dry ingredients into an ungreased 9-by-13-inch pan and mix with a fork. Pour the liquids into the dry ingredients and mix with a fork. Bake for 25 to 30 minutes.

That's it, but I should note that if you don't mix the dry ingredients enough, some of your guests may complain that the cake is salty, others may notice a pronounced baking-soda flavor, and so on. You might also find that parts of the cake have risen much better than other parts. That's probably O.K.; what point would there be in making a cake this way and having it turn out perfectly normal?

On the other hand, you might well ask, what point is there in making a cake this way at all?

Last and possibly least, if for no other reason than the elegance of its name, is a thing called Dump Cake.

I assume that the name derives from the cake's untraditional method of assembly—you more or less just dump the ingredients into a pan. I find the result pretty sweet but not bad, and it went over very well at the office. Those who don't care for it may feel that the name has more to do with what should happen to the cake *after* it is baked. That is certainly the interpretation that I would put on one version of this recipe that I heard on an Iowa radio station in 1967: Chocolate Blueberry Dump Cake. We'll skip that one.

Actually, I suppose Dump Cake doesn't really belong in this discussion at all. Although its preparation is indeed peculiar—you pour cherry pie filling into a pan, top it with crushed pineapple, then with dry cake mix and then with melted butter, nuts and coconut—nothing much happens to those ingredients while they bake. The finished product is cherry-pie-pineapple stuff on the bottom and what tastes like a thick layer of streusel on the top.

---

### *Pineapple-Cherry Dump Cake*

1 (21-ounce) can cherry pie filling
1 (20-ounce) can crushed pineapple
  (do not drain)
1 (18½-ounce) package yellow cake
  mix
10 tablespoons (1¼ sticks) butter, melted
1 cup flaked coconut
1 cup chopped nuts
Whipped cream or ice cream
  (optional)

Preheat oven to 350 degrees. Spread the cherry pie filling evenly on the bottom of a greased 9-by-13-inch pan. Layer the undrained pineapple on top of the cherries. (You needn't be too careful here. Some versions of the recipe have the pineapple on the bottom and the cherry on top, so any way that it all gets into the pan is probably fine.)

Sprinkle the cake mix over the pineapple. Cover with melted butter. Top with coconut and nuts.

Bake at 350 degrees for about 1 hour. Top, if you like, with whipped cream or ice cream.

---

### Little Mystery #3: Bananas

How come all of a sudden it's O.K. to put bananas in the refrigerator?

If even the question is a mystery to you, you must be under thirty. Ask an Old One to sing you the Chiquita Banana Song. Chiquita Banana wasn't always just a stylized cartoon character on a little blue label. She used to be a *person,* and she had all sorts of banana hints. Her biggest hint was that you must *never* put bananas in the refrigerator.

More recent banana commercials haven't included that warning, and occasionally one hears suggestions that bananas can be refrigerated if they're ripe but you're not ready to use them.

One such suggestion is contained in a publication of the banana industry's public-information outfit, The Banana Bunch, headquartered in New York. I called The Banana Bunch to straighten this matter out, but I had a little difficulty. After explaining who I was, running through the history of Chiquita and asking my question, I was told I was talking to a dental office. It seemed that, having said in black-and-white that it's O.K. to refrigerate bananas, The Banana Bunch went into hiding.

Thanks to a little help from colleague Mary Hart, who remembered the name of the public-relations firm that handled the banana account (Mary remembers everything) I finally got in touch with The Banana Bunch. It seems that some time after issuing the press release with the refrigeration note, they moved.

In any case, I have an answer. I'm not at all sure I believe it, but here it is, straight from the banana's mouth:

**Solution:** When the Chiquita Banana jingle was written, they needed a word to rhyme with equator and threw in a line about the refrigerator.

That's the whole explanation.

So for all those years we let our bananas rot just for the sake of a jingle?

Well, not really, said the bananaperson. "All fruit is better if you don't refrigerate it. But you can refrigerate bananas if they're beginning to get too ripe. However, the peel will get black, and that isn't very attractive."

O.K., now that we've heard that, whether or not we believe it, why not a little nostalgia trip for the Old Ones present? Here are the complete lyrics to the original Chiquita Banana song:

---

*I'm Chiquita Banana and I'm here to say*
*Bananas must be ripened in a certain way.*
*When they are flecked with brown and have a golden hue,*
*Bananas taste the best and are the best for you.*

*You can put them in salad*
*You can put them in a pie-yi!*
*Any way you want to eat them,*
*It's impossible to beat them.*

*But bananas like the climate*
*Of the very, very tropical equator,*
*So you should never put bananas*
*In your refrigerator.*
*Oh, no, no, no!*

# The SPAM Dinner

On June 6, 1944, Allied forces landed on the Normandy coast of German-occu-pied France.

Of the military struggle of those times much has been written, and it is fitting that we remember it today. It was a time of great national and personal sacrifice, the like of which we have not seen since.

It is also fitting, however, that we recognize that those soldiers were bringing to the yearning millions of Western Europe not only the breath of freedom but also, incidentally, American chocolate bars, chewing gum and, perhaps least con-sciously, SPAM.

SPAM, that much-maligned but much-eaten canned-meat product of the Geo. A. Hormel Co., Austin, Minnesota, was an inseparable element of the Allied advance. Where there were GIs, there was SPAM.

Not that all of them were thrilled about it, you understand.

If it were subjected to a rational evaluation, SPAM would surely have done quite well. It's nutritious, it's really quite tasty and it keeps almost indefinitely, which makes it an immensely practical food in wartime situations—and in many others.

But familiarity breeds contempt, and by the time of the invasion of Europe, our boys were mighty familiar with SPAM and the other government-supplied culinary staples. Whatever they thought about SPAM by then, it was not that it was fantastic.

There is a second side, however, to the matter of the desirability of sitting down to some SPAM.

Of the two men I know who served in France around the end of the war, both have told me much the same anecdote. On the basis of that small sample, I assume that it happened to others, too.

A bunch of Yanks were going somewhere or other and stopped at a French farmhouse or inn. The French folks could provide shelter but could offer little in the way of food because their larders were almost empty. The Americans said all they had was @%*# canned rations. The French took the SPAM and whatever and transformed it into the best food the Americans had ever eaten.

Well, friends, that's a challenge if ever I've heard one, even more than forty years after the fact.

Could I equal the French artistry with SPAM? Could *I* turn it into a truly memorable dish? I decided to give it a try, despite giggles from colleagues.

It might be true that you can't make a silk purse out of a sow's ear, but canned pork shoulder, it seemed to me, was another thing altogether.

(To be perfectly accurate, SPAM consists of "chopped pork shoulder meat with ham meat added and salt, water, sugar, sodium nitrite," but you can't turn very many clever phrases with a list like that.)

The Hormel folks, incidentally, insist that SPAM is spelled in capitals. And I have to go along, because it is *their* name for *their* product (and it is not to be used for just any luncheon meat).

A word about those giggles: Without help from me or the creative cooks of France, SPAM continues to sell quite nicely. On SPAM's fiftieth anniversary, Hormel put U.S. sales at 110 million cans a year.

But I think it's safe to say that it isn't being consciously merchandised as a potential ingredient in gourmet cooking.

Although the folks in Austin, bless 'em, put recipes on the SPAM cans, they tend to be for things like "SPAM Picadilly," a sandwich spread consisting of SPAM, cream cheese and pickle relish.

It may be that fancier recipes just wouldn't fit on the cans, but I suspect that we don't find them there largely because the SPAM folks don't have the audacity to suggest them.

Well, if they don't, I do.

In my usual burst of excess, I have produced an excellent garlic-laden SPAM-and-avocado appetizer, a creamy and delicate (and beautiful) SPAM mousse, an incredibly tasty SPAM-and-spinach gratin, a very mellow sauce for thin slices of SPAM, and a glazed dessert bar in which SPAM contributes to a sort of mincemeat mixture.

You could, it is true, make any of these recipes with ham (some of them were ham recipes before I got to them). But not only is SPAM rather good, and not only does it have almost no waste (a can of it contains no bones, no fat—nothing, other than the tiniest amount of gelatin, but SPAM), it also costs about half as much as canned ham.

You could also, it is true, make any of these recipes with some other brand of canned luncheon meat. I can't stop you.

But if you want the authentic experience, complete with knowing chuckles from ex-servicemen, genuine SPAM is what you need.

This first recipe is so uncomplicated that it could easily fit on a SPAM can.

And, containing as it does one of nature's two most perfect foods, garlic (the other is chocolate), it is a sure winner.

---

### Avocat au SPAM
(Avocado with SPAM)

2 avocados
1 small clove garlic
1/2 cup mayonnaise

About 1/2 (12-ounce) can SPAM, or 1 (7-ounce) can

Halve but do not peel the avocados, and remove the pits. Put the garlic through a garlic press or very finely mince it, and add it to the mayonnaise.

Cut the SPAM into small dice (1/8 inch to 1/4 inch on a side).

Thoroughly combine the SPAM and the mayonnaise, coating the SPAM cubes well, and put a mound of the mixture into each avocado half. Serves 4 as an appetizer.

---

The next dish uses a lot of pretty fancy ingredients almost certainly not found in the almost-bare French pantries of World War II. So what? It's delicious.

The recipe wouldn't fit on a can of SPAM (unless they make it in fifty-pound cans), but take my word; it's very, very good.

---

### Cold SPAM Mousse

2 (12-ounce) cans SPAM
1/2 cup water
2 tablespoons oil
4 1/2 tablespoons flour
1 1/2 (1/4-ounce) envelopes unflavored gelatin
Dash of salt
Dash of cayenne pepper
1 1/4 cups milk
2 sticks (1/2 pound) unsalted butter
1 teaspoon tomato paste
3 tablespoons sherry

2 egg whites
1 cup heavy cream

ASPIC (OPTIONAL):

1 (1/4-ounce) envelope unflavored gelatin
1 (10 3/4-ounce) can chicken broth
1 tablespoon tomato paste
1/4 cup sherry
Optional decorations with aspic (see text)

Put the SPAM through a grinder or food processor until it's finely ground (or finely chopped).

Put the water and oil in a small saucepan. In a small bowl, mix the flour, the 1 1/2 envelopes of gelatin (it's an approximate measure; don't worry about being exact—something like a rounded tablespoon), the salt and cayenne. Stir this dry mixture into the water until the

*(Continued)*

mixture is smooth. Slowly stir in the milk and heat the mixture on a medium-high burner, stirring constantly, until it just boils.

Pour it onto a large dinner plate or serving platter, cover it with plastic wrap and chill until it is cold and set. (This mixture serves to bind the other ingredients in the mousse. You can prepare it in advance.)

Cream the butter (don't substitute salted butter; with this much of it you'll really make the final product salty instead of creamy). Add the chilled gelatin mixture a little at a time, continuing to beat. Stir in the ground SPAM.

In a small cup, dissolve the tomato paste in the sherry and stir it into the mixture.

Beat the egg whites until they are stiff but not dry. Whip the cream. Fold the beaten egg whites into the cream and the whole thing into the SPAM mixture. Taste it (ain't that good?), and adjust seasonings if necessary.

This has been a fair amount of effort, and it tastes wonderful, but so far it doesn't look like much. Splashy presentation is a big help for something that can be described like that.

Affix a collar to a 1½-quart soufflé dish, or another round dish of similar capacity: Tear off a sheet of waxed paper long enough to go around the dish and overlap a bit. Fold it in half along its length. Brush one side of the paper with oil, and wrap it, oiled side in, around the dish; the paper should extend at least 2 inches above the top of the dish. Tie the collar tightly around the dish with string, or use rubber bands.

Pour the mousse into the dish, smooth the top against the collar and chill at least 2 hours. (Take the collar off the dish before serving.)

For an even more glamorous appearance, top with a little pale aspic (maybe with a few decorations): Soften the gelatin in ½ cup of the chicken broth. Combine the remaining broth with the tomato paste and sherry, and heat. Stir in the softened gelatin and cook over medium heat, stirring, until the gelatin is fully dissolved.

We're leaving out all the messy straining through beaten egg whites that fancy chefs insist is part of making aspic, so strain instead by pouring the mixture through a funnel or strainer lined with a tea towel. Refrigerate or freeze until the gelatin is syrupy. (If you waited too long, heat it again, very briefly.)

Put the soufflé dish on a plate to catch any aspic that leaks past the collar. Pour the aspic over the top of the mousse and spread it evenly. If you want to throw in a few decorations (slices of hard-cooked eggs or olives, maybe, turned into flowers with stems of green onion or dill), pour on less than half the aspic, let set briefly in the refrigerator, place the decorations and pour on the remaining aspic. Chill at least another hour. Now it's delicious and gorgeous, too.

Serves 10 to 12 (it's very rich).

---

Next the SPAM-and-spinach gratin. This recipe, too, takes a little time. But even without the SPAM it's excellent, and the SPAM improves it.

2 (10-ounce) packages frozen chopped
   spinach
4 tablespoons butter
Salt, pepper
3 tablespoons flour
1 (10½-ounce) can consommé

½ (12-ounce) can or 1 (7-ounce) can
   SPAM, diced into ¼-inch cubes
1 (6-ounce) package grated Swiss
   cheese (1½ cups), divided
4 tablespoons dry bread crumbs
3 tablespoons melted butter

## Gratin d'Epinards au Fromage et SPAM

(Spinach gratinéed with cheese and you-know-what)

Prepare the spinach according to package directions. Drain well. Really well. Squeeze it.

Heat the 4 tablespoons of butter in a 5-quart Dutch oven over moderately high heat. When the butter is bubbling, stir in the spinach. Continue stirring 5 to 10 minutes until all the moisture from the spinach has evaporated. The spinach will start to stick to the pan. Add a little salt and pepper.

Lower the heat to medium, sprinkle on the flour and stir for 2 minutes.

Stir in the consommé, bring to the simmer and cook over medium heat, stirring occasionally, for 15 minutes. Stir in the diced SPAM. Cook 5 to 10 more minutes, stirring occasionally, until the mixture has some body and is no longer liquid.

Stir ¾ cup of the cheese into the spinach, and pour the mixture into a well-buttered 2-quart baking dish. Mix the rest of the cheese with the bread crumbs and sprinkle it over the top. If you're preparing ahead, stop at this point.

When ready to go, preheat the oven to 375 degrees. Sprinkle the melted butter over the cheese and crumbs.

Bake 30 minutes in the upper third of the oven. You've probably never had better-tasting spinach. Serves 6.

Now to the sauce for thin-sliced SPAM. I don't know what to say here except "Wow!"

2 (12-ounce) cans SPAM, sliced thinly
3 tablespoons butter
1 tablespoon oil
2 tablespoons minced shallots
3 tablespoons flour
1 cup (most of a 10½-ounce can)
   consommé

½ cup sherry
1½ tablespoons tomato paste
Pepper
No salt
1½ cups heavy cream
4 tablespoons Cognac

## Sliced SPAM, Splendid Sauce

Note: This sauce has plenty of salt on its own. Don't add any in the course of routine seasoning.

Brown the slices of SPAM lightly in the butter and oil. Cook each side only a minute or so. Set the SPAM aside.

Add the shallots to the fat in the skillet and sauté until they are translucent. (If necessary add another tablespoon or so of butter.) Then add the flour and cook over low heat, stirring, 1 minute.

Combine the consommé and the sherry. Add the liquid to the flour mixture a little at a time, stirring constantly, until it is smooth. Add the tomato paste and pepper. Stir in the cream. Simmer 4 or 5 minutes, until the sauce coats a spoon.

Stir in the Cognac.

Add the SPAM slices (maybe cut in strips as a further disguise) and stir to cover them with sauce. Simmer slowly for a few minutes to heat the SPAM. Serves 8 to 10.

And last we come, as always we must, to dessert. Yes, SPAM in dessert.

It's kind of a mincemeat bar cookie. Some of you will recall that mincemeat used to be made with meat in it, instead of coming, meatless, from jars or boxes found on supermarket shelves. Return with us, now, to those thrilling days of yesteryear. Real meat in mincemeat!

Under another name, and made with lean ground beef instead of SPAM, this recipe won first prize in a contest sponsored by the National Live Stock and Meat Board. The meat board sent it to me, and I had my way with it.

## *Goodness Gracious, Great Bars of SPAM!*

FILLING:

2 (12-ounce) cans SPAM
1 (16-ounce) can whole-berry
   cranberry sauce
1¼ cups brown sugar
1 cup seedless raisins
¾ cup coarsely chopped walnuts
½ cup orange marmalade
½ teaspoon salt
1 orange

DOUGH:

4 cups flour
2 tablespoons baking powder
2 teaspoons salt
1⅓ cups milk
⅔ cup oil

GLAZE:

1½ cups confectioners' sugar
3 tablespoons milk
1 tablespoon rum

Prepare the filling: In a food processor or meat grinder (or with a knife, if you have some time) chop the SPAM until it is the consistency of hamburger. Put the SPAM, cranberry sauce, brown sugar, raisins, walnuts, marmalade and the ½ teaspoon of salt in a Dutch oven.

Grate the peel of the orange into the mixture, then squeeze in the juice of the orange (catching any seeds in a strainer or your hand). Stir well.

Cook, stirring, over medium heat until the mixture boils. Continue cooking 20 minutes, stirring very often. Cool.

Prepare the dough: Combine the flour, baking powder and the 2 teaspoons of salt in a bowl. Add milk and oil, stirring until the flour is fully moistened. Knead the dough briefly on waxed paper, and divide in half.

Roll half the dough between 2 sheets of waxed paper until it is slightly bigger than a 17-by-10-inch cookie sheet or jelly-roll pan. Peel off the top sheet of waxed

paper, invert the pan over the dough and invert the pan and dough together. Peel off the other sheet of waxed paper. Press the dough so it covers the bottom and goes up the sides of the pan.

Spoon the filling evenly over the dough.

Preheat the oven to 425 degrees.

Roll the second half of the dough between 2 sheets of waxed paper to the same dimensions—slightly larger than the pan. Remove the top sheet and quickly flip the dough onto the filling. (He who hesitates is in trouble here. Once it starts falling off of the waxed paper, there's no reasonable way to catch the dough.)

Remove the backing sheet and press the top and bottom layers of dough together at the edges. Don't worry if the top layer doesn't quite make it to the edge; it'll be fine. Make 4 long diagonal slashes through the top layer to minimize shrinkage.

Bake 25 to 30 minutes, until the crust is golden brown.

Remove from oven and prepare the glaze: Combine confectioners' sugar, milk and rum. Mix until smooth.

When the bars have cooled slightly, drizzle the glaze over them and spread evenly with a knife or spatula.

Allow to cool, and cut into bars.

---

### Little Mystery #4: Bananas

Not long ago we looked into the Chiquita Banana jingle that for years advised people:

*Bananas like the climate of the very, very*
*    tropical equator,*
*So you should never put bananas in your*
*    refrigerator!*
*Oh, no, no, no!"*

I could barely believe what I'd been told—that for years, all over this great land of ours, people were letting bananas rot for lack of refrigeration, just because some jingle writer couldn't come up with anything other than "refrigerator" to rhyme with "equator."

To demonstrate that there are other easy rhymes that would not have wasted so many bananas, I have constructed these alternative last verses for the Chiquita Banana Song:

---

*Bananas like the climate of the very, very tropical equator,*
*And you should never take bananas into an elevator!*

Or:

*Bananas like the climate of the very, very tropical equator,*
*But you should never give bananas to a right-wing dictator!*

Or:

*Bananas like the climate of the very, very tropical equator,*
*But you should never boil bananas inside your percolator!*

# A Burger and a Cherry Coke

A lot of American life seems to consist of stumbling across things you didn't know you needed until you saw them. Suddenly, inexplicably, there's another thing you've got to have.

Lots of folks have this problem at stores; I have it at flea markets.

I don't have the vaguest idea why my hidden needs seem to center on old things instead of new ones. I don't think I'm trying to get my childhood back—my adulthood is pretty nice. Lots of the stuff I find myself craving isn't even something I had when I was a kid. It is, though, always something that invokes those more carefree times.

That's the way it was when I read an article in the paper a couple of years ago about a fellow in Edina, Minnesota, who had assembled an entire soda fountain and counter in his basement. I really don't want to have a soda fountain in my basement (if you think I'm fibbing you haven't seen my basement), but suddenly I longed to recapture the experience of going into Pete's Drugstore in Milwaukee on a summer afternoon and having a chocolate phosphate while I pondered whatever one ponders at age eight or nine. (Maybe it was which of Pete's many candy bars I might buy if only I had another nickel.)

Today's kids probably wouldn't be able to understand what was so appealing about the drugstores of my youth. Why, they didn't even have Pac-Man or Donkey Kong. But there *was* an appeal. Armed with only a nickel you could while away most of an afternoon at Pete's (if you didn't bother the other customers by slurping forever at the last bubbles of phosphate or idly kicking the counter).

Pete didn't have a grill, but there was a Walgreen's nearby that did, and when I got a little older and began to have real pocket money some of us would occasionally go to Walgreen's for a hamburger. They weren't great hamburgers, but they were great *drugstore* hamburgers, a special class of burgers that, along with chocolate phosphates, cherry Cokes and not-particularly-thick malts made with honest-to-Pete (or honest-to-Walgreen) ice cream, constitute a kind of endangered species: drugstore food.

In the spirit of 1950, and with no apology to those who prefer a Big Mac and a "thick shake" (made with who-knows-what) it seemed appropriate to try to recreate just a few drugstore favorites.

No, there will not be included any of the elaborate sundaes whose appalling names ("Idiot's Delight," "Fat Man's Misery") decorated the wall above the inevitable Bastian-Blessing fountain. They're easy enough to make up yourself, though; just assemble umpteen scoops of various flavors of ice cream, a banana, lots of whipped cream, a little caramel sauce, hot fudge, some nuts and a maraschino cherry in a dish that can't possibly hold it all once the ice cream starts to melt.

Maybe I continued to like drugstores when I was a teenager because I wanted to be a soda jerk. If you weren't muscular enough to make the football team, you could still aspire to being a soda jerk, and, wearing your natty paper hat and expertly manipulating the gleaming silver tools of your trade, you could dream of winning the affection of the nubile head cheerleader by favoring her with an extra-large swirl of whipped cream atop the Fat Man's Misery you made for her.

To what can today's scrawny but oversexed teenagers aspire? No self-respecting head cheerleader can be won over with an extra pickle slice on a Quarter Pounder.

(Yes, yes. We'll get to the recipes eventually, but I have a little more I have to get off my chest.)

Whenever I attempted to discuss drugstore food with the folks at work, the conversation did not stay long with hamburgers and ice cream but always shifted rapidly to candy. Unlike the selection available at even the largest drugstore candy counter these days, drugstores used to have lots of inexpensive candy in addition to the standard candy bars. Although some of these candies are still around—especially, for some reason, in theaters—most have bitten the dust. Whatever, they seem to hold a special place in lots of hearts, even though the coating on some of them tasted like soap and others would stick in your teeth for half an afternoon. Who could forget:

Snaps and Nibs, as well as licorice whips; Jujubes, Dots, Black Crows and the little hard dots on paper strips; thin, striped, coconutty strips that looked like watermelon slices or rainbows; little molded candies that for some unfathomable reason were made to look like babies, and especially the variously shaped wax items containing a few drops of flavored liquid. My favorite of that sort was what appeared to be five tiny bottles of pop, each a different flavor. The whole thing cost five cents and was called Nik-L-Nip. If it's still around somewhere, which I doubt, it's probably called Dol-R-Nip.

You were supposed to be able to chew the wax from which these things were made, but it seldom congealed—it just hung around in your mouth in several flaky lumps. But everybody said it worked, so I always tried.

I recently visited the last place I knew about that had large amounts of this kind of stuff, and the space has been taken over by imported chocolate bars at $1.75 a whack.

Folks also remembered regional candy bars that they miss, including: Giant (a Milwaukee alternative to Mr. Goodbar, in case you're looking), Look and Big Hunk (West Coast goodies), Sugar Daddy (a Slo-Poke), Slo-Poke (a Sugar Daddy) and Snirkles, a large, rectangular spiral of white and brown caramel (CAHR-mul, or as they say on television, CARE-a-mell, or, as they say in a town in California, cahr-MELL).

O.K., I'm done reminiscing. On to the recipes.

Drugstore hamburgers are not at all like fast-food hamburgers. They are also not at all like the half-pound cutely named theme-burgers with avocados or sprouts or Monterey Jack and mushrooms that are served at restaurants decorated with packing-crate strips and ferns growing out of light fixtures removed from British trains. (These restaurants invariably have been converted from warehouses or automobile dealerships or mine shafts, a history that is supposed to add a certain *je ne sais quoi.* I certainly don't know *what.*)

The true drugstore hamburger is a flat, slightly crisp slab of well-done ground beef, served on an inexpensive but nicely grilled bun, with the option of cheese (Velveeta or the equivalent, not Monterey Jack) and maybe fried onions. That's it. Ketchup, mustard and pickles are not recommended, but they can be added by the diner if absolutely necessary.

The difficulty in preparing drugstore hamburgers at home is only that you need several large frying pans to take the place of the grill. Don't eliminate grilling the bun—it's a must.

---

### Drugstore Hamburgers

4 tablespoons butter or margarine, divided
1 medium onion
1 pound ground beef

5 or 6 inexpensive hamburger buns
5 or 6 slices pasteurized process cheese (optional)

In a small saucepan, melt 1½ tablespoons of the butter over low heat.

Coarsely chop the onion and stir it into the butter. Let the onion just cook away on the back burner, turning translucent and maybe a little brown. Add a little more butter if necessary. If it gets really brown, turn off the heat.

Set aside a large pan for frying the hamburgers.

Spread the cut surfaces of the buns with the remaining butter and set them in a very large pan, over low to medium-low heat. Check on them often, to make sure that they're grilling but not burning. (We're starting this early because you'll have to do it in shifts unless you have a huge pan. When the first buns are done, plop in the next ones. You could use the broiler in a pinch, but it tends to dry out the buns.)

Now the burgers. Heat the large frying pan, ungreased, over low-medium heat for a couple of minutes. While it's heating, divide the ground beef into 5 or 6 equal portions. Shape them by flattening each on a counter top and pressing it out until it is about 6 inches across. Really. They should be *thin.* (If you like, you can do this ahead of time; if so, stack the patties, separated by waxed paper or plastic wrap, in the refrigerator.)

When the pan is hot, arrange the patties in it, turn the heat up to medium and let them fry for a couple of minutes, pressing down on them occasionally with a spatula.

(They're not supposed to be thick and juicy; they're supposed to be thin and almost crunchy.)

When the bottoms of the burgers are fully browned (not just gray), flip them with a spatula. Press down again and fry the other side. (Drain off any very large accumulation of grease; a small amount should be left for authenticity.) When the second side is almost done, put a slice of cheese on any burger that is supposed to have it, add a heap of the nice, slightly greasy onions to each burger that is supposed to have them (in a real drugstore every hamburger got onions unless you practically screamed your refusal), and in any case cover each burger with the top of a bun. A burger with neither cheese nor onion should probably get a tiny bit of butter before the bun goes down, just for grease.

When the bottom of the burger is done (and the cheese, if any, is melted), slide a spatula under the whole thing and plop it onto a grilled bun bottom. As they never said in any drugstore I attended, "Voilà!"

---

To go with the drugstore hamburger, we have to make French fries, which isn't too easy to do well at home. There is no alternative side dish. Certainly not yogurt or a salad. And let's not even mention the "fries" that you get by baking some potatoes on a cookie sheet.

It's not that there's anything really difficult about the process of making French fries; it's just that there's a temperature-control problem. Your usual cooking pot doesn't hold very much oil—nothing like what a commercial deep-fryer holds. The result is that when your pot of oil gets to the right temperature for frying and you dump in a bunch of potatoes, it cools off nastily and the potatoes get greasy instead of nicely fried.

Well, you don't want to buy a commercial deep-fryer, and the prospect of minimizing the cooling effect by cooking one serving of fries at a time while the gang is at the table is more than a little off-putting. Happily, there is an approach that isn't too bad. The process isn't absolutely authentic, and it takes a little extra time, but the result is a whole lot better than anything you're going to get by baking potatoes in the oven. (Yuck.)

## Double-Cooked French Fries

**4 or 5 medium potatoes**
**Cooking oil**

**Salt**

Peel the potatoes if you like. (Washed but unpeeled is fine, too.) Cut them into ¼-inch slices, stack the slices and cut them into ¼-inch strips. These thin fast-food-style fries are easier to make decently at home than the larger, more-authentic drugstore model because they cook through more quickly, so if you're in doubt, slice thinner, not thicker.

Soak the potato strips in water—not cold and not in the refrigerator—for about an hour. Drain the strips and pat them dry with toweling.

Meanwhile, pour the oil into a large, deep pot. Don't fill it to closer than a couple inches from the top, because the oil will foam up. Heat it to 390 degrees. (If you don't have a deep-fat thermometer, you're in a little trouble here. You can use 1-inch squares of bread to measure temperatures approximately—at 390 degrees, it takes a bread square about 40 seconds to brown.)

Lower about half the potatoes into the oil (on slotted spoons or a strainer or in a basket if you have one). This overload of potato will cause the temperature of the oil to drop to about 350 degrees, which is what we want to maintain. (Adjust heat to maintain that temperature if you have a thermometer.) Cook the potatoes for about 4 to 6 minutes, moving them around occasionally, until they are softened but not brown. Remove them to drain on paper towels, reheat the oil to 390 degrees and cook the second batch the same way.

When both batches have been cooked, raise the oil temperature to 390 degrees again and fry the potatoes a second time in smaller batches (about one serving at a time). This time the oil temperature should be maintained at 390 degrees. (This won't be too hard, as the load of potatoes is smaller and they should still be warm.) Fry each small batch for 2 or 3 minutes until the potatoes are light golden-colored. Drain, salt and, if necessary, keep warm in a slow oven until the other batches are done.

And to go with burgers and fries you must have a chocolate malt. Or at the very least a cherry Coke.

First the malt. This method makes a malt that fills about 2 standard drinking glasses. It's not very thick, but you could make it thicker by cutting down the amount of milk or increasing the amount of ice cream. A blender is the ideal tool (short of a malt mixer) for making a malt. A food processor tends to liquefy the ice cream. An electric mixer is a little sloppy because of the open bowl, but it works adequately if you cut the ice cream into small pieces.

## Chocolate Malt

**1 cup milk (or ½ cup, for thicker malt)**
**¼ cup chocolate syrup**

**2 tablespoons malt powder**
**3 or 4 scoops vanilla ice cream**

If you're working with a blender, put in the milk, syrup and malt powder, then add the ice cream in half-scoop chunks and blend only until smooth.

If you're using an electric mixer, put in a quarter of the milk, and add the syrup and malt powder. Then, with the mixer at low speed, add the ice cream in small chunks (start with several) and add more milk only when necessary until all the ice cream is in. (Too much milk too early will splatter badly.)

These days you can buy cherry Coke already made, but you can also get hamburgers and French fries at McDonald's. That's missing the point. You want to make cherry Coke the way they did it at the drugstore. That is comparatively easy or a little difficult, depending. Do you have (or can you get) cherry syrup? Then it's easy. If you have to make the syrup, it's a little harder (see below). Don't be tempted just to add unsweetened cherry flavoring to the Coke. The real thing was made with syrup, which made the Coke a whole lot sweeter.

Once you have the syrup, pour a couple of tablespoons of it (more or less, to taste) into the bottom of a glass. Pour a little Coke into the syrup and stir until it's thinned and bubbly. Authenticity would require a needle spray of Coke at this point. If you want to make a stab at it, one of those plant-spraying bottles with the adjustable nozzle isn't bad. Either spray or pour in the remaining glassful of Coke, and stir once more.

If you can't get cherry syrup ready-made, making syrups really isn't all that hard. The trick is to avoid having them crystallize when they cool. To that end, follow the rather peculiar directions below more carefully than you might otherwise.

Once you've made the syrup, of course, nothing requires you to confine yourself to adding it to Coke.

One thinks immediately of cherry malts and of cherry (or other flavor) phosphates.

Make the latter like cherry Coke, by stirring a glug of club soda or fizzy mineral water into the syrup, filling the glass with poured or needle-sprayed fizz water and stirring again.

And, if you have something that crushes ice, pour some syrup over a hunk of it and you've got one of those flavored ice things that drips all over small children at fairs and carnivals. If, as seems likely, you don't have any conical paper cups, make it in a regular cup or a glass.

(I must admit that the conical paper water cup is one of the things I dearly loved about drugstores. It held an endless fascination for me. I really don't know why that might have been; it was certainly no more remarkable a feat of engineering than television, radar or Dynaflow—or, for that matter, the flat-bottom paper cup, which didn't leak, either.)

Back to phosphates. The needle spray is kind of pointless with a cherry Coke or cherry phosphate, but it's swell with a chocolate phosphate, made with regular canned chocolate syrup and club soda or fizzy water, because the spray really makes those big bubbles pop up.

(Several readers took me to task some time ago for not mentioning the availability of soda siphons in a discussion of making one's own carbonated drinks. Well, I'll mention them now. Soda siphons are gadgets that turn water into carbonated water with the aid of a $CO_2$ cartridge. They didn't stop making them when the Marx brothers quit making movies, and they work just fine.)

## *Cherry Syrup*

**2½ cups sugar**
**2 cups water**

**3 to 4 tablespoons cherry flavoring**
**Food coloring**

Combine the sugar and water in a saucepan over low heat, stirring only until the sugar is fully dissolved. Wet a paper towel and wipe the sides of the pan above the surface of the liquid to remove any grains of the sugar. Then cover the pan and bring to a gentle boil. Boil 5 minutes.

Allow to cool. When the syrup is not much more than lukewarm, stir in the flavoring and coloring. Use plenty of coloring (maybe half a teaspoonful—at least enough to make the syrup quite dark) in case you wind up using the syrup in something besides Coke. A pale phosphate is not appetizing.

Pour into a jar that has been carefully washed, and store in the refrigerator. Makes enough for maybe 18 cherry Cokes.

You can make other flavors of syrup, of course, and you can use real fruit ingredients instead of artificial flavors if you like. For lemon, lime or orange syrups, for example, put 3 tablespoons of lemon, lime or orange rind in the sugar and water and boil together. Some juice will help, too, but it isn't as potent as the rind. (Additional boiling time will help the flavor but runs an increased risk of crystallized syrup.)

You'll have to strain the bits of rind out of the syrup before you put it in the jar—well, you won't *have* to, but to leave them in would be tacky. Add the coloring after the syrup has been strained and cooled.

Another reason not to stint on the coloring is that it seems to have as much to do with the experience as the flavoring itself. When I made my first attempt at syrup, I used orange rind for flavoring, but all I had was green food coloring. I used it, and I could have sworn that the result tasted not like orange but like Green River, the lime-flavored pop once sold widely from machines in theater lobbies.

You can, if you like, add booze-based flavoring ingredients to the syrup after it cools. Kirsch, for example, makes a heck of a cherry Coke or a cherry malt.

If your recollections include lime rickey (the drugstore fountain item, not the collins or sour mixed drink), you can make one, knowledgeable sources indicate, with shots of lime and cherry syrup in fizzy water. My own favorite phosphate (other than, of course, chocolate) was made with vanilla syrup and orange syrup, a combination that tasted like circus peanuts. Alas, when I tried to duplicate it recently it tasted more like circus-tent sweepings.

No invocation of drugstore food would be complete without a hot fudge sundae. The aroma of a real drugstore counter around the afternoon snack hour is a complex blend of coffee and hot fudge with a little tang of hamburger grease, and it must not be allowed to disappear from our lives.

You know how to make a hot fudge sundae, of course, but let's depart from authenticity in the direction of deliciousness by making a hot fudge sauce that's heavier on the chocolate and butter than any you'll find ready-made.

### Hot Fudge Sauce

1 (6-ounce) package chocolate chips
4 tablespoons (½ stick) butter
2 cups confectioners' sugar

1 cup heavy cream
1 teaspoon vanilla

Melt the chocolate and butter over very low heat. Stir in the sugar and cream and bring to boiling, stirring constantly. Boil about 5 minutes—the sauce should be dark, smooth and thick. If you boil it too long the butter will begin to separate out (it will still be delicious but a bit greasy). Stir in the vanilla. Consume as Nature intended. Makes about 2 cups.

---

### Little Mystery #5: Artichokes

How do we get artichoke hearts? Are there artichoke-heart-recycling programs in artichoke-packing country in which you eat the artichoke leaves and put the hearts on the porch for somebody to pick up?

**Solution:** A spokesperson for the California Artichoke Advisory Board, Castroville, California, (no, they advise *about* artichokes), said the term "artichoke heart" is a misnomer. The marinated and frozen "artichoke hearts" are really baby artichokes that are trimmed of their outer leaves and tops.

That doesn't sound like it makes much economic sense, given what you can get for a full-grown artichoke. Why sell them when they're little?

No, said the chokesperson. See, the artichoke plant puts out all different sizes of artichokes. The biggest one is at the top, then there are what are called "secondaries," which are somewhat smaller, and baby artichokes—which grow further down and in the joints of the plant. The baby artichokes just don't get any bigger.

They *can* be cooked fresh, of course, the artichoke lady said, and lots of trendy Californians do just that—sautéing them and tossing them into everything imaginable (she mentioned spaghetti sauce)—but there is very little demand for fresh baby artichokes elsewhere, so most of them are sold as "hearts."

Artichoke bottoms, which she noted are also called "crowns," are, she said, the bottoms of large artichokes, completely trimmed of leaves.

So *that's* where the artichoke-recycling program is used—people eat the leaves and return the *bottoms?*

No again. The artichokes that are used for bottoms are culls—maybe they have some cosmetic damage or an insect hole in a leaf or whatever, so they can't be sold as artichokes, but the bottoms are still good.

That makes sense, but I've never heard them referred to as anything but bottoms. Who calls them crowns?

"Snobby people call them crowns," she said. "After all, a bottom is a bottom." Words to live by.

# *Wrong Way Corrigan Dinner*

We're well into the tornado and mosquito seasons, which means we're also well into the picnic season. I haven't been to a sponsored picnic in some time, but I do recall the picnics that my father's Masonic lodge had when I was a kid in Milwaukee.

I remember those picnics for two reasons: First, whoever was responsible for the soft drinks every year managed to get them in a very wide assortment. There would be flavors of pop (we called it soda water, but you know what I mean) that you never saw anywhere else: pineapple, banana, grapefruit—and chocolate.

The chocolate pop was actually rather unpleasant, but it was so much fun to look at that I usually didn't decide I didn't like it until late in the day.

The other memorable thing about those picnics—and all organized picnics—is the games for kids. When you go on a regular picnic, you might bring along a thing or two to keep kids occupied, but chances are you don't set up several hours of activities for them. Such things are standard, though, at sponsored picnics, and I remember the looks of weary bewilderment on younger kids' faces when, after an hour or so of frenzied activity, they began to fall apart.

Invariably in some sack race or spoon race or whatever, some kid would get turned around and head for the starting line, bringing whoops and cheers from the spectators and a hesitant smile to the kid's face—probably hesitant because he couldn't believe he was winning.

One of the things that people always shouted at that juncture was "Wrong Way Corrigan!" This, of course, only puzzled the poor kid, who had never heard of Wrong Way Corrigan. I only figured out later what that was supposed to mean. (Yes, dear reader, I was often that poor kid.)

I haven't heard anybody shout "Wrong Way Corrigan" in a long time. How soon they forget.

Corrigan came to mind recently when I was puzzling over how to enhance an already weird dinner idea.

I got a suggestion in the mail (of course I've misplaced it since, so I can't tell you who it was from) that I put together a meal of foods like tomato-soup cake—foods in which there is an ingredient that doesn't seem to belong there. The letter writer (who *was* that masked reader?—I wanted to thank her) noted that most such recipes seem to be desserts (sauerkraut cake, pork-sausage cake, etc.) but she was sure I could think of enough non-dessert items to put together a whole meal of recipes each of which had an odd ingredient.

It became clear after a bit of recipe pondering that the field was too wide. I needed some second constraint on my fevered brain. That's when I thought of Douglas Corrigan.

Corrigan, you may or may not remember, was a flier who, in 1938, was refused clearance to fly alone in his dilapidated monoplane from New York to Europe in an attempt to duplicate the Charles Lindbergh flight. So he said he was going to go back to California. The next thing anybody knew was when he landed in Dublin, Ireland, almost twenty-four hours later and asked the astonished officials, "Is this Los Angeles?" He claimed that his compass (his only instrument) got stuck.

He earned instant fame, including a ticker-tape parade down Broadway and a starring role in a movie about his life; and the sobriquet Wrong Way Corrigan passed into the language—at least for a while—as something to holler at drivers who ignored one-way signs, and at hapless children at picnics.

(Corrigan continued to maintain that he really was trying to get to California. Interviewed on the twentieth anniversary of his flight, he said, "That's my story. I've been telling it so long I'm beginning to believe it.")

Back to food. (You thought I'd lost my way, didn't you? Never. My compass was just stuck briefly.) What occurred to me was that as long as I was going to put an unlikely ingredient in each recipe, maybe I could put some coffee in the appetizer, a dessert ingredient in the salad, and so on—have the weird ingredients running the wrong way through the dinner.

It worked out rather well, I think. So well that if you are strange enough to want to duplicate this entire menu (rather than an individual item or two), you wouldn't necessarily have to explain anything to the guests. It's all nice food. If you want to drop a hint, though, you might consider serving Tums at the beginning of the meal.

For the appetizer, as I said, I wanted to use some coffee. So I made a coffee-flavored spread. With a little bacon on top, the whole thing was kind of like breakfast.

As with any other appetizer involving cream cheese spread onto crackers, don't assemble these far in advance. Moisture migrates from the cream cheese into the crackers, drying the cream cheese and making the crackers soggy. Nice folks won't ask me how I know this.

---

### *Java Sunrise Appetizers*

About 1/2 pound sliced bacon
2 1/2 teaspoons instant coffee
2 teaspoons hot water
2 teaspoons sugar
1/4 teaspoon salt
1/4 teaspoon pepper
1 (8-ounce) package cream cheese, softened
Crackers

Cut each strip of bacon into 4 or 5 pieces and fry them until they are crisp. Drain on paper towels.

Dissolve the instant coffee in the hot water, then stir or beat the coffee mixture, sugar, salt and pepper into the softened cream cheese.

Shortly before serving, spread the cream cheese mixture onto the crackers and top each with a piece of bacon. Makes about 4 dozen appetizers.

---

For the salad, as I said (if you expect to get anything more than a barely passing grade, you have to pay attention), I wanted to employ a dessert ingredient.

The obvious solution—obvious to those of us who hang on every word from the world's trendy-eating capitals—was one of those nouvelle-cuisine combinations now no doubt already passé: lobster in vanilla sauce on spinach leaves.

This being the Midwest, we'll ignore whether it's passé in New York.

This not being funded by a grant from the Mobil Oil Corporation, we'll switch to crab instead of lobster—and mock crab at that. (As much as my mind rebels at the idea of pollock flavored and shaped to look like crab legs, I must admit that it's very pleasant to eat.)

And this being me, and liking the flavor of sauces a whole lot, we'll mix the sauce and "crab" together instead of following the nouvelle-cuisine practice of setting unsauced food down in pretty puddles of sauce.

I must say this went over very, very well. If I had had more "crab" in vanilla sauce I could have peddled it easily.

This reinforces my lifelong contention that there is no situation in which dessert is inappropriate. Next come brownies in roast beef. (Only kidding.) (Well, maybe . . . )

2 tablespoons finely chopped shallots
3 tablespoons butter, divided
1/4 cup dry white wine
1/2 cup condensed chicken broth
1 cup heavy cream
5 teaspoons vanilla, divided

Salt, pepper to taste
1 (8-ounce) package mock crab legs
  (or mock crab "salad pieces"),
  thawed
1 (10- to 12-ounce) bag fresh spinach

*Vanilla*
*Mock-Crab Salad*

Briefly cook the shallots in a saucepan over medium heat with 1 tablespoon of the butter. Add the wine and cook down, stirring, until almost all of the liquid has evaporated. Add the chicken broth, raise the heat to high and cook down, stirring, until the liquid is reduced to about 1/2 its original volume.

Reduce the heat to medium, stir in the cream and 4 teaspoons of the vanilla and cook about 15 minutes, stirring, or until the mixture has reduced to about 1 cup.

Stir in the remaining 1 teaspoon of vanilla and pour the sauce through a sieve into another saucepan.

Press the shallots in the sieve to get all the lovely sauce out of them, then discard them. Add salt and pepper to the sauce and bring to the boil. Remove from heat.

Cut the remaining 2 tablespoons of butter into 3 or 4 pieces and swirl them into the sauce one at a time until each is melted and absorbed.

Cut the mock crab legs into bite-size pieces (if using "salad pieces," you're all set), and stir them into the sauce.

Rinse the spinach leaves and remove tough stems.

Make a foundation of spinach leaves on 6 salad plates or in a large salad bowl.

Rewarm the "crab" and sauce over very low heat, stirring, then spoon over the spinach.

Serves 6. Nummy!

If you followed the discussion of how the Wrong Way Corrigan principle would apply to this meal, you might have wondered what would happen in the middle, when the dishes going forward (appetizer, salad, main course, vegetable, dessert, coffee) met the odd ingredients going the other way (coffee, dessert, etc.).

What happened in this case, partly because I got confused as to which course which odd ingredient was to go in, was that I wound up trying to put a second meat into the meat course. That's not so odd, when you think about it. Lots of restaurants serve steak-and-lobster combinations (admittedly not rolled together, but on more or less the same plate). So if you can have surf 'n' turf at a nice restaurant, what's wrong with some chicken breast rolled around some hamburger at home? Nothing, so let's get into the restaurant spirit and call it:

## Chuck 'n' Cluck

¾ pound ground beef
1 small onion, chopped
Salt, pepper
2 to 3 tablespoons red wine
2 tablespoons Worcestershire sauce
1½ tablespoons cornstarch
¼ cup water
1 egg yolk, beaten
6 skinless, boneless chicken-breast
  halves

6 tablespoons butter or margarine

SAUCE:

¼ cup white wine vinegar
1 tablespoon minced shallots
1 teaspoon crushed dried tarragon
¼ teaspoon pepper
2 egg yolks
¾ cup (1½ sticks) butter

Break up the ground beef in a frying pan and brown along with the chopped onion, salt and pepper. Drain off fat. Add the wine and Worcestershire sauce. Cook 2 or 3 minutes. Dissolve the cornstarch in the water, stir in the beaten egg yolk and add that mixture to the ground beef. Cook briefly until the liquid has thickened. Adjust seasoning and set aside. After a few minutes, pour off any fat that has separated out.

Pound or roll out the chicken breasts lightly to flatten and enlarge them. Roll each around a portion of the beef mixture and fasten shut with toothpicks. (To allow the chicken to be fried easily, make the toothpicks run along, rather than across, the length of the chicken roll. Where that isn't possible, break off any protruding pieces of toothpick.) Salt and pepper the rolls.

Melt the 6 tablespoons of butter in a large skillet or electric frying pan and fry the chicken rolls, over medium heat, about 5 minutes on each of 2 opposite sides and 2 or 3 minutes each on the in-between sides. Remove the toothpicks, cover the chicken and keep it warm.

Meanwhile, prepare the sauce: In a medium saucepan, boil the vinegar, shallots, tarragon and pepper until there is only about a tablespoon of liquid remaining. Cool the liquid slightly, then beat in the egg yolks. Over very low heat or in a double boiler, stirring constantly, stir in the ¾ cup of butter a tablespoon at a time, making sure each piece has been fully incorporated into the sauce before the next one is added.

Serve the sauce over the chicken rolls. Makes 6.

If you elect to serve this whole thing on toast, you could call it Chuck 'n' Cluck on a Mukluk.

For a vegetable containing a salad ingredient, the obvious candidate is peas French-style (braised with lettuce). Except for two things: We used that in another article, and it is too obvious.

So how about *corn* braised with lettuce?

Not a bad combination at all, it turns out, and rather delightfully springlike in color. (Like the *season,* you difficult person, not like the thing that's rusting under your car.)

**Corn Française**

2 (10-ounce) packages frozen corn
1½ to 2 cups coarsely torn lettuce
⅓ large onion, cut into rings
1½ teaspoons sugar

½ teaspoon salt
¼ teaspoon pepper
3 tablespoons butter

Cook the corn according to package directions, but only until it is thawed. Drain.

Put half the lettuce in a large saucepan. Add the corn and the onions. Sprinkle with sugar, salt and pepper and dot with butter. Top with the other half of the lettuce, cover and cook over low-medium heat 8 to 10 minutes, until the lettuce on top is hot. Stir and add salt and pepper if needed.

Serves 6.

What do we have for the people now, Johnny?

We've got dessert, Bob! Lots and lots of dessert! And not just *any* dessert . . . It's dessert with an appetizer ingredient in it!

Shouldn't some nonvegetable course have had a vegetable in it by now, Johnny?

We got kind of confused, Bob. But we're pretty sure the folks will like this one anyway.

**Chocolate Mousse Sandwichettes**

1 (12-ounce) package semisweet chocolate chips
¾ cup (1½ sticks) unsalted butter
8 eggs, separated

3½ tablespoons granulated sugar
1 (13-ounce) box Triscuits
1 or 2 ounces semisweet chocolate (optional, for decoration)

Melt the chocolate chips in a double boiler or over very low heat. Cut the butter into 1-tablespoon chunks. Remove the chocolate from the heat and stir in all the butter until it is fully melted. (Reheat briefly, if necessary.) Allow to cool completely, then stir in the egg yolks, one at a time.

In a large bowl, beat the egg whites until they are just foamy. Gradually beat in the sugar, then beat the whites until they form stiff peaks. Stir about ¼ of the whites into the chocolate mixture to lighten it, then gently fold in the remaining whites. (The mixture probably won't get fully blended without excessive folding. Quit when it's evenly speckled, with no patches of white.)

If the mousse is not thick, allow it to chill an hour or so.

Assemble the sandwichettes: Spread a big, thick blob of mousse onto a Triscuit. Top with another Triscuit, pressing down slightly. If you're "that sort of person," you'll want to even up the sides so they look like little ice-cream sandwiches. If you're not "that sort of person," you won't. This has been a test.

If you like, melt an ounce or so of semisweet chocolate and dribble it across the tops of the sandwichettes. Refrigerate until serving time. Makes about three dozen.

Now to coffee. What could we put in coffee? Even forgetting what course the weird addition represents, what could we possibly use?

I spent some time fooling around with things that didn't work at all, and when I hit on this one, which I thought worked well enough that it wasn't repulsive, I quit.

Imagine my surprise when, although I offered plain coffee too, about half the folks asked for seconds of the doctored version.

---

### Peanut-Butter Coffee
(That's right!)

**6 cups brewed coffee**

Put the peanut butter and a cup or two of the coffee in a blender. Whomp until it's

**About 1 tablespoon peanut butter**

well blended, then stir back into the rest of the coffee. Serves 6.

---

### Little Mystery #6: Bananas

I couldn't believe the rhyme explanation to the mystery referred to on previous pages—that we were told for years not to put bananas in the refrigerator because the jingle writer needed a rhyme for equator. So I've done some more digging. It doesn't get better.

Some of the digging involved cleaning off my desk, where I found a 1981 press release from Chiquita Brands, Inc., about refrigerating bananas. The release claims that the jingle "at the time was most accurate."

"At the time of Miss Chiquita's debut in 1945," the release says, "bananas arrived green at your local grocer on stalks, which he would then hang from the ceiling. When you bought these bananas, it would take a while for them to ripen. The act of putting them in the refrigerator would halt the ripening process, and hence the line forbidding refrigeration went into Miss Chiquita's song.

"Today . . . Chiquita bananas are shipped from the tropics in cushioned cartons and then taken to special warehouses to be ripened under careful temperature and humidity conditions. When you purchase bananas in your supermarket, they are most likely yellow with green tips—practically ripe. Most consumers let them sit for a day or two, until the peel has brown flecks in it. When they reach this stage (or the stage you like), feel free to put them in the vegetable compartment of your refrigerator for storage."

If that all leaves you feeling a little confused, you're in good company. Just because in 1945 bananas mightn't have been very ripe when you brought them home, why was it a bad idea to refrigerate them when they *had* ripened?

If we can understand today that we should wait until they are ripe before we refrigerate them, why was it "most accurate" to say in 1945 that they should never be refrigerated?

(And, for that matter, who says bananas in supermarkets today are generally only a day from full ripeness? I've seen piles of bananas so green they look like long limes.)

Well, phone calls and press releases have an ephemeral quality—you can say almost anything in them and hope nobody will remember. That's why my eyes lit up when I found a book, a 1974 paperback called *The Chiquita Banana Cookbook,* prepared and produced by Chiquita Brands.

When they realized they were committing ink to paper that might be saved and looked at for years, what did Chiquita Brands have to say about the great turnaround on the refrigeration issue? Here is the complete text:

"Recent research now shows that the fact is that once bananas have ripened at room temperature to the point you like to eat them, they may be kept several days longer in the refrigerator."

It's difficult to imagine what the "recent research" involved. Possibly putting a banana in a refrigerator.

# Stewing in My Own Au Jus

One day some time ago, when my kids were in town for a visit, we were driving around near the University of Minnesota and passed the two-story McDonald's that, for some reason, exists in Dinkytown.

Dave, who was nine at the time and perfectly normal but occasionally lapsed into a second personality rather like that of Eddie Haskell on *Leave It to Beaver* ("That's a beautiful dress you're wearing, Mrs. Cleaver"), noticed the McDonald's out the window, shifted into smarmy and remarked:

"Why, what a charming restaurant. I'll bet it's lovely in there. They probably don't even have tin ashtrays!"

Even for Dave, who plays a mean game of Highway Alphabet, that was an unusually insightful remark.

There *are* little touches that instantly convey something about the tone of a restaurant, and the disposable ashtray is certainly one indicator of a bargain-basement beanery.

Dave has always had a good eye for restaurant detail.

Several years ago, when he was quite small and could not yet read, the neighborhood Red Barn introduced a salad bar. There were posters and mobiles all over the walls and ceilings of the place, raving about this development. They featured photos of a jumble of salad ingredients—things like pieces of lettuce, slices of cucumber and onion, tomato wedges and globs of salad dressing.

Dave pointed to one of the posters and said, "Look, Dad! They have garbage!"

My thought exactly. Dave is a (chocolate) chip off the old block.

Anyway, after I made much of the ashtray remark, both Dave and his older brother, Joe, who is no slouch in the observation department himself, began pointing out other indicators of restaurant class, such as the presence or absence of plastic water tumblers, whether you have to bus your own tray, and, moving up several notches, how many forks there are at a place setting.

I myself have always been put off by eating places that put lemon in your iced tea even if you don't ask for it, but that is neither here nor there.

(This whole *thing* is neither here nor there, and I recognize that, but bear with me; I'm beginning to come to the point.)

It is possible, of course, to have *wonderful* food at a restaurant that has foil ashtrays, plastic glasses and the disposable spoon-and-fork combination that I've never known whether to call a spork or a foon.

And it is certainly *very* possible to have lousy food at a restaurant where the tableware is real.

So these are not indicators of the quality of the food, but of how tony the place is.

A dinner date at a two-fork restaurant is more likely to impress some sweeties (even if the food is reminiscent of college dorm cafeterias) than is a mess of really excellent ribs thrown onto a paper plate by a surly guy who needs a shave and can't seem to make change.

Another such indicator, and the focus of today's sermon, is the number and severity of misspellings and other amusements on the menu.

The "roast beef au jus with gravy"—or "roast beef served with au jus gravy"—may be terrific, but you probably will lose points if your boss, mother-in-law or other severe critic notices many entries of that sort on the menu of the restaurant you have selected.

I have long been a fan of such menu irregularities, and after a recent encounter with a particularly outrageous spelling of zucchini I decided it was time to put together some kind of salute to them.

So here, at last, it is: The Bad Menu Dinner.

The first entry is a generic, not a specific, dish:

Wet Your Appetite with
Our Selection of Hor Derves

True, many restaurants (to their credit) would never even attempt to spell a term like hors d'oeuvres, but there are also lots of places at which you are encouraged to "wet" your appetite with an appetizer.

Despite straining what we like to call my brain for five or ten minutes, I couldn't think of a specific appetizer that is commonly misspelled.

But it doesn't seem fair not to give you a recipe, so here's one that isn't misspelled.

This is the kind of thing often served in very large restaurants, where they seat a whole group of folks in a kind of waiting area off to the side with a basket of crackers and some kind of spread and hope you'll buy some drinks.

*That* is wetting your appetite.

---

## Ham or Shrimp Butter

1 (6½-ounce) can ham chunks or 2 (4½-ounce) cans shrimp or 1 (6-ounce) bag frozen cooked shrimp
2 shallots
¾ cup (1½ sticks) unsalted butter, divided

2 tablespoons lemon juice
1 tablespoon dry sherry
½ teaspoon tarragon
Salt, pepper
Pinch of cayenne pepper
Crackers

Note: This spread is best if it is refrigerated a day or two before serving.

Thaw the shrimp if they are frozen. Mince the shallots. Melt 2 tablespoons of the butter, add the shallots and cook until they are soft. Put the shallots, ham or shrimp, lemon juice, sherry, tarragon, salt, pepper and cayenne in a food processor or blender.

Melt the remaining butter and pour it into the processor or blender while it's whomping the shrimp or ham around. Taste and fiddle with the seasonings if you like. Pour into an attractive (clear glass?) bowl and refrigerate.

For spreadability, take it out of the refrigerator half an hour before serving. Serve with crackers. Makes about 1 cup.

---

Next, a multiple winner:

The Soup de Jour of the Day:
Clam Chowder Soup

I've always been partial to a little redundancy now and then; I've been known to repeat myself redundantly myself. And I am quite fond of the story of the widow woman who had a big St. Bernard dog and used to take him for a walk on Easter Sunday until she met a Jewish rabbi.

This particular dish is about as far as menus generally go in that direction. The added touch of the misspelling of Soup du Jour is my own—*I've* never actually seen both "Soup de Jour" and "of the day" on the same menu, but I'm sure that even as we speak somebody somewhere is staring over "our bottomless cup of coffee" at those very words.

Anyway, here's the soup. It's New England style, but not so thick that your spoon stands up in it. If you prefer your chowder to resemble pudding, throw in more potatoes or use less half and half or milk. That way you can eat it with the fork de jour of the day.

### Clam Chowder

2 medium onions
2 large potatoes
2 slices bacon, cut into 8 or 10 pieces
  each
2 cups water
2 (8-ounce) bottles clam juice, or 2
  more cups water

3 (6½-ounce) cans minced clams, not
  drained
1 teaspoon salt
¼ teaspoon pepper
1½ tablespoons butter
1½ tablespoons flour
2 cups half-and-half
1 cup milk

Peel and chop the onions. Peel and cube the potatoes.

In a Dutch oven, fry the bacon pieces until they're almost done. Add the onions and sauté gently 3 or 4 minutes. Add the water, clam juice (or use 2 extra cups of water instead, if you prefer), clams, potatoes, salt and pepper.

Cover and simmer 1 hour. (Yes, that's a long time, but it's sure good.)

Melt the butter in a small saucepan. Stir in the flour and cook, continuing to stir, for 30 seconds. Slowly stir in about a cup of the hot chowder and cook briefly until the mixture is smooth and thick.

Pour this white sauce slowly into the clam chowder, stirring, and bring the chowder slowly to the boil. Stir in the half-and-half and the milk and simmer 5 minutes.

Serves 8 to 10.

Next a little greenery:

Our Famous
Ho-Made Cold Slaw

There's really nothing more wrong with "Ho-Made" than there is with any other cutesyism like "Lip-Smackin' Good" (except if you live where the street usage would indicate that ho-made slaw was prepared by someone you wouldn't want your son bringing home to dinner). It is a phenomenon of life, though, that terms like this usually spread until they make no sense at all.

On a recent vacation trip, for example, I saw a sign outside a restaurant advertising "Ho-Baked Pies."

Moving right along, here's the recipe, which cheats a little because it uses bottled salad dressing, but I did an exhaustive survey of menus before I did the cooking for this article, so I was exhausted.

The recipe produces a slightly orange and nicely creamy cole slaw.

### Cole Slaw

1 medium head cabbage, finely
  shredded
1 small onion, finely chopped

½ cup French dressing
¼ cup dairy sour cream
1½ tablespoons chopped chives

Place all the ingredients in a large bowl and toss thoroughly. Cover and refrigerate 2 to 3 hours. Stir before serving.

Makes 4 to 6 servings.

For a vegetable dish, there can be no contest. It's got to be your favorite squash and mine, in a nice combination with some Italian sausage.

### Zuhccinni Medaly

Have you ever wondered what we ate twenty or more years ago, when nobody had ever heard of zucchini?

For that matter, have you ever wondered what the Italians put on noodles before the tomato was brought back from the New World?

We'll have to look into that sometime.

For now, let's make some zucchini.

---

*Zucchini Medley*

1 pound Italian sausage, sliced ½ inch thick
2 tablespoons oil
½ small onion, chopped
4 small (bratwurst size) zucchini, thinly sliced
½ medium head cabbage, sliced thin
½ teaspoon sugar
Salt, pepper

Brown the sausage 15 to 20 minutes, until it is cooked through.

Meanwhile, in a small Dutch oven, heat the oil. Sauté the onions for a few minutes. Add the zucchini, cabbage, sugar, salt and pepper and stir well.

Cover and continue to cook, stirring often, about 10 minutes, until zucchini and cabbage are somewhat tender and the cabbage has lost its shape.

Add the cooked sausage pieces and cook, uncovered, about 10 minutes more.

Serves 4 to 6.

---

This next dish might seem an obvious candidate—right up there with the au jus gravy—but it's not. In fact, it doesn't belong here at all, except that everybody thinks it does. (Consider this exposition one evidence of the educational mission of the newspaper.)

### Macaroni "n" Cheese au Gratin

(I threw in the "n" instead of 'n'—or even *and*—just to make it look normal.)

The heavyweights of the cooking biz (by which I mean those with prestige, not those who need to go on a diet) will tell you that *au gratin* does not mean "with cheese." The French word for cheese is fromage, not gratin. *Au gratin* means that the dish in question is topped with bread crumbs and/or grated cheese, and usually some melted butter, and is then subjected to high heat in the oven or broiler to produce a crust.

So there is macaroni and cheese, like it comes out of the box, and there is macaroni and cheese au gratin, which gets additional treatment to make the top crusty.

There. Now that you have a fascinating fact with which to bore somebody at a cocktail party, let's make some macaroni and cheese au gratin.

Regular readers (both of them—Hi, Dad) know that I believe in making things from scratch, with more or less real ingredients, so that's what I did to make the macaroni and cheese. In the process, I acquired tremendous respect for the boxed macaroni and cheese dinner, which costs *much* less and, I must admit, tastes at least as good as the recipe I followed.

I'm not in love with boxed M&C dinners, having subsisted on them for much of a year in my college days, but I think that this first production of M&C from scratch will also be my last.

The gratin part, on the other hand, was pretty good—after one very bad try with a recipe that had four times more bread crumbs than it needed. (I *knew* it sounded wrong. I've got to learn to trust me.)

I'd suggest trying out the gratin on some boxed M&C. But here's the entire recipe, for those of you who just won't take my word. I repeat: The recipe is fine, but the boxed product is easier, much cheaper and no less tasty. If you don't think so, you can add Worcestershire sauce, dry mustard and chopped onions to *that,* too.

## Macaroni and Cheese au Gratin

7 ounces (2 cups) elbow macaroni
1 tablespoon butter
1 medium onion, chopped
1 tablespoon flour
1/4 cup milk
1/2 teaspoon seasoned salt
Pepper
1 1/2 cups (6 ounces) shredded Cheddar cheese or pasteurized process cheese

1 tablespoon Worcestershire sauce
1/2 teaspoon dry mustard

TOPPING:

1/4 cup dry bread crumbs
1/2 cup (2 ounces) shredded Cheddar cheese or pasteurized process cheese
3 tablespoons butter

Cook the macaroni according to package directions. Drain.

Melt the 1 tablespoon of butter in a saucepan, stir in the onions and sauté until they are translucent. Stir in the flour and cook a minute or so, stirring. Slowly add the milk, stirring constantly.

When all the milk is in and the sauce is smooth and creamy, stir in the salt, pepper, the 1 1/2 cups of cheese, the Worcestershire and dry mustard. Reheat a bit if necessary to melt all the cheese. Stir in the cooked macaroni.

Now comes the au gratin part:

Turn the macaroni and cheese into a greased 2-quart casserole. Combine the bread crumbs and the 1/2 cup of cheese and sprinkle over the surface of the M&C.

Melt the 3 tablespoons of butter in a small pan and drizzle over all.

Bake at 350 degrees for 10 minutes or so (unless the mixture had gotten cold before it went into the oven, in which case make it 20 to 30 minutes), and run it under the broiler quickly at the end to brown the top. Serves 6.

For dessert there are many choices, but I kind of like this one for its general appeal:

Our Own Banana Cream Pie,
Made with Fresh Banana's
and Piled High with
Real Whip Cream

Part of the charm of this entry is its application of the maxim apparently taught to menu writers, produce-counter clerks and sign painters: When in doubt, throw in an apostrophe.

As for the whip cream, it is from the same school of thought that gives us mash potatoes and ice tea.

This is quite a nice recipe. There's nothing wrong with straight banana cream pie, of course, but it's even better with a layer of a different flavor under the banana.

Those who cannot guess what flavor I used should consider a course in remedial eating.

Those who guessed carob should sign up immediately for "Eating as a Second Language."

---

## Black-Bottom Banana Cream Pie

**BOTTOM FILLING:**

1 1/2 (1-ounce) squares unsweetened
   chocolate
6 tablespoons milk
1 egg yolk
2 tablespoons sugar
1 1/2 teaspoons cornstarch
1/8 teaspoon salt

1 baked 9-inch pie shell

**BANANA FILLING:**

1/2 cup sugar
6 tablespoons flour
1/4 teaspoon salt
2 1/2 cups milk
1 egg plus 1 egg yolk
1 tablespoon butter
1/2 teaspoon vanilla
3 ripe banana's (or bananas)

1/2 cup heavy cream, whipped

Prepare the bottom filling:

Melt the chocolate in a small saucepan; set aside.

Scald the milk in a saucepan. In a mixing bowl, beat together the egg yolk, sugar, cornstarch and salt. Gradually beat in the scalded milk.

Pour the mixture into the saucepan in which the milk was scalded and cook over low heat, stirring constantly, until the custard is smooth and thick—don't boil it.

Stir in the melted chocolate and spread over the baked pie shell.

Prepare the banana filling:

Combine the sugar, flour and salt in the top of a double boiler over boiling water.

Gradually stir in the milk and cook, stirring constantly, until the mixture is thickened. Cover and cook 10 minutes more, stirring occasionally.

Beat the egg and egg yolk and beat in a small amount of the hot milk mixture. Lower the heat under the double boiler

(Continued)

so that the water stops boiling.

Pour the diluted egg into the hot milk mixture, stirring it in rapidly. Allow the mixture to cook over the hot water for two minutes, stirring constantly.

Remove the mixture from the heat and stir in the butter and vanilla. Cool.

Slice 1 banana and arrange on the chocolate layer.

Immediately slice a second banana into the warm custard mixture and pour into the shell. (If you wait a long time before you cover them, the first banana slices will darken.) Chill.

Just before serving, whip the cream and pipe or spoon it over the top of the pie.

Slice the last banana and arrange the slices around the edge of the pie, inserting them into the whipped cream at a slight angle. Serve immediately. Serves 6 to 8.

---

I passed up the opportunity to make expresso, lemonaid and consumme. Another time.

# National Hot Dog Month

Quick. What comes after the third of July?

If you said the Fourth of July, give yourself five points. If you said the fourth day of National Hot Dog Month, give yourself 25 points, for having read the big print, for being fairly weird, or both.

There are many edibles whose existence is observed in national weeks or months. We have noted here in the past such distinguished festivals as National Potato Lovers Month and National Sauerkraut Week. But none really feels quite so American—or so appropriately timed—as National Hot Dog Month.

All right, so frankfurters come from Europe, not America, and the stories about how they got to be served in buns are a little suspect. The fact remains that, wherever they came from and however they got to be the way they are, they are now a very American institution. Almost as much as baseball, apple pie and the Chevrolet Motor Division of General Motors.

And the Fourth of July, even more than Memorial Day, is when the hot dog is really in flower. Except for those of us with small children (kids can be counted on to eat hot dogs when nothing else will work), many of us deal with hot dogs mostly on special occasions: Fourth of July, Labor Day, Twins games, State Fair and Resident Cook Gone to Visit Mother.

The National Hot Dog & Sausage Council (yes, there is a National Hot Dog & Sausage Council—you read it here first) is no doubt aware of this phenomenon and is quite anxious to make sure that you miss no opportunity to consume mass quantities of tube steaks. To this end, it has sent forth across this great nation any number of peculiar recipes.

I hesitated at first to involve myself in so relentlessly cylindrical a venture as testing lots of frankfurter recipes. I have a reputation to maintain, after all, and—odd as it is—it has not to this point included a dinner in which everything I made looked the same.

I realized, though, after a moment's thought, that not every wiener recipe had to involve whole wieners (I'm a little slow sometimes), so I decided to have a go at it.

An aside about nomenclature: According to the National Hot Dog & Sausage Council (let's just call it the NHD&SC, shall we?), the U.S. Department of Agriculture makes no distinction, in its regulations, between the terms "hot dog," "frank," "furter," "frankfurter" and "wiener."

I'd never even *heard* of "furter" (I think it's a sly attempt by the NHD&SC to emulate "burger"), but I had been carelessly using the other terms interchangeably, and I was glad to learn that, at least according to our federal government, I had not committed a grease misdemeanor.

In selecting the food for the Wonderful Wiener Wepast, I decided not to commit the kinds of culinary outrages that seem so possible when one's main ammunition is the frankfurter. For example, I did not use wieners to prepare the Viennese veal delicacy Wiener Schnitzel. In fact, three of the recipes I used came straight from the NHD&SC, although I fiddled with them a bit, just to keep things honest.

I served the food with fairly little comment, but my smart-aleck guests were in absolutely revolting form. I will pass along some of their choicer remarks, but, to save these folks from being pilloried by friends and neighbors, I will not reveal their identities.

The appetizer was a dip containing ground hot dogs (my own innovation—the NHD&SC folks had suggested using hot-dog pieces as dippers.) It was nice and smoky and actually pretty darn good, but it looked a little odd.

Guest 1: "This isn't bad if you're hungry."

Guest 2: "Well, I ate two days ago, so I'm going to pass."

## Hot Dog Dip

½ pound frankfurters
1 tomato
1 sweet red pepper
½ cup drained and pitted green olives
2 (3-ounce) packages cream cheese, softened

2 teaspoons Dijon mustard
Onion salt or onion powder to taste
1 to 1½ pounds assorted raw vegetables for dipping (carrot sticks, broccoli and cauliflower florets, etc.)

Finely chop the frankfurters (by hand or in a food processor). Core the tomato and the pepper. Cut both into chunks and coarsely chop them and the olives.

Cream the cream cheese and stir in the mustard and the chopped meat, tomato, pepper and olives. Add onion salt to taste.

Serve with raw vegetable dippers. Serves 6.

---

Getting folks to eat a salad containing hot dogs presented something of a challenge. But, as Guest 3 and Juwius Caesar put it, "Wienie, widi, wici."

I thought the result was very respectable, particularly after my substitution of refried beans for chili beans, but to be perfectly frank it would have been almost as good without the hot-dog component. I did slice the hot dogs thin instead of putting them in in big chunks as recommended, a move that made them not quite so obvious. The furter you got from the salad, the better it looked.

---

## Mexican Hot Dog Salad

DRESSING:

⅔ cup salsa or red taco sauce
⅓ cup mayonnaise
⅓ cup dairy sour cream

SALAD:

1 medium avocado
Lemon juice
½ head of lettuce

2 medium tomatoes
3 cups tortilla chips (about 4 ounces of chips)
1 (16-ounce) can refried beans
1 pound hot dogs
1 (8-ounce) jar pasteurized process cheese spread
1 (4-ounce) can chopped green chilies, drained
2 teaspoons chili powder

Prepare the dressing in advance: Combine salsa, mayonnaise and sour cream; cover and refrigerate until serving time.

Peel and pit the avocado, cut in slices and dribble lemon juice over them to keep them from discoloring. Chill until serving time (or, as I did, until 2 days later, when I found them in the refrigerator).

Shortly before serving time, shred the lettuce and make a small mound of it on each salad plate. Chop the tomatoes and sprinkle them on the lettuce. Put about ½ cup of tortilla chips in the middle of each salad. Heat the beans in a saucepan, slice the franks into the beans and simmer until heated through.

Meanwhile, in another saucepan, heat the cheese spread (Guest 4: "Mmm. What kind of cheese is this?" Host: "Whiz.") until it is just melted, then stir in chilies and chili powder. Pour ¼ cup of the cheese mixture over the chips on each salad, and top with about ½ cup of the beanie wienie. Garnish with avocado slices, if you remember, and serve with the dressing in a bowl. Serves 6.

As we moved toward the main course, I brought out the special wine I had purchased for this occasion: a Binger St. Rochuskapelle Kabinett. It's a nice little wine, produced in Bingen, West Germany, which is about thirty miles from a much larger city. Given that thirty miles isn't very far as these things go (if somebody from, say, Elk River, Minnesota, were traveling in West Germany, he might well identify himself as a Minneapolitan), I feel justified in calling this a Frankfurter wine.

Guest 3 immediately began referring to it as "wieno."

For the main course, frankfurters in their entirety (finally), each nestled in a boat crafted from a scooped-out zucchini half. I found all of the items on the menu quite respectable, but I thought this one *really* cut the mustard.

These hot dogs contain cheese, prompting Guest 4 to ask, "This recipe isn't called 'Easy Cheesy something,' is it?" No. It is one of my very few rules that I do not prepare recipes called "Easy Cheesy something."

(Another is that I do not prepare recipes called "something Surprise." When I sit down to eat, I don't *want* to be surprised. Pleased, yes; surprised, no. Things called "something Surprise" remind me of a business firm in Milwaukee with a very jarring slogan: Blau's Sudden-Service Plumbing. Every time I see it, I picture plumbers bursting into the house at three in the morning, while searchlight-equipped helicopters hover outside.)

Well, now that I have *that* off my chest, let's get back to our main course. It's not "Easy Cheesy Zucchini," it's not "Zucchini Surprise," it's:

---

## Wienie Zucchini

4 (8- to 10-inch) zucchini (1½ to 2 pounds)
½ cup chopped green onions
2 tablespoons chopped parsley
½ teaspoon oregano
¼ teaspoon tarragon
¼ teaspoon basil

Dash pepper
2 tablespoons butter
2 tablespoons oil
1 cup bread crumbs
½ teaspoon garlic salt
Oil for brushing
1 pound cheese hot dogs

Preheat the oven to 350 degrees. Cut the ends off the zucchini, then cut each in half lengthwise and scoop out each long zucchini half (reserving the scoopings) to leave boats with sides about ½ inch thick.

Chop the part of the zucchini you scooped out of the boats, combine it with the green onions, parsley, oregano, tarragon, basil and pepper, and fry in the butter and oil. Stir in the bread crumbs.

Sprinkle the hollowed-out zucchini boats with garlic salt and fill each with the fried zucchini mixture. Put the filled zucchini boats in a shallow pan, and brush the tops with oil. Bake for 25 minutes, then put a cheese hot dog on each one and bake 7 or 8 minutes more, until the hot dog is heated through.

Makes 8, and they're quite good.

---

As good as these hot-dog items sounded—and as well as they turned out—I couldn't see serving a hot-dog vegetable. That, I figured, would be the wiener of our discontent. So I made my favorite spinach recipe, which you've already seen (with the SPAM recipes). You don't need to see it again, do you?

Thanks. You're a nice person.

It was when dessert approached that my guests got really restless. "What's it going to be?" inquired one uneasily. "Hog 'n' Dazs?" "No," responded another, "probably Pudding on the Dog."

They needn't have worried. Dessert, believe it or not, was not a difficult place to use up some hot dogs in a reasonable manner—it is not unheard of for meat to appear in a sweet item. Usually it's not hot dogs, but that's only a small additional stretch.

Mincemeat pie with hot dogs instead of beef was slightly smoky-tasting, but I didn't find that at all unwelcome. Maybe I was just relieved that it wasn't worse, but I don't think so. Several folks took seconds.

---

### Hot-Dog Mincemeat Pie

**1/2 pound hot dogs**
**3 medium apples**
**1 cup raisins, or 1/2 cup raisins and 1/2 cup currants**
**1/2 cup fruitcake mix (candied fruits)**
**4 tablespoons butter**
**1 cup packed brown sugar**
**1 cup apple cider**
**1/2 cup apple jelly**
**2 tablespoons molasses**
**1 teaspoon salt**
**1 teaspoon cinnamon**
**1/2 teaspoon cloves**
**1/2 teaspoon nutmeg**
**1 tablespoon lemon juice**
**Dough for 2-crust pie**

Chop the hot dogs quite fine. Wash, peel, core and chop the apples. Chop the raisins, currants, and fruitcake mix.

Melt the butter in a Dutch oven and add the hot dogs, apples, raisins, currants, fruitcake mix, brown sugar, cider, jelly, molasses, salt, cinnamon, cloves and nutmeg. Cook slowly, uncovered, 1 hour, stirring occasionally, until most of the liquid is absorbed. Add the lemon juice.

Preheat oven to 425 degrees. Line a 9-inch pie pan with one crust, fill with mincemeat, top with second crust, crimp edges and cut a few slashes in the top.

Place pie on a cookie sheet to catch any drips, and cover the edges of the crust with strips of foil to prevent burning.

Bake 25 to 30 minutes, removing the foil strips after 15 minutes. Serves 6 to 8.

---

When dinner was over, guests helped themselves from a candy dish full of antacid tablets.

# *Food in a Cloud*

I was watching television one Sunday when Bill Cosby interrupted rather a fine session of *Wonder Woman* to extol the virtues of Coca-Cola. Or was it Pepsi?

That reminded me of Jell-O Pudding Pops, whose merits Cosby had been praising not long ago, and of Pudding in a Cloud, which he'd been enthusing about before that.

Remember Pudding in a Cloud? Cosby told us how to make it. Often. Just swirl a ring of Cool Whip into a dessert dish and then fill the center with Jell-O Pudding (another General Foods product). Bring it out, grinning, and listen to the kids go "Yaaaay! Pudding in a Cloud! Ummmmm!"

Cosby has become sort of a television junk-food institution.

Sigh. Whatever happened to "I Spy"?

Anyway, Pudding in a Cloud sort of stuck in my mind, and I began to muse about it, to the point that I never did find out how *Wonder Woman* prevented the destruction of IRAC, the smart-aleck computer. If pudding in a cloud of Cool Whip was so great, I figured, surely there were possibilities in other food in clouds of other stuff.

After the idea had echoed around in my head for a while, I had a number of cloudy possibilities. One, chestnut mousse in a cloud of meringue, was a disaster, and I'll spare you the recipe. (You can look it up yourself if you like; make it only if you're really fond of bland.)

The rest were pretty good. The clouds added contrasts in texture, flavor, color and temperature, and in no case were difficult to supply.

Although I served a number of cloud dishes at the same meal, that probably isn't the best idea, as it tends to diminish the dramatic effect of any one of them. (I've looked at clouds from both sides now, but it's clouds' profusion I recall.)

Here are some possibilities for you to ponder. Others will certainly suggest themselves, perhaps while you're trying to fall asleep (be sure to write them down). In almost every case you can add to the fanciness of the presentation by piping the cloud material out of a pastry bag.

Appetizers:
*Herring in a cloud (of blended sour cream and yogurt)*
*Hard-cooked eggs in a cloud (of mayonnaise)*
Soup:
*Chilled zucchini-dill soup in a cloud (of sour cream)*
Main courses:
*Moussaka in a cloud (of egg-yogurt custard)*
*Shepherd's pie in a cloud (of mashed potatoes)*
Dessert:
*Brownie in a cloud (of whipped cream, topped with hot chocolate sauce)*

The first dish is the most peculiar. You can buy herring already packaged in sour cream sauce. Why would you bother to serve it this way instead? First of all, in honor of Bill Cosby. Second, because this way you get to glop up the herring with as much sour cream as you like.

I tried this with one big dish, as a sort of community dip. It doesn't work nearly so well as providing individual dishes, with individual little clouds of yogurty sour cream, each with its herring center. That way every guest gets his or her own cloud with a herring lining.

---

### Herring in a Cloud

1 (8-ounce) carton dairy sour cream
½ cup plain yogurt

1 (8-ounce) jar herring in wine sauce, well drained

Blend sour cream and yogurt. Swirl a small circular ridge of the mixture onto each of 4 small saucers.

Into the hole in the sour cream, place a small mound of drained herring, onions and whatever else came out of the jar. Eat with crackers or with fork. Serves 4.

---

Oeufs Mayonnaise (halved hard-cooked eggs topped with mayonnaise) is a standard appetizer in France. Oeufs en Nuage (eggs in a cloud) is only the merest perversion of that classic: instead of topping the eggs with mayonnaise, top the mayonnaise with eggs.

### Oeufs en Nuage
(Eggs in a cloud)

4 lettuce leaves
1 cup mayonnaise

4 to 6 hard-cooked eggs

Arrange a lettuce leaf on each of 4 salad plates. Spoon or pipe mayonnaise into a small mound.

Halve the eggs and arrange 2 or 3 halves on each mound of mayonnaise.

If you have 10 minutes and some oil, homemade mayonnaise is delicious and not very difficult at all:

### Mayonnaise

1 egg yolk
3/4 teaspoon Dijon mustard
Salt and pepper
Pinch of sugar
Generous 3/4 cup oil (olive oil is best,

others are perfectly fine)
1 tablespoon tarragon vinegar (or other vinegar if you don't like tarragon)

Put the egg yolk in a medium-size bowl. Add the mustard, salt, pepper and sugar and stir with a whisk or wooden spoon. Add a few drops of the oil and stir until it is fully incorporated and the mixture is absolutely smooth. Add more oil, a little at a time, stirring hard after each addition, to incorporate the oil fully.

When more than half the oil is in, you can add it a bit faster, but never add oil until the last batch is fully incorporated, or you can kiss your mayonnaise good-bye.

When all the oil is in, stir in the vinegar. Makes about 1 cup.

You can probably do this more easily in a blender. On the other hand, you can do it still more easily by buying a jar of mayonnaise at the supermarket.

The zucchini-dill soup can be served either hot or cold, and either way the cloud of sour cream would be nice. A hint is in order, though: This is a very filling soup. It's more like a whole lunch than it is like part of dinner.

### Zucchini-Dill Soup in a Cloud

4 tablespoons butter
2 medium onions, cut into rings or coarsely chopped
1 clove garlic, put through a garlic press
1 (10 3/4-ounce) can chicken broth, diluted with only 3/4 cup water

1 pound zucchini
2 medium potatoes
1 teaspoon salt
1/8 teaspoon pepper
1 1/2 teaspoons dill weed
1 cup heavy cream
2 cups dairy sour cream

Melt the butter in a 5-quart Dutch oven. Sauté the onions and garlic in the butter until the onions are translucent. Add the canned broth and the 3/4 cup of water.

Wash the zucchini and peel the potatoes. Grate or slice the zucchini and potatoes and add them to the broth, along with the salt, pepper and dill.

Simmer 15 to 20 minutes, until the vegetables are tender.

*(Continued)*

Pour, half at a time if necessary, into the food processor or blender and purée. Add cream and stir. Chill thoroughly or heat (but not to boiling).

Divide sour cream equally among soup bowls, swirling a ridge of it below the rim of each bowl.

Ladle the soup into the bowl, being careful not to spill any on the sour cream. Serve immediately. Serves 8 to 10.

---

Here's a recipe that almost didn't need any fiddling to turn it into something in a cloud. The only departure from standard moussaka is that, instead of pouring all the sauce over the moussaka and letting it wind up who-knows-where, you provide a margin in the pan for the sauce to gather and form the cloud. (I can hear those kids now: "Yaaaay! Moussaka in a Cloud! Ummmmm!")

---

### Moussaka in a Cloud

1 tablespoon oil
3 cloves garlic, put through a garlic press
2 large onions, chopped
1½ pounds ground lamb
1½ teaspoons salt
Pepper
Dash paprika
Dash cinnamon
2 pounds eggplant, peeled and cut in ½-inch slices
Flour for breading
Oil for frying
3 eggs
1½ cups unflavored yogurt
1 cup shredded Swiss cheese
Pinch nutmeg

Heat the oil in a large frying pan, and sauté the garlic and onions until the onions are translucent. Add the ground lamb and salt, pepper, paprika and cinnamon. Break up the lamb and cook until the pink color is gone.

Using a slotted spoon so the fat stays behind, transfer the lamb-onion mixture to a bowl and set it aside. Heat the fat remaining in the frying pan, adding oil if necessary.

Meanwhile dredge the eggplant slices in flour. Fry them lightly on both sides, adding oil to the pan when necessary. Set fried slices aside.

Place a layer of eggplant slices in a 9-by-13-inch baking dish, leaving a 1-inch margin around the sides. (For the cloud, remember?) Top with about half the meat mixture. Place a second layer of eggplant slices on top of the meat mixture, and top with the remaining meat. Finish off with a third layer of eggplant slices. The last may be only a partial layer of eggplant. That's O.K.; just make it look like that's what you intended.

Preheat the oven to 375 degrees.

Thoroughly beat the eggs, and slowly add the yogurt to them. Mix in the cheese and the nutmeg.

Spoon the yogurt mixture into the 1-inch border, and dribble a bit of it across the top of the moussaka as well.

Bake about 45 minutes, until the top of the yogurt is golden brown. Serves 6 to 8.

---

If lamb is not your cup of meat, how about Shepherd's Pie, which is made, in this version, with ground beef? The mashed-potato cloud is a standard part of this dish.

### Shepherd's Pie

2 cups mashed potatoes (instant spuds work fine)
2 eggs, separated
Dash salt
2 tablespoons butter, divided
1 medium onion, chopped fine
1 pound ground beef

Salt and pepper
1 teaspoon Worcestershire sauce
$\frac{1}{2}$ cup prepared gravy (or $\frac{1}{2}$ cup canned consommé in which 2 tablespoons cornstarch has been dissolved)
1 tablespoon grated cheese (optional)

Add the egg yolks to the prepared mashed potatoes. Beat the egg whites with the dash of salt and fold them into the potatoes. Spread half of the mixture in a 9-inch pie pan, building up the rim.

Heat 1 tablespoon of the butter and fry the onions in it until they are translucent. Add the ground beef, salt, pepper and Worcestershire sauce and cook until the meat loses its pink color. Drain off the fat. Add the gravy or the consommé-cornstarch mixture and cook until well mixed and thickened.

Preheat the oven to 400 degrees.

Fill the potato cloud with the meat mixture and top with the remaining potatoes, leaving a ring of meat peeking out, if you like. Dot the mashed potatoes with the remaining butter and/or cheese.

Bake for 35 minutes. If not nicely browned, run it under the broiler for 30 seconds or so.

Serves 6. Eat with caution, because the middle stays *hot!* (Leftover mashed potatoes might be the very thing we need to replace urea formaldehyde foam insulation.)

---

Dessert time. What could be a more appropriate dessert cloud than whipped cream? And what could it better surround than something chocolate?

I toyed with the idea of chocolate mousse in a whipped-cream cloud, as the grown-up-and-moved-to-a-better-neighborhood version of pudding in Cool Whip, but I decided that it would be better to go for something with the possibility of temperature variation (always nice at dessert time). So ladies and gentlemen, for our closing number this evening we proudly present Warm Brownie in Cold Whipped Cream, topped with Hot Chocolate Sauce.

This excellent brownie recipe (from *Best Loved Recipes of the American People,* by Ida Bailey Allen) calls for chocolate chips, but you could use 1-ounce semisweet chocolate squares instead. Half of the chocolate gets melted; the other half gets stirred in at the end as whole chips, so if you substitute block chocolate you'll have to break it up. (The advantage is that you can break it in fairly big pieces, which are a *real* treat when you hit them in the brownie.)

**BROWNIE:**

**12 ounces semisweet chocolate (chips or 1-ounce squares), divided**
**⅓ cup butter or margarine**
**½ cup sugar**
**2 eggs**
**1 teaspoon vanilla**
**½ cup flour**
**½ teaspoon baking powder**
**¼ teaspoon salt**
**½ cup chopped walnuts**

**CHOCOLATE SAUCE:**

**4 (1-ounce) squares semisweet chocolate**
**6 tablespoons water**
**¼ cup sugar**
**2 tablespoons butter**
**1 egg yolk, lightly beaten**

**CLOUD:**

**3 cups heavy cream**

Over low heat, melt 1 cup of the chips (or 6 one-ounce chocolate squares) with the butter in a saucepan. Remove from heat and pour into the bowl of a mixer. Beat in the sugar, then the eggs one at a time, beating well after each. Stir in the vanilla.

Sift together the flour, baking powder and salt and add the mixture to the chocolate; mix well. Stir in the nuts and the remaining cup of chips (or the remaining 6 one-ounce squares of chocolate, broken into chunks).

Preheat the oven to 375 degrees.

Oil an 8-inch square pan, and spread the brownie batter in it evenly. Bake 25 to 30 minutes. (When testing for doneness with a toothpick, try several places; if you stick the toothpick into one of the chips or chunks of chocolate it'll come out gooey even if the brownies are done.) Cool to warm.

While the brownies are baking, prepare the chocolate sauce. (You've seen this sauce before, but it's worth repeating. It's good.) Put the chocolate and water in a saucepan and melt over very low heat. Stir until the mixture is smooth. Add the sugar and stir until it is dissolved, then boil gently for 4 minutes. Remove from heat and stir in the butter, stirring until it is melted. Cool slightly.

Beat a spoonful of the chocolate into the egg yolk, then stir the yolk into the chocolate mixture.

If the brownies aren't still warm when you're ready to serve them, you might return them to a 250-degree oven for 10 minutes. Meanwhile, whip the cream (unsweetened—there's enough sugar in the brownie and sauce to sink a bismarck).

If the chocolate sauce has cooled, warm it gently, stirring.

Swirl a cloud of whipped cream in each dessert dish, plop a brownie in the middle and spoon hot chocolate sauce over it. Makes 9. You'll never be tempted by Pudding in a Cloud again.

# *A Midsummer Night's Dinner*

There are many, many things to enjoy about England, as any evening with American public television will surely demonstrate. There are also many things that you can be glad did not fully make the leap across the Atlantic with the Pilgrims.

Like British place-name spelling, or pronunciation—or actually the combination. Norwich, pronounced "norridge." Worcester, pronounced "wooster." Leicester, pronounced "lester."

And then there is the British habit of observing peculiar holidays. How dare they? Boxing Day, Michaelmas, St. Swithin's Day. You might have heard of them, sure, but when they show up in a critical passage in a nice, blood-curdling mystery, do you have the least idea when they are? Would a pie left on the window ledge at Michaelmas freeze solid or curdle? Why don't they just celebrate the Fourth of July and Thanksgiving, like everybody else?

Take, for a more detailed example, Midsummer Day, and the night before it (variously called Midsummer Night, Midsummer Eve, St. John's Night and St. John's Eve). First of all, only the British would have four names for the same evening (and they probably pronounce them all "splunge"). Second, this Midsummer Night is not in the middle of the summer. It's the 23rd of June, for goodness sake—the very beginning of summer!

If a sensible person were to celebrate the middle of summer, he or she would do so halfway between the beginning of summer (in late June) and the beginning of fall (in late September). The middle of summer, by such ruthlessly practical American standards, is 6½ weeks after the beginning of summer—or about August 6.

This might not be exactly the right time to celebrate it, but in observance of midsummer, *whenever* it is, let's have a dramatic celebration—a meal based on *A Midsummer Night's Dream.*

That was kind of a short introduction, so may I add a brief reminiscence about my own stage experience? (If you'd rather I wouldn't, you lose. But you can skip over it easily enough.)

When I was a squeaky-voiced lad of ten or eleven in Milwaukee, our fifth-grade class put on a performance of Humperdinck's *Hansel and Gretel.*

It would have been fairer to Humperdinck, I think (or I thinck), not to have mentioned his name, as he surely would not have recognized in our performance much of anything he wrote.

History hasn't been all that kind to the old composer anyway. Who would have guessed that many years after his death his name would be stolen by some British pop singer who looks, in concert, like he's going to take his clothes off any minute? That the singer remains better known than the composer is perhaps a testament to the power of looking like you're going to take your clothes off. (I'm sure that the composer didn't look like that—even when he was going to take his clothes off.)

Be all that as it may, for our fifth-grade production I was chosen to play the part of Hansel. "What an honor," you might well be thinking. Well, sort of. In order to distribute the glory, our teacher had selected an entirely different cast for each of the three acts. I didn't think that was great, but I didn't think it was terrible, either. After all, even a third of Hansel is a big deal, right? Second-act Hansel. Pretty nice.

Except, as it turned out, for three things: The audience was not informed that there would be any switches of performers. My appearance on the stage was the first of any of the second set of players. And my opening line, as someone whom the audience would have no way of knowing was supposed to be Hansel, was "Cock-a-doodle doo!"

It was absolutely humiliating. I firmly believe that that one experience accounts for the fact that I am not now the Toast of Broadway, but am instead the Cupcake of Minneapolis.

And now let us return to the Midsummer Night's Dinner. (And hello again to those of you who skipped the fascinating Al's Childhood anecdote.)

You might notice, if unlike me you're at all practical, that three of the Midsummer Night's Dinner items require baking in the oven. A bit hot for that at midsummer, you might huff.

Well, now, calm yourself, sweetie. It's true that *I'm* not very practical, but let's face it: You're not really likely to get around to trying these recipes for months anyway. In October or November they'll be fine.

For an appetizer, let's have some little rolls with a nice sausagy filling. (A food that contains another food is an appropriate beginning for a dinner in honor of a play that contains another play, no?)

I must say that the filling, despite some of my best efforts at seasoning, tasted a little more like summer sausage than I would have preferred. On the other hand, some people really like the distinctive flavor of summer sausage. This is for them. Hint: If you aren't one of those people, try something more like kosher salami.

But not in a dinner with this theme.

Read the title of this recipe with a German accent, to honor Mr. Humperdinck. (The first Mr. Humperdinck.)

## Rolls
### Midsummer Sausage

ROLLS:

2 (¼-ounce) envelopes active dry
   yeast
½ cup warm water
Pinch of sugar
½ cup butter
1 tablespoon salt
⅓ cup sugar
1 cup dairy sour cream

5 to 5½ cups all-purpose flour
2 eggs

FILLING:

4 slices bacon
2½ tablespoons butter
1 medium onion, chopped
About 4 ounces summer sausage,
   finely diced
1 egg, lightly beaten

Stir the yeast into the warm water in a cup with the pinch of sugar. Set aside.

Cream the butter in the large bowl of an electric mixer. Add the salt and gradually add the ⅓ cup of sugar, continuing to beat until the mixture is smooth.

Beat in the sour cream, followed by 1 cup of the flour. Add the eggs, one at a time, beating well after each addition. Beat in the yeast mixture, which should be foamy. (If it's not, start that part again, with newer yeast.)

Using a large wooden spoon, beat in enough of the remaining flour to make a dough that is soft and easy to handle. Turn the dough out onto a lightly floured surface and knead it until it is smooth.

Wash and grease the mixer bowl. Roll the dough into a ball and put it into the bowl, turning it so that the surface that is up is well greased. Cover and let it rise in a warm place until it is doubled in volume, about 1½ hours.

Meanwhile, prepare the filling:

Fry and crumble the bacon. Drain on paper towels. Melt the butter in a frying pan and sauté the chopped onion until it is translucent. Stir in the bacon and summer sausage.

Punch the risen dough down and divide into 32 pieces. Roll each piece into a rough ball.

Holding a dough ball in the palm of your hand, make a large indentation in the center and spoon in about 1 teaspoon of the filling. Close the dough firmly around the filling and set the roll on a greased cookie sheet. (Keep rolls about 2 inches apart.)

Cover the rolls lightly and let them rise until doubled, about 45 minutes. Preheat the oven to 400 degrees. Brush the tops of the completed rolls with beaten egg, avoiding letting the egg run down onto the baking sheet.

Bake for 10 minutes, or until the rolls are golden brown. Serve hot. Makes 32 appetizer rolls.

---

Do you like the artichoke bottom? (Or, as the French say, "Fond d'artichaut?") (The French say that when they are referring to the artichoke bottom, not when they are asking whether you like it. The French have lots of other words that mean "to be enamored of something.") (The French have lots of other words for "bottom," too. Never mind.)

In any case, if you like the artichoke bottom you should enjoy Artichoke Bottom Soup. So, I'd guess, would Bottom, a character in *A Midsummer Night's Dream.* He winds up wearing a donkey's head, but I mention that merely for identification, not to suggest anything about those who are fond of the artichoke bottom.

Confused enough? Then let's have some nice soup.

3½ tablespoons butter, divided
1 (14-ounce) can artichoke bottoms
  (7½ ounces drained weight)
2 medium onions
2 tablespoons flour
2 (10¾-ounce) cans chicken broth

1 egg yolk
1 cup cream
Rind of ½ orange, grated
1 tablespoon brown sugar
Tabasco to taste
Salt, pepper to taste

## Artichoke Bottom Soup

Melt 1½ tablespoons of the butter in a frying pan. Drain and rinse the artichoke bottoms, slice them thin and add them. Slice the onions thin and add them, too. Sauté the vegetables gently for 10 minutes, remove from the pan and set aside.

Melt the remaining 2 tablespoons of butter in a small Dutch oven. Add the flour and cook, stirring, 1 minute. Slowly add the chicken broth, stirring constantly until the mixture is thickened and smooth.

Beat the egg yolk in a medium bowl and stir in the cream. Stirring constantly, add a cup of the hot broth mixture to the egg mixture. Pour the diluted egg mixture into the broth, stirring well.

Add the artichoke mixture, grated orange rind and brown sugar, and Tabasco, salt and pepper to taste. Serves 4.

---

Now for a pleasant midsummer vegetable. I thought this was a much more than adequate way to dispose of a few pesky zucchini.

2½ pounds zucchini
1 medium onion
1 small clove garlic
¼ cup (½ stick) butter
½ teaspoon salt

⅛ teaspoon pepper
½ tablespoon dried dill or 1
  tablespoon fresh dill
1 cup dairy sour cream

## Midsummer Squash with Dill Sauce

Wash the zucchini and cut on the diagonal into ½-inch-thick slices.

Cut the onion into thin slices and cut them in half. Chop the garlic fine. Melt the butter in a large skillet and sauté the onion and garlic until the onions are translucent.

Stir in the sliced zucchini, salt, pepper, and dill. Cook, covered, over low heat, 10 to 15 minutes, or just until the squash is tender. Stir occasionally. Stir in the sour cream and heat gently, stirring, until the sauce is heated through. Serves 6 to 8.

---

The main dish for a meal at this level of culture ought to nod to the playwright, wright? Or write? Or right?

You bet. So let's have some very pleasant chicken that does just that.

Is it fried chicken?

"Nay, sirrah! Never was it fried! It is Shakespeare 'n' Bake. And I assisted!"

## Shakespeare 'n' Bake Chicken

1 egg, beaten
¼ teaspoon paprika
¼ teaspoon salt
½ cup crushed saltine crackers (10 single saltines)
½ cup crushed potato chips

1 teaspoon Italian seasoning
¾ teaspoon garlic powder
½ teaspoon onion powder
1 teaspoon basil
1 tablespoon grated Parmesan cheese
4 chicken breast halves, skin removed

Preheat the oven to 400 degrees.

Combine the beaten egg, paprika and salt in a shallow bowl. Combine the cracker crumbs, potato-chip crumbs, Italian seasoning, garlic powder, onion powder, basil and cheese in a large, clean paper bag. Dip the chicken pieces, one at a time, in the egg mixture, then shake them in the crumb mixture, coating well.

Place the chicken pieces in a single layer in a greased baking pan. Bake 20 minutes, turn and bake 20 minutes more, or until done.

Serves 4.

Dream bars would have been the obvious dessert choice here, but for two things: They were *too* obvious; and I had just made a batch and didn't want them again so soon. (Or did I dream that?)

Instead, here's a dessert that stems from one of the best parts of camping out—that moment late in a midsummer night when the foolhardy begin to roast marshmallows around the campfire (getting icky, sticky goo all over themselves in the process) and the smart foolhardy begin to assemble chocolate bars, graham crackers and melted marshmallows to make S'mores (getting icky, sticky goo all over themselves in the process but getting a much better deal when all is said and done).

This is the adult version of that messy treat. In contrast to the S'more, the S'nore is not tricky to eat.

You could do it in your sleep.

## S'nore

2 cups graham-cracker crumbs
½ cup (1 stick) butter, melted
1¼ cups granulated sugar, divided
3 (8-ounce) packages cream cheese, softened
2 teaspoons vanilla extract

3 eggs
1 cup dairy sour cream
1 (7-ounce) jar marshmallow creme
1 (12-ounce) package semisweet chocolate chips
¼ cup milk

In a large bowl, blend the crumbs, butter and ¼ cup of the sugar. Press the mixture firmly against the bottom of a lightly greased 8-inch springform pan and an inch or two up the sides. Preheat the oven to 350 degrees.

Beat the cream cheese until it is fluffy. Gradually add the remaining 1 cup of sugar and the vanilla extract.

Beat in the eggs, one at a time, and the sour cream. Stir in the marshmallow creme; don't beat it in fully, but leave a small chunk of it here and there in the batter.

Pour the batter into the crumb-lined pan. Bake 70 minutes, or until the filling is firm. Turn off the oven. Leaving the oven door slightly ajar (prop it open with a wooden spoon, if necessary), allow the cheesecake to remain in the cooling oven for 1 hour. Then chill it in the refrigerator.

Just before serving, melt the chocolate chips in a saucepan over very low heat, stirring, and stir in the milk. Spoon as sauce over individual servings of cheesecake.

Makes 12 servings.

---

The writer is expecting a midsummer visit from the Bard of Avon Lady.

# The Raw Dinner

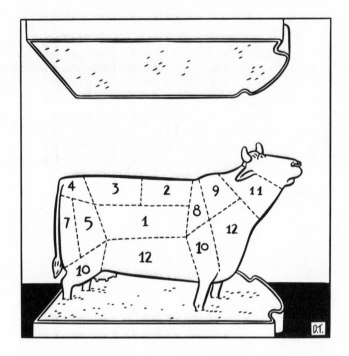

On a recent plane trip I was paging listlessly through the in-flight magazine (I had forgotten my list, and I figured the magazine was a better choice than either the cheap thriller I had grabbed at the airport bookstore or my well-thumbed copy of *How to Face Death in the Air),* when what to my wandering eyes should appear but one of those city-profile articles that in-flight magazines seem to love—and it was about the city I grew up in! (And the city in which I learned not to end sentences with prepositions. And not to write sentence fragments.)

What a chance, I figured, to catch the slick magazine writer with his adjectives down! I just knew that he would attempt to paint Milwaukee as either a gloomy industrial town or the Beverly Hills of Wisconsin, bustling with goat-cheese and raspberry-vinegar parties.

There was, in fact, a hint of the latter suggestion, but I was disappointed to find that, by and large, the city described in the magazine was fairly closely related to the actual place. What fun is there, I began to grumble, in reading an article like that?

The only thing I carried off the plane (beyond my luggage, a bag of peanuts and a slight headache) was a bit of puzzlement that the author of the article had mentioned, as an interesting fact, that Milwaukeeans (that's the term of choice—not Milwaukeeites or Milwaukeeoids) like to eat raw ground beef.

Well, sure, I thought. But so do other people. Steak tartare or variations of it are eaten around the world. When I mentioned this peculiar magazine assertion to various folks who aren't from Milwaukee (or as natives pronounce it, Mwaukee), they allowed that, although they might have eaten steak tartare at a few fancy parties, they really didn't have it very often at all. They didn't remember, for example, ever eating raw ground beef on rye bread as an after-school snack. I didn't do that all the time, but I certainly did once in a while. It was pretty good, too.

Well, then, maybe Milwaukee consumption of what we used to call cannibal sandwiches does exceed the national average. (Or at least eastern Wisconsin consumption—the only one of my friends who had fond recollections of this snack is from Sheboygan).

That, as we like to say, set me to thinking. ("Thinking" is sort of a grand description of what it set me to doing, but it will have to suffice. We don't have a concise term for saying "uhhh . . ." a lot.)

(Gee. Maybe I could tone up these articles if I used *lots* of more elegant phrasing. If I larded each opus with things like "I found the resulting tuna casserole wholly admirable" and "peanut butter has a special affinity for jelly," would I sound like Craig Claiborne? Probably not, but I don't have anything better to do.)

Anyway, spurred by the discussion of cannibal sandwiches, I decided for lack of a better idea to prepare a dinner of uncooked foods.

Sushi, the Japanese delicacy consisting largely of various kinds of absolutely raw fish, entered my mind, but I showed it right back out because, unless you have excellent assurances about your suppliers—as restaurants should—raw fish can contain parasites that you wouldn't care to read about, much less consume.

Gravlax, the Scandinavian dish consisting of salmon cured in a dill marinade, also occurred to me, but only when it was too late to marinate it. Maybe the next time we do raw food.

"What do I care what he didn't make?" you are probably asking.

"What do I even care what he *did* make?" you are possibly asking.

Just simmer down, now. If yours was the first question, we're merely clearing the decks for the goodies to come. If yours was the second question, you have clearly mistaken this for some other section of the newspaper. Might I recommend the entertainment or travel sections, which are very nice today. (My name is Al; I'll be your obsequious servitor. If you have any questions, I'll be happy to answer them. Is everything O.K. here? You can just pay me when you're ready.)

All right, then. If you're all set, let's hear it for dinner. Raw! Raw! Raw!

Regular readers will know that I am not the man to whom one should turn for ideas on the consumption of raw vegetables. I'm not so fond of cooked vegetables that I am eager to deal with them before they got to be *that* good.

But in a dinner like this one, one appetizer has got to be raw vegetables and a dip. So here goes. The dip is very nice; you can pick your own raw vegetables to dip in it.

---

### Mexican Cheese Dip

¼ cup (½ stick) butter or margarine, softened
8 ounces (2 cups) shredded Cheddar cheese
1 tablespoon chopped parsley
1½ tablespoons chopped canned hot peppers
½ teaspoon or more Tabasco (to taste)
1 tablespoon steak sauce
½ teaspoon salt
Assorted raw vegetable dippers

Cream butter or margarine. Add cheese, parsley, peppers, Tabasco, steak sauce and salt, and beat until smooth.

Serve with assorted vegetable dippers. Serves 6 to 8.

---

On, now, to what started all this, the cannibal snadwich. No, that's not a typographical error. Somewhere in the dim past, somebody in my family saw "snadwich" on a sign, and that became a preferred family pronunciation. So, as long as we're having this recipe from my past, that's how we're going to spell it.

---

### Cannibal Snadwiches

¾ pound lean steak, ground
1 egg yolk (optional)
½ cup chopped onion
Salt to taste, but be generous
Pepper
Slices of cocktail rye bread

You can certainly start with plain ground beef (that's certainly what we did), but starting with steak and having the butcher grind it assures you of less fat—and of ground beef that hasn't been exposed to air (and spoilage potential) for as long.

Work in the egg yolk (if you like—it adds some body and richness) and the onion, salt and pepper.

Spread thick on slices of cocktail rye bread and serve open-faced.

If there's one ingredient that's really necessary to successful cannibal snadwiches, it's plenty of salt. I underdid it when I served these, but that's easy enough to fix. Just have the salt shaker handy next to the plate of snadwiches.

Makes about 16 appetizer snadwiches.

---

I must confess to splendid ignorance about seviche, although I've eaten it several times. The first time I had it was in an Italian restaurant, and that fixed it in my mind as an Italian dish. When I couldn't find it in any Italian cookbooks, I tried French, too, figuring it might have been just southern European.

It turns out, as all of you no doubt know, that it is part of the local cuisine from Mexico to the tip of South America, and it is said to be of Polynesian origin.

Here, technically minded readers will note, we stretch the definition of raw, because although the scallops are not cooked they are marinated in a citric-acid mixture which performs a similar function. (The scallops turn white and opaque in acid just as surely as they do when cooked with heat.)

## Seviche

1 pound bay scallops (or quartered sea scallops)
½ cup chopped onion
1 clove garlic, put through a garlic press
1 medium tomato, chopped
1 tablespoon chopped canned hot peppers
¾ cup lime juice
3 tablespoons olive oil
2 tablespoons white wine
Dash Tabasco
1 teaspoon salt
½ teaspoon pepper
¼ teaspoon crushed basil
¼ cup chopped parsley

Note: This recipe requires marinating time.

Discard any liquid from the scallops and put them in a small bowl. Stir in the onions, garlic, tomato and chopped peppers.

Combine in a jar the lime juice, olive oil, wine, Tabasco, salt, pepper and basil. Shake well.

Pour this marinade over the scallop mixture and turn the scallops in it. If there isn't enough marinade to cover the scallops completely, add more lime juice and oil, roughly 4 parts lime juice to 1 part oil. (If you're running out of lime juice, you can use a little lemon juice; nobody will sue.)

Cover the bowl tightly and refrigerate at least 6 hours, stirring once in a while.

Drain before serving, and sprinkle with parsley. Serves 6 as a first course or 12 as an appetizer.

---

Here's another raw-meat appetizer or light main-dish item. Unlike seviche, which (my ignorance not to the contrary) has fairly deep roots, carpaccio is apparently a Johnny-come-lately, traced usually to Harry's Bar in Venice in about 1961. I suppose that makes it a Harry-come-lately. Anyway, it's paper-thin slices of un-cooked lean beef with a tangy dipping sauce.

Several of my guests liked it just fine; a few others had a little of it raw and said that it was O.K., but they wouldn't mind a little more of it cooked. That's easy enough, since paper-thin beef cooks in a little oil in almost no time. So you might want to be adventuresome and try it raw but have the old frying pan standing by to turn it into Familiar City if that doesn't work out.

---

## Carpaccio

1 pound top round steak, all fat removed
½ cup mayonnaise
6 tablespoons Dijon mustard
¼ teaspoon crumbled basil
¼ teaspoon crumbled tarragon
2 teaspoons lemon juice
Wedges of lemon or lime

Slice the meat paper thin. (That's easier to do if you freeze it an hour or two first; not so it turns into a brick, just so it isn't squidgy.)

Meanwhile, combine the mayonnaise, mustard, basil, tarragon and lemon juice, cover and refrigerate.

Once the meat is sliced, put a few slices at a time between sheets of plastic wrap and roll or pound them out until they are even thinner. (Novice carpaccists might want to skip this step, as it is a considerable pain. If it turns out you love the general idea of carpaccio but wish the meat was a bit easier to chew, pound it out like this the next time.)

Arrange the slices prettily on a large platter (you might even want to roll a few up into roses), serve with the sauce and garnish with the lemon or lime wedges.

For those who turn out not to be remotely carpaccoid, sauté the slices ever-so-briefly in hot oil.

An appetizer or very light main course for 8.

---

More often lately than I care to discuss in the public prints, I find myself admitting either that I hadn't really read a recipe before I started to prepare it, or that I read it but I hadn't fully grasped it.

I am a bad example. Please don't do that.

The next dish was just fine—quite good, in fact—but I realized as I was about to prepare it that it wasn't going to wind up one bit raw. It was simply going to wind up cold. If you're willing to handle that admission gracefully, I'll pass along the recipe.

If you're going to gloat, on the other hand, we'll print it in disappearing ink, and after you cut it out and paste it on one of those cute little cards with the bunnies in the corner it will simply fade away.

So be nice.

---

## Cold Pasta and Asparagus Salad

1 (7-ounce) package elbow macaroni
4 tablespoons olive oil, divided
1 pound fresh asparagus
1/2 pound mushrooms
2 medium red or green bell peppers
1 small clove garlic
6 or 7 pimiento-stuffed ripe olives
1 lemon
1 teaspoon salt
1/4 teaspoon freshly ground pepper
1/2 teaspoon sugar
1/4 teaspoon crumbled oregano
1 1/2 teaspoons sesame oil (the oriental kind, not the health-food-store kind)

Prepare the macaroni according to package directions; drain. Toss the drained macaroni with 2 tablespoons of the olive oil.

Cut the asparagus into 1-inch pieces, slice the mushrooms, seed and slice the bell peppers, put the garlic through a garlic press and slice the olives.

Heat the remaining 2 tablespoons of oil in a Dutch oven and add the asparagus, mushrooms, peppers and garlic. Cook over medium heat about 15 minutes, stirring occasionally. Drain off the liquid. Stir the vegetables into the macaroni in a large bowl.

Grate about 1 tablespoon of lemon peel. Add the grated peel, the juice of the lemon and the olive slices, salt, pepper, sugar, oregano and sesame oil to the macaroni-vegetable mixture. Toss well, cover and refrigerate at least an hour. Serves 8.

---

For dessert, there is one obvious candidate. So I made it. Raw chocolate-chip cookie dough.

You certainly don't need a recipe for it (if you do, it's on the bag of chocolate chips [and in the next chapter]). But how about a Serving Suggestion? (You always see illustrations labeled "Serving Suggestion" on cans and frozen-food packages. Soup might be shown in a bowl, for example, to keep you from pouring it into people's hands.)

Serving Suggestion: A scoop of chocolate-chip cookie dough can be plopped in a dish and topped with whipped cream or warm chocolate sauce.

Or not. Any way you serve chocolate-chip cookie dough is deliciously naughty. With every bite you can imagine your mom hollering at you not to do it.

We should have a dessert *recipe,* though, for those who insist on cutting things out and leaving them around the house.

You're never going to actually make most of these things, you know.

Oh, well, if it makes you happy. How about a sort of thin fruit-based mousse?

---

### Banana or Mango Stuff

3 bananas (or 2 mangoes and a banana, if you like mangoes and can find them)

Juice of 1 1/2 limes or 1 lemon
1 1/2 cups heavy cream
1 1/4 cups plain yogurt

Peel the fruit and mash or purée it with the lime or lemon juice. Whip the cream. Blend the yogurt and fruit together; fold in 1/2 cup of the whipped cream and divide among 6 serving dishes. Top with remaining whipped cream. Chill.

Serves 6.

---

How about a little something raw for *after* dinner?

When I was growing up skinny, and hating milk, eggs and all the various healthy foods that the American Heart Association is now telling us to cut down on, my mother used to sneak eggs and milk into things that I *would* eat.

To turn one of these child-fatteners into an acceptable after-dinner drink might have been difficult a few years ago. People would have said it was too sweet.

But these days, when Bailey's Irish Cream and other cream-and-booze mixtures are doing so well, it's just one of the crowd.

---

### Al's Milwaukee Cream

8 heaping teaspoons chocolate malt powder
2 cups milk
1 small banana, sliced

1 egg
1/2 cup or so brandy
2 scoops vanilla ice cream

Combine all ingredients in blender. Whomp lightly, until ice cream is broken up and mixture thickens.

Makes enough to fill 6 small drinking glasses.

# The Language of Cookies

Not long ago a friend was down in the dumps and I asked her if there was anything I could do to help.

"No."

"Wanna talk?"

"No."

"Wanna drink?"

"No."

I played my trump card. "Want me to make some oatmeal cookies?"

That did it. "Would you?"

I made a batch of oatmeal cookies and brought them to her still warm. She was deeply grateful, and it improved her mood for at least five or ten minutes. (You can't expect a plate of cookies to work miracles, after all.)

You must understand something. I didn't suggest oatmeal cookies because I like them. I don't care for them much at all—they are singularly lacking in chocolate. But I know they're her favorites, so that's what I offered.

In that way, cookies are like flowers. A bouquet of carnations is a bunch of flowers to some people but a special thing to those who really love carnations. Getting the right kind of flowers gives the gift extra meaning.

In addition, of course, if you want to really get specific with a floral tribute, there is a whole language of flowers. I don't know where it came from, but reference books and florists have lists of what each flower means.

Some are kind of strange. Azaleas, according to one list, are for transitory passion; red carnations for admiration; dahlias signify treachery (one assumes that it is on the part of the recipient, not the sender, as a treacherous person would be unlikely to telegraph his deceit—even if he did telegraph the flowers). Orange lilies are for hatred; yellow roses speak of infidelity or jealousy; and asphodels mean "my regret follows you to the grave."

Well!

That language of flowers probably comes in handy sometimes. Say a woman has attracted the attention of a particularly obnoxious individual and is having difficulty letting him know that she'd prefer no company at all to his. Saying so outright is difficult, and even a letter to that effect can be kind of cruel. But sending him a mixed bouquet of petunias (anger) and meadow saffron ("let us part"), with a note saying "Look them up, stupid," cushions the blow because the flowers come before their full import is realized.

It occurred to me that, in the same way, a language of cookies might be a good idea. If cookies, like flowers, can be a gift of love, why shouldn't cookies be able to communicate as specifically? There are certainly enough kinds of cookies around that assigning a meaning to each type would provide a very large range of messages.

The only problem I could see was finding some authority to impose the meanings on various cookies, so I began skimming cookbook indexes to see if there were many cookies whose names might already imply specific messages. I found so many that I think we don't need the cookie-meaning czar—a language of cookies already exists.

**Date Cookies,** for example, mean "Will you go out with me?"

**Date-Honey Cookies** are a somewhat bolder statement: "Will you go out with me, *honey?*"

**Hermits,** of course, mean "Leave me alone," while **Molasses Cookies** indicate "I want to stick to you."

Actually, those are fairly general messages, like those conveyed by red roses (love and desire). There are a number of cookies that get pretty specific. If asphodels can go so far as "my regret follows you to the grave" (something you don't hear every day, although you heard it twice already this morning), cookies can do no less.

For example:

**Poppy Seed Cookies** are for when you want to say "Your father is becoming disheveled."

**Cherry Bars** mean "You stay out drinking so much that your nose is turning red."

If you send somebody a **Sand Tart** or two, that means "If you wear such a skimpy bathing suit to the beach, people will get the wrong idea about you."

Want your roommate to fork over for half of the groceries? Make some **Toll House Cookies.**

**Sugar Nut Cookies** mean "I'm nuts about you, sugar," while any of the wide variety of **Refrigerator Cookies** signifies an intention to give the recipient the cold shoulder.

As a reward for those of you who have endured this far without mailing a batch of **Drop Cookies** to the newspaper's Circulation Department, let's stop just chatting about communicative cookies and start making some.

Our first cookie, far easier to make than I would have guessed and really exceptionally good, is for a message of gravity: You deserve to be hit on the head.

---

**Fig Newtons**  (Immediate apologies are due Nabisco, as Fig Newton is that company's trademark for a fig bar cookie. I'm sorry.)

(It just wouldn't have worked to write "For a message of gravity, send a Fig Bar Cookie.")

| | |
|---|---|
| **3 cups sifted flour** | **1 teaspoon vanilla** |
| **$1/2$ teaspoon salt** | **About 1 pound dried figs** |
| **$1/4$ pound (1 stick) plus 3 tablespoons butter or margarine** | **1 cup water** |
| **1 cup packed brown sugar** | **2 tablespoons sugar** |
| **2 egg whites** | **2 tablespoons lemon juice** |

Note: This cookie requires a refrigerated rest, so it can't be made in a hurry.

Sift the flour and salt together.

Cream the butter and brown sugar until the mixture is very light and fluffy. Beat in the egg whites and vanilla and then gradually add the flour mixture, beating constantly. The dough is quite thick.

Wrap it in waxed paper and put it in the refrigerator for at least 2 hours.

Meanwhile, make the filling. Cut off the stems and hard ends of the figs. Chop the figs quite fine (you should have about 2 cups of chopped figs). Combine the figs, water, sugar and lemon juice and, if you have a blender, blend them briefly to break up the figs even more. (If you don't have a blender, it'll work O.K. if you just skip that step.)

Pour the fig-water-sugar-juice mixture into a pan and bring it to the simmer (stirring continuously, until it is thickened—6 to 7 minutes).

Set the filling aside to cool (don't refrigerate it).

When the dough has chilled, preheat the oven to 350 degrees.

Cut a 2-by-3-inch rectangle from a piece of paper to use as a guide in cutting the dough.

Lightly flour your work surface and a rolling pin. Break the dough into 6 roughly equal pieces. Leave 5 of them in the refrigerator.

Roll the dough out into a rectangle about $1/4$ inch thick. Using the paper guide, cut the dough into 2-by-3-inch pieces (return the scraps to the chunk of dough in the refrigerator). Plop a generous (but not heaping) teaspoon of the filling into the middle of each rectangle and spread it so that it forms a band about an inch wide, running across the rectangle the short way all the way to the edges (the filling should fill the middle third of the cookie).

Use a metal spatula to lift one side of the uncovered dough, and fold it about two-thirds of the way across the filling. Then flip the cookie over onto the rest of the uncovered dough. (The dough should overlap.)

Place the cookies, seam side down, on an ungreased baking sheet and flatten them slightly with the back of the metal spatula. (They don't spread at all while baking, so you needn't leave much room between them.)

Repeat with remaining dough and filling.

Bake them about 12 minutes, until they are just slightly brown and seem to have a bit of firmness—they'll firm up more as they cool.

Cool them on racks.

Makes 30 to 36 cookies.

---

Next, an old favorite, the Chocolate-Chip Cookie, updated by making a sandwich cookie out of two of them, with peanut butter or chocolate frosting in between.

Since this Chocolate-Chip Sandwich Cookie has neither top nor bottom, it is the appropriate vehicle for the following message: "Any way I look at it, you seem to have a chip on your shoulder."

---

## Chocolate-Chip Sandwich Cookies

1 cup plus 2 tablespoons flour
1/2 teaspoon salt
1/2 teaspoon soda
1/2 cup softened butter or margarine
3/8 cup (6 tablespoons) white sugar
3/8 cup (6 tablespoons) brown sugar
1/2 teaspoon vanilla
1 egg
1 (6-ounce) package chocolate chips (1 cup)
1/2 cup chopped nuts (optional)

or
1 cup golden raisins (optional)

FILLING:

Chunky peanut butter
  or frosting made with:
2 (1-ounce) squares unsweetened chocolate
2 cups confectioners' sugar
2 tablespoons milk (approximately)

Make the cookies:

Preheat the oven to 375 degrees. Combine the flour, salt and soda. Cream the butter and beat in the white sugar, brown sugar and vanilla. Beat in the egg.

Gradually beat in the flour mixture, then stir in the chocolate chips, and the nuts or golden raisins if you like. I vote heavily for golden raisins, because they make the cookies chewier, which is the way I like them. If you like 'em crisp, avoid the raisins. Drop by rounded or heaping teaspoonfuls onto ungreased cookie sheets and bake 8 to 10 minutes.

Now choose your filling. If you like both peanut butter and chocolate, don't miss the opportunity to try chunky peanut butter in this application.

If you're not such a goober fan, the chocolate filling is quite fine.

Either way, you can't lose. If it were me, I'd make some of each. And since it *was* me, I did.

To prepare the chocolate filling, melt the chocolate in a double boiler or over very low heat in a saucepan. Stir in the confectioners' sugar and gradually stir in the milk until a thick but spreadable frosting is achieved.

Whichever filling you chose, spread a nice thick blob of it on the bottom of one cookie and cover with another.

Makes 20 to 24 sandwich cookies.

To my surprise, the next message unit (as they say in the telephone biz) might require some explanation to some readers.

I made the cookies and brought them to a party (and brought more to work a day or two later), and fully half the people who asked what meaning they were supposed to convey just looked puzzled when I told them.

The message is "I think you're fibbing."

Maybe you have to be a little older, or to have come from east of the Mississippi or something, to recognize the name of this pleasant, soft cookie as the exact equivalent of "baloney," as in "Awww, baloney!"

Some of us do. Trust me. I'm not fibbing.

---

### Applesauce Cookies

| | |
|---|---|
| ½ cup butter or margarine | 1 teaspoon baking powder |
| 1 cup sugar | ½ teaspoon cinnamon |
| 1 egg | ¼ teaspoon allspice |
| 2 cups cake flour | ¼ teaspoon cloves |
| ½ teaspoon salt | 1 cup unsweetened applesauce |
| ½ teaspoon soda | |

Preheat oven to 375 degrees. Cream the butter and sugar. Beat the egg and blend it in.

Sift together the cake flour, salt, soda, baking powder, cinnamon, allspice and cloves and add these dry ingredients alternately with the unsweetened applesauce.

Grease cookie sheets well, and drop the batter onto them by rounded or heaping teaspoonfuls. Place the cookies fairly far apart, as they spread.

Bake about 15 minutes. Makes 36 to 48 cookies (depending on the amount of batter you use for each).

---

Now for a *pleasant* cookie message. (About time, right?) Here's one that's sure to please: "I'd like to be macarooned on a dessert island with you."

And, as long as we're about it, let's go ahead and be both coconut macarooned and chocolate-coconut macarooned.

---

### Coconut or Chocolate-Coconut Macaroons

| | |
|---|---|
| 4 egg whites | 2 cups (less than a 7-ounce bag) flaked coconut |
| ¼ teaspoon salt | 2 ounces unsweetened chocolate (optional) |
| ¼ teaspoon almond extract | |
| ½ teaspoon vanilla | |
| 1⅓ cups sugar | |

Preheat the oven to 325 degrees.

Beat the egg whites with the salt, almond extract and vanilla until soft peaks form (peaks form when you lift out the beaters, but the tops flop over). Add a few tablespoons of the sugar at a time, beating after each addition, and beat until stiff peaks form (the tops no longer flop over).

Fold in the coconut.

If you want the chocolate version, melt the chocolate in a saucepan over very low heat and fold it into the macaroon mixture.

Grease cookie sheets and drop the batter onto them by rounded teaspoonfuls. Leave room, because these cookies spread a little more than one would hope, but they're quite tasty. (The chocolate versions spread somewhat less and have a bit more body.)

Bake 18 to 20 minutes, until they acquire a light-golden-brown color and are no longer at all mushy when touched.

(You'll have to go by feel with the chocolate ones.)

Cool them briefly on the cookie sheets (you'll never get them off otherwise), then put them on wire racks to cool.

Makes about 30 to 36 cookies.

---

I've saved the most potentially dangerous cookie for last, just to keep hotheads from stumbling across it. You wouldn't want to send this improvement on the oatmeal cookie without thinking about it first, because if you give a lady one of these you're saying "I've just heard about your reputation, so get lost!"

---

### Dropped Chippies

1 cup sifted flour
2 teaspoons baking powder
1/2 teaspoon salt
1/2 cup butter or margarine, softened
1 cup packed brown sugar

1 1/2 cups quick-cooking oatmeal (the dry flakes, not the cooked product)
2 eggs
1 teaspoon vanilla
1 (8-ounce) package pitted dates

Preheat the oven to 350 degrees.

Sift together the flour, baking powder and salt.

Cream the butter with the sugar and beat in the flour mixture and oatmeal. Beat the eggs lightly with the vanilla, then beat them into the batter.

Chop the dates and stir them into the batter.

Grease baking sheets and drop the batter onto them by rounded teaspoonfuls. Bake 10 to 15 minutes. The cookies should spring back when the tops are touched. Cool on racks. Makes around 40 cookies.

---

The writer is sending his boss some butter cookies, hoping that if he butters her up enough she'll send him to do research in the Sandwich Islands.

# Little Brother

Well, by now you've had enough of George Orwell to last until 2084, right? It's amazing how much analysis can be wrung out of one work of literature.

Actually, I don't understand what all the fuss is about. I've read *lots* of funnier books.

And, if the truth were told, Orwell kind of missed the boat on the real menace of the all-seeing television camera. In the worst of all possible worlds, as many children know, it wouldn't be Big Brother watching you.

It would be Little Brother.

That's a *really* chilling possibility. "AN-drew! Who said you could play with that? That's MINE! I'm gonna tell Mom!" "BET-ty! You're not doing your homework! Come here and look at what I drew!"

And there would be nowhere to hide.

Little brothers, of course, didn't ask to be little brothers. But once they figure out what Nature has done to them, most of them tend to take their revenge in this classic fashion.

Wise (but possibly foolhardy) is the parent who decides to create a momentary gap in the sibling rivalry by giving Little Brother or Little Sister something special to do. I'm not exactly recommending this, you understand (my degree in child psychology having been revoked by Kay Kyser and the entire Kollege of Musical Knowledge), but if you've already decided to try something of the sort might I suggest a small cooking session?

What follows is a selection of recipes that might entertain a little nipper who has a vague interest in hanging around in the kitchen with you.

These recipes might require some, a little or a lot of help from an older person (depending on the age of the nipper), but none requires any chopping or slicing.

Avoiding knifework was about my only negative guideline in recipe selection, so some of the recipes involve stovetop cooking and moving things into and out of the oven. If that bothers you considering the size and other peculiarities of your nipper, look over the recipes first.

I did try to choose recipes that have an element that would be kind of fun: One involves making a white sauce, which is kind of remarkable when you first see it; one involves shaking chicken pieces in a bag with potato chips; in one you shape little balls of spinach in your hands like modeling clay; in one you just mix a whole bunch of things and bake them for an appetizer-snack, and for the dessert you have to crush some cookies and scoop ice cream into glasses. Sounds messy but fun, right? Ideal for Little Sibling.

Two of these recipes also have the additional feature of using up some of the Girl Scout cookies/crackers that *other* little nippers sold you. (This is yet another example of the endless cycles of Nature.)

With one exception, I did not have kids actually prepare these recipes. I did an article like *that* once before. It involved three young neighbor kids, who spent as much time giggling and getting in each other's way as I did crying in the corner. I haven't gotten over it yet.

The exception is the spinach balls, which are either an appetizer or a peculiar vegetable course. The recipe is from my own younger kid, David, who has prepared them himself on several occasions starting when he was nine, including once on a visit with me. I have no idea where he got the recipe, so my apologies to whomever it is stolen from.

An aside: David's Big Brother, Joe, is an excellent speller. Little Brother David is an excellent logician, card player and reteller-at-length of movie plots, but he is not much, right now anyway, in the spelling department. I mention this because David mailed me the recipe, and his spelling of the name of this dish is so weird that I have to pass it along to you. (I asked him if I could.)

He called it Recepy for Spinich Balls. He added that even Joe loved them, "and he hates helth food."

Spelling, I guess, is like greatness: some are born spellers and some have spelling thrust upon them.

And some are more equal than others, which brings us back to George Orwell and ties this whole thing up in a nice, neat package.

Except for the recipes.

Which follow.

Starting now.

Here is the recipe that David sent me. I have altered it a tad, to put it into traditional recipe style, and I've added lots of comments, which is my way. I've also fixed the spelling, so that it will make sense years later to those of you who insist on clipping out the recipes without the introductory text. You probably would have had some difficulty, for example, with "½ cup graded cheese."

---

### Spinach Balls

½ stick (4 tablespoons) butter
1 (10-ounce) package frozen spinach
1 egg
1 cup crumb-type stuffing mix (or crushed croutons)

½ cup grated or shredded Cheddar or Swiss cheese
Seasoned salt
Pepper

Preheat the oven to 350 degrees.

Wash your hands.

Melt the butter in a small pan. In another pan, prepare the spinach according to package directions, and drain it well.

(Here's a very important lesson to teach beginning cooks: Open frozen-vegetable packages carefully, so you don't rip through the instructions just to get the stuff out. And don't throw the box away until you have memorized the instructions or cooked the stuff.)

Put the egg in a large bowl. (David points out that you have to crack the egg first.) Now beat the egg a little with a fork. That makes it easier to add other stuff to it, because otherwise the egg white is sort of icky.

Stir the stuffing mix into the egg. Stir in the cheese, melted butter, cooked spinach, seasoned salt and pepper (one or two hearty shakes of each is a reasonable measure). Let it cool a few minutes.

Wash your hands again, just to be sure. Grease a cookie sheet. (That's always fun.)

Shape the spinach stuff into bite-size balls, about an inch across or so (that's even *more* fun if you can get into it) and put them on the cookie sheet.

Now put the cookie sheet in the oven and bake about 10 or 15 minutes.

When the balls are baked, get them off the cookie sheet with a metal spatula and put them on a serving plate or tray.

(These can be frozen before baking, according to David. Add a few minutes' baking time if you do.)

When everything is done, wash the dishes—a very important step.

Makes about 24 balls.

Note: Do not allow Little Brother, or anybody else, to attempt to juggle or play catch with the spinach balls. They don't hold up well under impact.

---

This appetizer-snack mix calls for Golden Yangles, the Girl Scouts' little cheese crackers. You could use other little cheese crackers, too, but why would you? You could also leave out the bacon, if you don't have any or you don't like it or you don't want to have your youngster fry it and maybe get spattered. It'll be fine either way.

**Snack Mix**

4 slices bacon
2 tablespoons butter or margarine
2 cups thin pretzel sticks (about ⅓ of a 9-ounce bag)
2½ cups Girl Scout Golden Yangles or other small cheese crackers

1 (3-ounce) can French-fried onion rings
About ¾ cup chopped walnuts or pecans (about 3 ounces)
1 teaspoon Worcestershire sauce

Preheat the oven to 325 degrees.
  Wash your hands.
  Fry the bacon until it is crisp. Put it on paper towels to drain. Pour off the bacon fat, but save about 2 tablespoons of it in the pan. Melt the 2 tablespoons of butter in the same pan. (If you're not using the bacon, melt 4 tablespoons of butter.)
  Break the pretzel sticks in half.
  In a big bowl, mix the pretzel sticks, cheese crackers, onion rings, chopped nuts and Worcestershire sauce. Pour the melted fat over and stir up with a spoon.
  Spread the mixture out on a cookie sheet and bake for 15 minutes, stirring it around now and then.
  Take the mixture out of the oven, let it cool and pour it into a bowl. Crumble the bacon and stir it in.
  Wash the dishes.
  Serves 10 to 12.

Now for a nice main dish. There's nothing particularly kidlike about this one, but it's awfully easy, and shaking chicken in potato chips is fun.

**Chicken in the Chips**

1¼ sticks (10 tablespoons) butter or margarine
About 4 or 5 ounces potato chips

3 tablespoons sesame seeds (optional)
1 cut-up broiler-fryer chicken

Preheat the oven to 350 degrees.
  Wash your hands.
  Melt the butter in a large frying pan. Let it cool briefly.
  Crush the potato chips to cornflake size while they are still in the bag. This is not only less messy than other methods, it's more fun. (Poke a small air-escape hole in the bag first; then it will be easy.) Pour the crushed chips into a big, clean grocery bag. Put the sesame seeds in the grocery bag, too.
  Turn a piece of chicken in the melted butter to coat it completely. Then drop it into the grocery bag of potato chips, close the top well and shake the chicken a few seconds. Put the chipped piece of chicken in a 9-by-13-inch baking pan. Repeat with the other pieces of chicken. Drizzle 2 to 3 tablespoons of any leftover butter over the chicken.
  If the chicken was quartered, instead of fully cut up, you probably didn't use up all the chips. You can sprinkle some of the leftover chips on the chicken, or discard them. (Don't eat them. Uncle Al knows best. Cooked chicken is great. Raw chicken is not, and stuff that's been kicking around with raw chicken is not good for you unless it gets cooked, too.)
  Wash your hands. And your face, for that matter.
  Put the pan of chicken in the oven and bake about 1 hour. Put the chicken on a serving plate.
  Wash the dishes.
  Serves 4.

Now a nice vegetable that's very little work but leads into the mysterious ways of the starch granule.

## Creamed Peas and Onions

1 (16-ounce) can tiny peas
1 (16-ounce) can or jar boiled whole
  small onions
1 tablespoon butter
1 tablespoon flour

2/3 cup milk
1/2 teaspoon salt
1/2 teaspoon garlic salt
Pepper

Wash your hands.
  Drain the peas and onions.
  Put the butter in a small saucepan and heat it over low-medium heat until it has melted. Stir in the flour, and keep stirring (use a wooden spoon because a metal spoon might get hot) while it cooks and maybe gets a little brown, for about a minute.
  Then add just a little bit of the milk and stir it in. Where did it go? Stir in some more milk. Isn't that amazing.?

Don't add too much milk at once, or you'll have to stir a lot longer before it works its way into the sauce.
  When all the milk is in, add the salt, garlic salt and a shake of pepper, then stir in the drained peas and onions. Heat, stirring once in a while, until the vegetables are heated through.
  Pour into a serving bowl.
  Wash the dishes.
  Serves 4 to 6.

Now for dessert. Ice-cream parfaits. This might be a little messy, but what the heck?
  The final assembly—which is most of the work—has to take place right before you serve them. If you make the parfaits ahead and keep them in the refrigerator, the ice cream melts; if you keep them in the freezer, the peaches freeze. But everybody can wait 5 minutes after dinner while you and Little Sibling assemble these goodies.

## Peach-Cookie Ice-Cream Parfaits

24 Girl Scout Thin Mint cookies
1 (16-ounce) can peach slices

1 1/2 quarts vanilla ice cream

Before dinner if you like (but it won't save much time) break up 12 of the cookies into small pieces (something like 6 or 8 pieces per cookie—not tiny crumbs). WASH YOUR HANDS FIRST!
  Drain the peach slices and put them in a bowl. Count them to see how many you have. Since this recipe makes 6 servings, divide that number by 6—that's how many peach slices you have for each parfait. It's probably between 3 and 4.
  When you're ready to assemble the parfaits, wash your hands again and divide the broken cookies into 3 equal piles.
  Divide the first pile equally into the

bottoms of 6 eight-ounce glasses (regular tall drinking glasses).
  Drop a scoop of ice cream into each. Top with a peach slice or two (about 1/3 of the peach supply).
  Sprinkle into each glass the pieces from the second cookie-piece pile. Top with another scoop of ice cream and another peach slice or two.
  Put in the last of the cookie pieces, the last of the peaches and one more scoop of ice cream, to fill each glass.
  Stick two mint cookies into the ice cream at angles to form a V.
  Serves 6.

The writer washed his hands before he set the table, too.

# Foods of the State Fair

There are some foods that are strongly associated with special occasions and are eaten at almost no other time: plum pudding at Christmas, for example; cranberry sauce at Thanksgiving; the traditional Tom and Jerry or champagne on New Year's Eve; the traditional aspirin, raw egg and Worcestershire sauce on New Year's Day; hot cross buns at Easter; stale egg-salad sandwiches for two weeks after Easter; and 24 hours of nothing at all on Yom Kippur.

Nothing stops you, of course, from eating cranberry sauce on the Fourth of July, or from hoisting a few Toms and Jerrys for Labor Day; it's just that almost nobody does it.

And there's no law against making a meal of a Pronto Pup, a pickle on a stick and bunch of tiny donuts when you're at home instead of at the state fair. But even if there were such a law, who would consider breaking it? The fair is *the* place to eat such stuff.

And anyway, how would you make all that stuff at home even if you wanted to?

You're in luck. Rising to just such pointless challenges is what makes me so peculiar.

In pursuit of this particular challenge, I visited the fair a few days ago and had a good time sampling some of the cuisine that you get almost nowhere else.

This means that I didn't get to eat the hot beef sandwich at the restaurant run by the Jehovah Lutheran Church of St. Paul, for example, or the pork tenderloin dinner served up by the Ramsey County Young Marines, although the food served in such places is very nice.

I concentrated instead on such stuff as fried cheese curds and mini-donuts. And I tried to capture, in my notes, some of the small things that would help you recreate the sense of the fair at home, as an accompaniment to the homemade versions of these fair foods. Here are some suggestions:

• Eat outside. If it's sunny, wear a hot raincoat. If it rains, eat outside anyway and don't wear a raincoat.

• Eat standing up. If you *must* sit down, get some neighbor's kids to stand and stare at you all through your meal. One of them can cry, if you like.

• Do not use plates, nor provide yourself with napkins or anything for cleanup other than waxed paper.

• Put small pebbles in your shoes and walk around the block before eating.

• Try to duplicate that elusive state fair atmosphere. Nothing can match the ultimate state fair taste sensation—a hot dog eaten at the concession stand just inside the swine barn—but you can get a little bit of Commonwealth Avenue in your own backyard if you're willing to work at it.

For example: A day in advance, empty a few cans of beer onto the ground where you'll be eating. At the same time, peel and slice several onions, and scatter them in sunny areas with bits of hot dog. If you must eat inside, pour smaller amounts of beer, onions and hot dog bits onto a kitchen counter or table.

(Now, let me save some of you the cost of a phone call or a stamp. I *like* the state fair. And a lot of what I like about it is that it *is* hot and greasy and redolent with the perfume of yesterday's Old Milwaukee.)

Back to duplicating the food. My fair-at-home meal consisted of imitation Pronto Pups, deep-fried cheese curds, mini-donuts, fried ice cream and a "health drink."

My first exercise was the ubiquitous Pronto Pup, also known at the fair as Poncho Pup, corn dog and hot dog on a stick.

If you don't know what this is, your stomach is probably in better shape than mine. It's a skewered hot dog, dipped in a batter containing cornmeal, and deep fried.

You can indeed make these guys at home, and very easily if you're willing to use a prepared mix.

Genuine Pronto Pup coating mix is sold in grocery stores, as is pointed out on a sign inside every Pronto Pup booth at the fair. (A sign outside every Pronto Pup booth at the fair defines this item as "A banquet on a stick," and much as I like Pronto Pups I think that gives new meaning to the word "banquet.")

You can also assemble a sort of Pronto Pup batter from scratch. The mix has the advantage of turning out to the proper consistency right off the bat, while the homemade batter must be tinkered with a bit.

And if you make your own you have to come up with the wooden skewers somewhere (the mix has a bunch thrown in). That's not as easy as it sounds. Despite their abundance at the fair, supporting not only hot dogs but pickles, pizza, steaks, pieces of cheese and slices of pineapple, I couldn't find them for sale at grocery stores. My best suggestion is to ask your butcher for some. This seems to work, but unless you're very friendly with your butcher I wouldn't rely on it if you plan to make enough corn dogs for your church picnic.

---

### Corn Dogs

**Oil for deep frying**
**1 cup flour**
**2/3 cup cornmeal**
**1 1/2 teaspoons baking powder**
**2 tablespoons sugar**
**1 teaspoon salt**

**2 tablespoons solid shortening**
**1 egg, beaten**
**3/4 cup to 1 cup milk**
**10 hot dogs**
**Mustard**

Heat the oil to 375 degrees.

Mix flour, cornmeal, baking powder, sugar and salt.

Cut in the shortening with a pastry blender or a couple of knives, until the lumps are the size of crumbs. Separately combine the beaten egg and 3/4 cup of the milk, add to the dry ingredients and mix well.

Add more of the milk if necessary to achieve the proper consistency. The batter should be mushy—not wet, but liquid enough to flow slightly (to coat the hot dogs more-or-less uniformly).

Unwrap the hot dogs, pat them dry, insert the skewers (you can do this after they're fried if you're using a mini-fryer and the skewers won't fit) and dip them into the batter one at a time, getting all sides well coated. Let each drip before inserting it slowly into the oil, and fry until golden brown, about a minute on a side. Drain and brush with mustard.

As with all deep-fried food, fry only a few at a time, and allow the oil to reheat to the proper temperature between batches if necessary.

Makes 10.

Special hint to fair-food lovers: If you don't want to strew the landscape with onion slices, you can achieve a bit of the same effect by frying the hot dogs, or other items, in oil that had been used previously to make onion rings.

Also, beer can be substituted for some of the milk in this batter (and for the water that's added to commercial Pronto Pup mix).

---

While we're on the subject of hot dogs at the fair, lovers of trivial details might be interested to note that the signs that advertise FOOT LONG HOT DOGS have a few words in smaller script above the word FOOT. If you read carefully, the signs really say *About a* FOOT LONG HOT DOGS. The result of some federal Truth in Hot Dog Act?

Apparently not. The signs that advertise MILE LONG HOT DOGS have not been amended.

Onward, to deep-fried cheese curds. I had to do these twice before I succeeded. With the first batter I tried, the result might be called cheese cruds—they came out soft and eggy, and the effect was like greasy French toast with cheese.

But batter No. 2 worked just fine.

---

## Deep-Fried Cheese Curds

Oil for deep frying
1 egg
1 cup milk
1 tablespoon oil
1 cup flour

1 teaspoon baking powder
¼ teaspoon salt
1 (9-ounce) package cheese curds, or
    bite-size chunks of cheddar cheese
Salt, if desired

Heat the oil to 390 degrees.

Beat together the egg, milk and the 1 tablespoon of oil. Add the flour, baking powder and salt and beat until well blended and smooth. Toss the cheese curds into the batter, separating them before they go in. (This works best with large pieces, so don't break up any big ones.) Let the cheese sit in the batter for a few minutes, and stir it around to make sure the pieces are all well coated.

Fry them rapidly, a few at a time, turning once, until they are light golden. These are a little tricky. First, because of the odd shapes of the curds, some of them tend to be what NASA used to call, in the days of ocean splash-downs,

"monostable." They will only float one way up. Tough. Just push them around in the oil as best you can and get them out of there.

The second tricky part: if they're in the oil too long, the cheese begins to boil inside and shoot out through the coating. If the surface of the oil begins to get covered by lacy gunk, that's what's happening. You have to cook them quicker, which means raising the temperature, or settle for less brown.

(Fish off the lacy gunk with a slotted spoon and try again.)

Cool a bit and salt if you like.

Makes lots.

---

If you have a mini-donut cutter, use it to make these mini-donuts—and tell me where you got it. The mini-donuts sold at the fair all get extruded out of machines, and I've never seen a cutter the right size to produce them.

If you don't have one, you can do what I did. Buy a small (5½- or 6-ounce) can of ready-to-drink fruit juice—not frozen concentrate, because those cans, while about the same size, are cardboard and won't hold up. Open the can, discard the top, drink the contents (you'll need your strength) and wash the can. This will serve as the cutter for the outside of the donut. To produce the hole in the donut, I used the cap from a bottle of reconstituted lemon juice. Any similar cap will do just fine.

(I'm using the spelling of "donut" that is favored at the fair. If you prefer "doughnut," you will find yourself offended by the "Tom Thumb Donuts," the "Tiny Tim Donuts," the "Tinkerbell Mini-Donuts," and the ones that everyone winds up asking for, "Those Little Donuts.")

Oil for deep frying
1 tablespoon butter
1 egg
1/2 cup sugar
2 cups flour

2 teaspoons baking powder
1/2 teaspoon salt
1/3 cup milk
1/2 teaspoon vanilla
Sugar for dipping

Heat the oil to 375 degrees. Melt the tablespoon of butter.

In a large bowl, beat the egg until it's lemon-colored. Gradually beat in the sugar, and continue beating until the batter is thick. Separately combine the flour, baking powder and salt. Add these dry ingredients to the egg mixture, alternating with the melted butter, the milk and the vanilla. Stir until fully blended.

This is a really tough, sticky dough, and it will make things a lot easier if you refrigerate it for an hour or so, if you have the time. Even if you do, flour your working surface rather well, turn the dough out onto it and flour the top of the dough, too. With floured hands, pat it out, flipping it often on the floured surface so that it doesn't stick. Finally roll it out with a lightly floured roller until it is between 1/8 inch and 1/4 inch thick.

Cut the donuts, punch out the center holes, and fry the donuts about 45 seconds on each side. Fry only 5 or 6 at a time to avoid cooling the oil excessively.

Drain and toss with sugar—put the sugar and the donuts into a paper bag and shake; it's a lot easier and neater than flipping them around in a dish of sugar.

You can fry the holes as a special homemade bonus (the donut machines at the fair don't produce holes).

As I was cutting donuts, I was reminded of a riddle my father once posed to me: A bum used to roll his own cigarettes out of butts that he found. It took 6 butts to make 1 cigarette. One day he had particularly good luck and found 36 butts. How many cigarettes did he get?

Seven, because he got 6 cigarettes out of the 36 butts, and when he smoked them he had 6 butts—enough to make another cigarette.

Anyway, I was able to make 22 donuts out of the dough as first rolled out, 9 from the scraps, 5 from those scraps and 2 from those scraps, for a total of 38 donuts, 38 holes, and some scraps that I finally threw out but that probably would have yielded a few more holes.

---

This recipe for fried ice cream is only my guess, but it turns out to taste virtually identical to what is served at the fair.

Besides, under the chocolate, whipped cream and cherry, it's darned hard to tell what you're eating.

## Fried Ice Cream

1 quart ice cream
1 egg
About 1 cup dry bread crumbs
Oil for deep frying

Canned chocolate sauce
Aerosol can of whipped cream
Maraschino cherries

Shape the ice cream (your choice of flavor) into 8 to 10 balls. Return them to the freezer for a few minutes, while you beat the egg and put the bread crumbs in a separate small bowl.

Place a cookie sheet covered with waxed paper in the freezer. Roll each ice-cream ball first in the beaten egg, then in the crumbs. Return to the cookie sheet in the freezer. Freeze again for an hour or more, to firm up the coating.

Heat the oil to 350 degrees. "Fry" the ice cream balls, one at a time, for about 3 seconds, turning rapidly in the oil to crisp all the sides. If you fry them much longer, the ice cream starts to melt and the whole thing falls apart. Remove the ice cream from the oil with a slotted spoon, rapidly drain the oil off the spoon and turn the ice cream into a bowl. Cover with chocolate sauce and whipped cream, and top with a cherry.

Special warning to fair-food lovers: After a night of eating food like this, you wake up very oily in the morning.

While I pondered, weak and weary, what were styled as "Exerps from the Poem 'Why,' by Evel Knievel," painted near the entrance of "The Incredible Show" on the Midway, I realized that I was in need of something not fried.

The fried zucchini (or zuchinni, depending on which sign you read) no longer tempted me, as it had earlier in the day. Nor did "Ice Cream on a Stick," which in my dazed condition I did not realize was simply an ice cream bar.

What I needed, I concluded, was to sit down under the grandstand and watch a health drink being made in the Vita-Mix 3600.

This kind of activity has been an essential part of fairgoing for me since I was a kid and my father wanted to watch all the cabbage-slicer salesmen while I wanted to go on the rides. We watched a lot of cabbage-slicer salesmen.

At the end of the Vita-Mix 3600 demonstration, everybody gets to try a little of the drink. I've never been convinced that the drinks made for these demonstrations are all that healthful, but at least they're not fried. And they're free.

If there is one aroma that, along with the beer, onions and hot dogs, would complete your backyard simulation of the fair, it is this drink. You never get enough of it in those little paper nut cups to really pin the flavor down, but it seems to combine all the lingering essences of the juice stands that line the fair's sidewalks. (If you don't want to drink it, just slop some of it on the ground.)

I wasn't too sure that I could duplicate the drink with the blender I bought at a garage sale, because the Vita-Mix 3600 is a very powerful machine. Its blades reverse instantly and seem to reduce the ice cubes to slush in nothing flat. But I was willing to take a lot longer to get results than the Vita-Mix man was, and to cut into small pieces the fruits that he threw in more or less whole.

By the end, my blender motor smelled like an electrical fire, but I succeeded.

1 orange
½ apple
1 ½-inch-thick slice of lemon
1 wedge of melon (Persian or
cantaloupe), with seeds
2 cups ice cubes or 1 cup cold water
⅓ of a banana
2 tablespoons honey

Remove only the zest (the bright orange portion of the skin) from the orange, leaving the thicker white portion. Cut the orange into quarters, holding it over the blender container to catch any juice. Squeeze the quarters into the container, then toss in one of the squeezed quarters. Blend at high speed until it is fully liquefied, then add the other 3 quarters, one at a time, liquefying each before adding the next.

Cut the half of an apple into chunks, without removing the peel or the seeds. (That's essentially what the Vita-Mix salesman did. I pitched the stem—I thought that was *too* much, even for a health drink). Add the chunks, one at a time, waiting for each to liquefy before adding the next.

Throughout this process, stop the machine occasionally and probe around with a spatula to make sure there are no hidden chunks. (The drink gets very opaque.)

As you did for the orange, remove only the bright yellow portion of the peel from the thick slice of lemon. Squeeze in the juice, then cut the remaining mess in half and add the pieces one at a time.

Remove the rind from the wedge of melon. Add the seeds to the blender, then throw in pieces of the melon, one at a time.

Now add the ice cubes. The following procedure worked in my blender, but check the instructions for yours to see if it will handle ice cubes. If you value yours a lot and you can't find the instructions (did you look under the sink?), maybe you should just add 1 cup of water and skip the ice cubes. If you're game: Get the blender going at its highest speed and drop the ice cubes into the vortex one at a time, waiting for the awful noises to subside before you go on to the next one. (The Vita-Mix 3600 took all 2 cups of ice cubes at once with equanimity, and it gave the impression of being up to eating a case of 10-penny nails if anybody wanted to add them.)

Let the blender run for a minute or two after the last ice cube is added, then toss the banana, in chunks, into the vortex. Finally add the honey.

For authenticity, serve in paper nut cups.

Makes 1 quart, enough for 64 itty-bitty servings.

As a result of this experience, the writer has thought about spending a few days in a degreasing tank at a Standard Oil station, and he is planning to have his kitchen hosed down with live steam.

# The Checkerboard Meal

I don't know why I'm on so many mailing lists; I don't buy very much by mail.

I have succumbed occasionally to the blandishments of the New Process Company, of Warren, Pennsylvania, (the outfit that sends you five pounds of little pieces of paper every month, each picturing some item of apparel and often accompanied by tiny swatches of crinkle-cut material), and I occasionally buy something from J. C. Whitney in the forlorn hope of sustaining the flickering flame that is my seventeen-year-old car, but that's really about it.

Still, almost every time I bring in the mail, expecting maybe a form letter from my congressman, an NSP bill or something equally cheering, I get at least one attempt to sell me something.

Some of that stuff is fun—I got one a while back that tried to interest me in furniture designed for "the new way of sitting." Others are merely insistent.

"Frankly, I'm puzzled. You have everything to gain and nothing to lose in taking our no-obligation offer [for pantyhose]."

Mostly what I get is catalogs. And that's a real problem for me, because I'm afraid to throw them out. I guess I figure I'll need to look in one for something someday, so I stack them up for a year or so until I can't stand it any more.

Then I throw them out, shortly before I really do need one of them. (I'm not quite to the throwing-out stage yet this year, so if you suddenly find that you need to order ugly salt-and-pepper shakers, publishers' overstock books or a reflecting telescope, I can probably help you out.)

One kind of mailing that is particularly compelling but particularly awful is the fancy-kitchen-accessory catalog. I find it depressing to page through endless arrays of very pretty but outrageously priced cookware and gadgets that might be used once every five years.

How many people in this economy are up to $120 stainless-steel fish poachers or $65 black-aluminum teapots?

One item that is showing up in lots of those catalogs these days is a pan for making checkerboard cake. Checkerboard cake is a two- or-three-layer cake, each layer of which contains two or three concentric rings of different-color batter.

You alternate the colored batters when you make the different layers, and the effect, when you assemble the cake and slice it, is a checkerboard pattern.

This is not a new idea. In fact, it's old as the hills.

And when your mother or grandmother made it, she didn't buy any special pan for it, either.

I don't bear any malice toward the kitchen-equipment-catalog folks, but I thought I'd save you the $13 to $20 they're getting for a checkerboard-cake pan by telling you how to make the cake without it.

While we're at it, let's take the theme to our usual ridiculous extreme by making some other checkerboard items.

Check?

Check.

Here's what I made:

*Checkerboard sandwiches*
*Checkerboard pizza*
*Checkerboard cake*
*Checkerboard ice cream*

I was tempted to take the checkerboard theme past the food itself and into decorations, but I kind of forgot about that until it was too late. All I did was alternate two colors of napkins around the table. A checkerboard tablecloth would have been nice. You could alternate the good dining-room chairs with the plastic ones that are usually on the back porch or in the basement. You could force alternate guests to drink different colors of wine or pop, you could wear a lumber-jack shirt with a checkered suit, and you might even prop bags of Purina Puppy

Chow, Cat Chow and Camel Chow in the corners of the room.

On second thought, though, all of that geometricity might overshadow the food, and, in these pages anyway, we try to avoid doing that.

Checkerboard sandwiches are sandwiches made on checkerboard bread. Checkerboard bread consists of two loaves of bread—one white, one rye—cut apart, reassembled checkerboard fashion (held together with cheese-butter) and refrigerated until it sets. If the entire idea strikes you as ludicrous, stop reading now because this article gets a whole lot worse.

Obviously you can put anything you want between two pieces of checkerboard bread. Since the opportunity seldom exists to have a sandwich on both white bread *and* rye, you ought to take advantage of it by having something nice. How about ham and cheese? Mustard goes with rye bread and mayonnaise goes with white, so mustardy mayonnaise seemed like a good idea for checkerboard sandwiches. It was.

---

## *Checkerboard Sandwiches*

**CHECKERBOARD BREAD (enough for 10 to 14 sandwiches):**

**3 sticks butter or margarine**
**6 ounces American cheese**
**1 (1-pound) loaf white bread, unsliced**
**1 (1-pound) loaf rye bread, unsliced**

**DRESSING:**

**½ cup mayonnaise**
**1½ tablespoons Dijon mustard**

**FILLING, PER SANDWICH:**

**1 large slice cooked ham**
**1 large slice Cheddar cheese**

At least 6 hours (or a whole day) before serving time, begin preparing the checkerboard bread:

Cream the butter and beat in crumbled American cheese. Beat until the mixture is quite soft.

Trim the top, bottom, side and end crusts from both loaves of bread. Cut each loaf into 6 lengthwise horizontal slices (about ¾ inch thick each).

Spread the cheese-butter fairly thickly on one horizontal slice of rye bread. Don't skip any areas, and go all the way to the edges. Top with a horizontal slice of white bread, butter it carefully, and continue alternating until you have a 6-slice alternating loaf, starting with rye and finishing with white.

Repeat, in the same pattern, to make a second loaf. You should have half the cheese-butter left.

Put both loaves back in their plastic bags, press down to help seal the layers together, and chill them at least 2 hours in the refrigerator.

When the ribbon loaves are quite firm, remove one from the refrigerator and slice it into six lengthwise *vertical* slices—each slice running the length of the loaf and containing 6 ribbons of alternating colors of bread.

Spread cheese-butter carefully on one slice. Turn the next slice end over end so that, if the first slice starts with a ribbon of rye and ends with white, the second starts with a ribbon of white and ends with rye. Butter that slice and put it next to the first one. Continue buttering and flipping until the bread is reassembled with half the slices inverted.

Repeat with the other loaf; bag, press firmly and chill again.

Prepare the dressing by combining the mayonnaise and mustard.

The cold bread does hold together fairly well when sliced (although the corner pieces have a tendency to loosen), but it begins to drift a bit when warm. Don't, however, slice the bread thin, or small defects in the adhesion of checkerboard pieces will cause the slices to fall apart.

You have a choice about how to proceed.

You can cut the bread, assemble the sandwiches and refrigerate them until serving time. But the chill diminishes the rather pleasant flavor.

Or you can cut the bread and assemble the sandwiches 15 minutes or so before serving and allow them to rest that length of time at room temperature (taking a very small risk that you've increased their propensity to explode on impact).

In either case, when you're ready, coat one slice of the bread generously with mayonnaise-mustard dressing, then layer in 2 half-slices each of cheese and ham (alternating cheese and ham, of course), and top with another slice of bread also well-coated with mayonnaise-mustard dressing. (The dressing helps hold the whole thing together as a sandwich, so don't eliminate it.)

Serve to a crowd of folks, who will probably say something like, "What in the world are *those?*"

---

In the planning stages, I thought of this next item, checkerboard pizza, as really looking like a checkerboard: red squares of tomato sauce, yellow squares of cheese—surely easy enough to pull off by "masking" parts of the pizza when cheese is sprinkled on.

I decided to make a rectangular pizza rather than a round one, to heighten the effect (a square one would have been even better but I didn't have a wide-enough pan to make a decent-size square), and to complete the image I got slices of pepperoni for the squares at one end and Italian sausage for the squares at the other end.

When the idea was actually executed, it suffered somewhat from the flowing characteristics of the mozzarella cheese, which tended to make the edges of the squares highly indistinct, but the effect was sort of there. Aesthetics aside, the pizza was quite good, and you can skip the checkerboard business if you like. Even the red squares tasted fine, because I blended the Parmesan cheese in with the tomato sauce before I spread it. The thin crust was nice and crisp.

For my taste, there should have been more sauce; others at the table disagreed.

I'll leave it up to you. If you like your pizza reasonably wet, I'd make half again the amount of sauce.

## *Checkerboard Pizza*

(Makes two 15-by-10-inch rectangular, 14-inch round or 12½-inch square pizzas)

**DOUGH:**

1 (¼-ounce) envelope active dry yeast
1 cup warm water
½ teaspoon sugar
3¼ cups flour
1 teaspoon salt

**SAUCE:**

2 (8-ounce) cans tomato sauce
1 tablespoon olive oil
2 tablespoons water
2 cloves garlic, put through a garlic
  press
1 teaspoon oregano

¼ teaspoon basil
¼ teaspoon crushed fennel seeds
  (optional but nice)
½ teaspoon salt
½ teaspoon sugar
Dash cayenne pepper
1 pound Italian sausage in bulk
3 ounces (½ cup) grated Parmesan
  cheese
2 (4-ounce) cans mushroom stems and
  pieces, drained (optional)
12 ounces (3 cups) shredded
  mozzarella cheese
1 (3½-ounce) package sliced
  pepperoni

Prepare the dough: Stir the yeast into the warm water; stir in the sugar and let stand 10 minutes.

Sift the flour and salt into a bowl, add the yeast mixture and stir with a heavy spoon, gathering in all the flour, until a stiff dough is formed (if the dough is wet, add up to ¼ cup more flour).

Knead the dough on a lightly floured countertop for about 5 minutes, folding, yanking, mauling and pummeling it as necessary to work out your hostilities and to make it smooth and elastic. Add flour only if you must.

Wash and grease the bowl and turn the ball of dough in it to coat it completely. Cover the bowl with a towel and let the dough rise in a warm place about 45 minutes, or until it has doubled in bulk.

After the dough has risen for 10 or 15 minutes, prepare the sauce: Combine tomato sauce, olive oil, water, garlic, oregano, basil, fennel, salt, sugar and cayenne in a saucepan. Cover and cook over very low heat for 20 minutes, stirring occasionally.

Break the Italian sausage into ½-inch-or-so chunks. (You may not find the sausage in bulk; if not, squeeze it out of the casings before breaking it up.) Fry

until color is gone from the meat; drain and set aside.

When the dough has risen, punch it down and divide it in half. (If you don't want to make both pizzas at once, you can refrigerate half the dough, wrapped, for a day or two.) Grease 2 pans of the shape you have selected, put the dough in them and stretch it out to fit. You can begin by rolling it with a rolling pin, but in the end you'll probably need your hands. Cut the edge even and fold up a small lip. The dough is very forgiving, so fill any rips or uneven edges with cut-away bits.

Stir the Parmesan cheese into the sauce and cover the dough evenly with the mixture. Sprinkle the mushrooms around.

Preheat the oven to 425 degrees.

If you don't really care about making the pizza look like a checkerboard, you're almost done. Just scatter the pieces of Italian sausage, strew with mozzarella cheese and toss on the slices of pepperoni. Or use whatever other pizza toppings you like.

But if you're going for the checkered flag, this is the tricky (or stupid) part:

Fold or cut 10 or 12 strips of waxed paper about 2 inches wide. Arrange pieces of Italian sausage in the centers of imaginary 2-inch squares at one end of each pizza. Lay strips of waxed paper lengthwise and others crosswise on the pizza, leaving equal-size empty spaces between them. Scatter about a third of the mozzarella cheese on each pizza, leaving a third of the cheese to take care of something peculiar:

You may have thought that this lattice of waxed-paper strips would create a checkerboard pattern, but if you think a little harder you'll realize that it doesn't quite. I didn't figure this out until I got to this point and really looked at what I had. Half the rows are checkered, O.K., where the waxed-paper strips cross them, but the rows in between those are completely covered with a strip of waxed paper.

To make it a checkerboard (and to get a decent amount of cheese onto it), the pizza should have cheese not only on the squares that have *no* waxed paper over them, it should also have cheese on the squares that are covered by *two intersecting* strips of waxed paper.
If you have a pizza in front of you, are inclined to doodle or are into Boolean algebra, you will probably see what

I mean. If not, take my word for it.

Tip the waxed-paper strips, so that the cheese on them falls onto the already-cheesed squares, and remove the strips. Now you can certainly see the areas of missing cheese. Don't bother repositioning the strips. Just drizzle the remaining cheese into those missing squares. If you're really into this, reposition the few shreds of cheese that have wandered where no cheese belongs and neaten up the edges of the squares. It won't avail you much once the cheese start to melt, but some people need to have things just so.

Deal the pepperoni slices onto squares at the opposite end of the pizza from the end with the pieces of sausage. (If the guests don't like the pizza they can play checkers with the pepperoni and sausage.)

Slip the pizzas into the oven and bake 20 to 25 minutes, until the cheese is bubbling and the edges are browned. Cut the pizza into squares and serve to a crowd of folks, who will probably say something like, "What in the world is *that?*"

---

Because this was supposed to be a piece about checkerboard cake, we'd better make one. It's not hard, and you really could use about any white or yellow cake batter you want, but I have provided here a very stiff pound-cake-like batter that worked quite nicely.

# Checkerboard Cake

### CAKE:

¾ cup (1½ sticks) butter
2 cups sugar
4 eggs
3 cups cake flour
4 teaspoons baking powder
1 cup milk

### FLAVORING FOR HALF OF CAKE BATTER (OR USE RED FOOD COLORING):

6 (1-ounce) squares unsweetened
   chocolate, melted
1½ teaspoons cinnamon
½ teaspoon ground cloves
1 teaspoon vanilla

### DARK FROSTING:

6 ounces cream cheese
4 (1-ounce) squares unsweetened
   chocolate, melted (or a few drops of
   red food coloring)
Dash of salt
5 cups confectioners' sugar, sifted
2 teaspoons vanilla
3 to 4 tablespoons milk

### CONTRASTING FROSTING (OPTIONAL, BUT WHAT THE HECK):

2 ounces cream cheese
1⅔ cups confectioners' sugar, sifted
1 teaspoon vanilla
2 teaspoons milk

Prepare the cake batter: Cream the butter, beat in the sugar and add the eggs one at a time, beating well after each.

Combine the flour and baking powder. Add that mixture to the batter in thirds, alternating with thirds of the milk and beating constantly.

Put half of the batter in another bowl and add the melted chocolate, cinnamon, cloves and vanilla and mix well. (The spices in addition to the chocolate add what I found to be a welcome sense of strangeness to the dark portions of the cake.)

Note: If you're using some other cake batter, prepare 1½ recipes of it. Divide it in not-quite-even halves—one half a little bigger than the other—and add red food coloring to one half. You might be able, instead, to add the chocolate flavoring above to your recipe, but there's no way I can say for sure. The red food coloring is a tasteless but sure-fire alternative. It's up to you.

Grease 3 eight- or nine-inch cake pans. The idea, in case you've forgotten, is to produce layers of cake, each of which consists of three rings of alternating colors.

The batter I used is so stiff that you might be able to get away without any dividers at all between the rings, but unless you've made this kind of thing before and are not likely to panic as you see batter oozing away from where it belongs, I wouldn't recommend that.

Instead, cut and fold a piece of foil into a strip about 2 inches high and about 20 inches long. Overlap the ends about 2 inches. Paper-clip them together and shape the strip into a rough circle a little less than 6 inches across. Take care that when the ring you've formed sits on a flat surface there are no large gaps underneath it. This is the ring that separates the outer circle of cake batter from the middle one.

Repeat with a strip about 12 inches long, overlapping the ends 2 inches and forming a ring a little more than 3 inches across. This is the ring that separates the middle circle of cake batter from the inner one. (For this ring you can substitute a very-well-washed tuna can or cat-food can with top and bottom removed.)

Preheat the oven to 350 degrees, or whatever is called for by your recipe.

Position the rings in the first pan.

*(Continued)*

When I made this cake, the batter measured 5¼ cups, and I divided it out for you so that you'd be able to add the batter to the rings with some confidence that you wouldn't come out wrong at the end. This is fairly unusual cake batter, though—there's not much of it and it rises quite a bit—so if you're using a different batter you'll probably have more than 5¼ cups of it. If you're handy with a pencil or a calculator you can figure out proportions similar to mine. If not, guesswork will probably turn out just fine.

Into the inner ring put ¼ cup of the chocolate batter (or, if you're using a different recipe, a proportionate amount of the larger "half" of your batter). Put ½ cup of yellow batter (or proportionate amount of the other batter you've prepared with your own recipe) into the middle ring and 1 cup (or proportionate amount) of the chocolate batter into the outer ring. Lift out the separators, rinse them off and dry them.

Note: This batter, as mentioned, has very little volume until it bakes, so it looks like there won't possibly be enough. There will; just spread it around each ring with a knife or narrow spatula so it's reasonably even and there aren't any gaps.

Put the separators into the next pan, but add batter in reverse order (vanilla, chocolate, vanilla). Repeat with the third pan, using the same order you used in the first pan. Put the pans into the preheated oven. This batter rises—and dries—quickly. Start checking in 15 minutes. (Or bake your recipe as long as it specifies.)

Prepare frosting:

Cream the cream cheese in the large bowl of an electric mixer.

Beat in the chocolate (or a few drops of red food coloring, if you prefer) and the salt, and add the confectioners' sugar, alternating with the vanilla and small amounts of milk, as needed.

Assemble (with lots of frosting between the layers and top and sides, of course) so that the two identical layers are top and bottom and the other one is between them. When you cut a slice of it, there you are. Checkerboard.

Let's checkerboard the frosting, too, as long as we're at it (although you certainly can skip this if you want to). Let the chocolate (or pink) frosting set on the cake for half an hour or so. Then prepare the small amount of contrasting white frosting by creaming the cream cheese and beating in the confectioners' sugar, vanilla and milk.

Cut a 2-inch-square piece out of a brown paper bag and cut a 1-inch-square hole out of the middle of it. When the main frosting is set, put 1-inch squares of white frosting on it with a spatula and the piece of brown paper as a kind of stencil. If you have enough frosting left, you can pipe a ring of it around the edge of the top.

When you set *this* in front of folks, they'll probably say something like "Enough is enough, already!"

---

What, dear friends, is checkerboard cake without checkerboard ice cream? I vaguely recall occasionally seeing some ready-made. If you can find that, you're home free. If not, this is the simplest of the bunch of recipes to put together.

---

**2 rectangular (not cylindrical) cartons ice cream (pints, quarts or half-gallons, as needed) in contrasting colors and flavors. (Vanilla and chocolate seem like** **reasonable choices, but you could certainly choose cantaloupe and blackberry or whatever else your heart desires.)**

*Checkerboard Ice Cream*

Turn your freezer up. That is, turn your freezer temperature down. That is, make it extra-cold in your freezer.

Let the ice cream rest in your cold freezer for at least 2 hours. Put a couple of wide spatulas where they'll be handy to grab and, if you have them, put on a pair of dishwashing gloves (they insulate the ice cream from your hot little hands).

Working rapidly, open the packages fully and, using a sharp knife, cut each brick into 4 lengthwise vertical slices. Separate the slices slightly, and rapidly transfer 2 slices from one brick into alternate spaces in the other one and vice versa. You now have 2 bricks, each of which has vertical stripes of alternating colors. Quickly repack and close the packages, then firm them in the freezer for another 2 hours.

Unwrap one brick and again cut into 4 lengthwise slices, only turn the brick onto its side before you cut the slices, so that each slice is four layers of alternating-color ice cream. Turn alternating slices end-over-end, and repackage and return to the freezer. Repeat with the other brick. Let freeze 2 hours before serving. When you serve checkerboard ice cream with checkerboard cake, your guests will king you.

This has not been the high point in the writer's checkered career.

# A Back-to-School Dinner

Am I preoccupied with the passage of time, or what?

Everything I touch lately seems to say something about the days flying by. And here, almost before I knew it, it's back-to-school time again.

I wasn't completely surprised, of course. There have been back-to-school advertisements since late June. On the other hand, those ads were from the same crowd who push Christmas merchandise before Halloween, and sensible people have learned long ago to ignore them.

Well, be that as it may, ready or not, it's another of those times of year that adults (some adults, anyway) envy kids. Groan and moan as kids might about it, a new school year is a whole new experience, quite unlike what an adult faces when he returns to work—from a much shorter vacation—to find his desk covered with half-done stuff.

One of my favorite parts of high school—and of college, even more—was going back in the fall. It was even better in college because, at least for those who lived away from home, there was a period between registration and the beginning of classes when all of the burdens of the world and Life were suspended. My old friends were back, too, full of tales of summer glory, and the only thing we had to do for three or four days was unpack stuff and buy books. For a few warm, shining days there were no responsibilities—and there was money from summer jobs. (We knew it had to last through June, but the bulk of it was there and a little splurge would hardly hurt it.)

The splurge seldom turned out to be anything more uninhibited than going to a couple of movies, but in that brief window of total freedom almost anything we did was really fun.

I never went to camp, but I bet it was kind of like that.

The other back-to-school memory I treasure is the first day of classes, filing into rooms that were steaming despite the open windows, seeing who else was there that I hadn't already seen, and hoping against hope to get the really good instructors—or at least not to get the really awful ones.

179

Those were the last few moments of such delight. I went to an engineering school, and once classes started, that was the end of carefree. Other people who went to other kinds of schools may have other recollections. A friend who is reading this over my shoulder says she always remembers kicking through leaves on the mall at the University of Minnesota and going to football games wearing mums—and then realizes that the mum part never happened to her. It happened to her mother, who went to school in California, but her mother's description was so vivid that my friend always pictures it for a while before she remembers that it's not her own recollection.

Surprisingly enough, there is a recurring dream shared by lots and lots of people, independent of what they recall about going to school. It concerns final exams.

One day at lunch several years ago a bunch of us were talking about dreams, and I mentioned that I have this one once in a while. So, it turned out, did everyone else at the table, including a colleague who had been out of college thirty-five years at the time!

Details of the dream vary, of course, but this is the general picture. It is the night before or the very morning of the last day of final exams, and looking through some list you suddenly realize that there is a course that you registered for months ago but never, *ever* attended. You don't even have the book, and now you have to take the final.

I don't know what it means that years later people are plagued by this dream of having once been irresponsible. But I suspect it indicates that doctors who do ulcer surgery don't have to worry about where their next bland meal is coming from.

On that note, let us try to remember that very little in life is worth more than a passing grump, and let us then have a back-to-school dinner—in which each course is based on a course, of course.

For an appetizer, I was propelled into a very special choice by a gift from one of my guests—a small tin of very nice caviar.

Well, you don't just shovel caviar into your face with a spoon; you make it last by making a production of it.

Russians eat it with sour cream, melted butter, chopped onions and blini, which are very much like thin buckwheat pancakes except that there's yeast and rising involved. I made blini once, and I made buckwheat pancakes the other day from a box of Aunt Jemima Buckwheat Pancake Mix, and unless you're a Russian— and maybe even then—I'm pretty sure you'll find the mix perfectly satisfactory and a lot less trouble.

So what course is involved with caviar? Contemporary Music Appreciation. (Like, what fish produces arguably the best caviar?)

---

*Like, a Sturgeon*

Buckwheat pancakes, prepared from 1
   package buckwheat pancake mix
1 medium onion
½ cup butter

1 cup dairy sour cream
1 (2- to 4-ounce) jar caviar, whatever
   sort you feel reasonably sinful
   buying

Prepare the batter for 12 to 14 pancakes according to package directions. But fry them up thin, as you would crêpes. Have you forgotten how? Like this. (Sigh.)

Heat a small skillet over low-medium heat and butter it lightly. Add about 2 tablespoons of the batter, tilting the pan rapidly to cover it with the batter. Cook each pancake about 1 minute, until the bottom is lightly browned. (Adjust the heat to make this take about a minute.) Cook the other side of the pancake briefly, and cool the pancakes on a sheet of waxed paper, overlapping them slightly. You'll get about 15 pancakes. Arrange them on a serving platter, overlapped, and keep them warm or reheat them in the oven just before serving.

Meanwhile, chop the onion and put it in a small dish. Melt the butter and decant it slowly into a small dish, leaving behind the milky solids. Put the sour cream in a small dish and the caviar in a small dish.

Provide spoons, knives and small plates or napkins. Then let guests go to it, spreading sour cream, caviar, onions and butter on the pancakes, rolling them up and downing them. Serves 4 to 6 folks, depending on their caviar hunger.

Those who are so inclined might like to provide small glasses and ice-cold vodka. This may either increase or decrease caviar consumption.

---

Plenty of folks, fully aware that caviar is expensive and much sought-after by the people who seek after that kind of thing, nonetheless wouldn't take caviar if you gave it to them. Even if you gave it to them with a nickel on the side. So if you plan to serve caviar for Music Appreciation, maybe you ought to take care of Math at the same time by serving something *everybody* likes—chips and dip (the Lowest Common Denominator).

Now that we have divided the class according to class, it's time to get back together for some nice cool soup. If it isn't warm enough today to make cool soup appealing, surely it will be some other day.

This is a version—a particularly tasty one, I think—of what many of you know as gazpacho. Others of you know it as Spanish soup (and still others have never heard of it, but they don't count right now), so we'll use it to introduce our course in Spanish.

¿Como está Usted? Una piña colada, por favor. Sessue Hayakawa habla mejor Español que Usted.

---

### Spanish Soup

2 tomatoes
1 green pepper
1 onion
1 cucumber
1/4 cup red wine vinegar
1/4 cup olive oil
1 3/4 cups tomato juice
1 clove garlic
1/4 cup chopped fresh basil (or, not as good, 1 1/2 tablespoons dried)
1 tablespoon lime juice
1 tablespoon lemon juice
2 (10 3/4-ounce) cans chicken broth
1 teaspoon Worcestershire sauce
Salt and pepper
Dash cayenne pepper

Core and finely chop the tomatoes and the pepper. Peel and finely chop the onion. Peel the cucumber; cut it in half along its length, scoop out and discard the seeds from each half and chop the cucumber.

*(Continued)*

Put tomatoes, pepper, onion and cucumber in a pan or bowl and stir to mix. Put just half the mixture in a blender (in more than one batch, if necessary) with all of the vinegar, oil and tomato juice. Peel the garlic, put it through a garlic press and add the pressed garlic to the mixture in the blender. Add the basil.

Purée the mixture.

Add the puréed mixture to the chopped vegetables remaining in the pan. Stir in the lime juice, lemon juice, chicken broth (first skim off any fat from the broth), Worcestershire sauce, salt, pepper and cayenne. Mix well and chill. Serves 8.

---

Let us now move along to a discipline in the human sciences, Anthropology, and attempt to discover the meaning of a collection of flint arrowheads found in the vicinity of some poultry bones.

Perhaps the students who took the last class could help us out, as this combination occurs often in the Southwestern United States and down into Mexico and Central and South America.

---

## Arroz con Pollo
(Rice with chicken)

3 strips bacon
2 tablespoons olive oil
1 cut-up 4-pound fryer
Salt
Pepper
1 onion
1 clove garlic
1 (28-ounce) can tomatoes
1 teaspoon dried rosemary
1/2 teaspoon dried oregano

1 (2 1/4-ounce) can sliced black olives
1 bay leaf
1 tablespoon chili powder
2 cups water
1 cup uncooked rice
1 (10-ounce) package frozen peas, thawed
1 (3 1/2- or 4-ounce) jar sliced pimiento

Dice the bacon and fry it in a Dutch oven. Remove the cooked bacon and set aside to drain on paper towels.

Add the olive oil to the bacon fat in the pan and heat. Meanwhile, season the cut-up chicken with salt and pepper. Brown the chicken on all sides over medium heat. Remove the chicken and set aside.

Chop the onion, put the garlic through a garlic press and sauté in the same fat until the onions are translucent. Coarsely chop the canned tomatoes and add them

and their liquid, along with some more salt, and the rosemary, oregano, olives and their liquid, bay leaf, chili powder and water. Bring to the boil.

Add the chicken, rice and bacon, reduce heat, cover and simmer for 25 minutes.

When the chicken is cooked, stir through. Add the peas and pimientos. Cover and cook another few minutes to heat through. Stir and serve.

Serves 6.

---

For a vegetable, we need some Literature! Not *Warren Peas,* though; we need to eat *this* week.

How about a dish based on a historical novel by somebody born in Hungary? Makes me hungary just thinking about it.

To catch the full literary significance of this dish, one must imagine being asked

what it is by the girlfriend of Dudley Do-Right of the Mounties.
"What is that interesting-looking red vegetable dish, Dudley?"

---

### Scarlet Pepper, Nell
(With cheese sauce)

2 red bell peppers (or green, but then it would be Verdant Pepper, Nell)
2 tablespoons butter
2 tablespoons flour
1½ cups milk
1 cup shredded sharp Cheddar cheese
½ teaspoon salt
Pepper
½ to 1 teaspoon dry mustard (to taste)
¼ to ½ teaspoon curry powder (to taste)

Core the peppers and cut them into strips about ⅛ inch wide and 2 inches long.

Bring 2 cups of water to the boil in a saucepan. Add the pepper strips and cook about 10 minutes. Drain.

Meanwhile, in a saucepan, melt the butter, stir in the flour and cook 1 minute, stirring. Slowly add the milk, cooking and stirring all the while. When the sauce is thick and smooth, reduce the heat and stir in the cheese, salt, pepper, mustard and curry powder.

Combine with the pepper strips, stir over heat briefly to heat through, and serve. Serves 4 to 6.

---

For dessert, as usual, there were many possible choices. I thought briefly about Ice Cream Social Studies, but I decided, as I usually do when it comes to dessert, to forgo making the best pun in favor of making the best food. So, for a course in English, we'll have English Trifle. And to make it better *(much* better), it will be *Chocolate* English Trifle, with raspberries here and there. (The raspberries are a nod to those troublemakers who always sat at the back of the room and made rude noises, while all of us sensitive types participated in word-by-word dissection and desiccation of poetry, an exercise led by a teacher who pronounced "poem" as "pwem." Never mind.)

I used pudding mix and cake mix and the result was tremendous. So good, according to one way of looking at things, that there's no need to improve it by using homemade pudding and cake. Or, looked at another way, this was so good using quickie ingredients that it would have to be stupendous with better ingredients.

Two different schools of thought. I will leave this problem to you for homework.

---

### Chocolate English Trifle

1 layer of chocolate cake (made from ½ of a full recipe or ½ of a standard cake mix or 1 small mix—or some leftover chocolate cake, if such a thing is possible)
Pudding made from 2 (3½-ounce) packages chocolate pudding mix (not instant; there's a limit)
About 4 ounces slivered almonds, divided
¼ cup seedless raspberry jam
¾ cup black raspberry liqueur
2 cups heavy cream
1 cup fresh raspberries or 1 (10-ounce) package frozen raspberries, thawed and drained

Prepare the cake. Bake, cool and remove from pan.

Meanwhile, prepare the pudding according to package directions and allow it to cool. Set a sheet of waxed paper on the surface to prevent a thickened layer from forming.

(You didn't forget to buy the eggs, oil and milk that making the cake mix and the pudding mix would require, did you? You know, I considered putting those in the ingredients list, but then I figured that if I spell everything out for you, you'll never make it in the real world. Ponder that as you go back to the store.)

Toast the almonds in a frying pan over very low heat, stirring more frequently as time goes by, until they have just begun to color and acquire an aroma (5 to 7 minutes). Set aside.

Paint the cooled layer of cake with the raspberry jam and cut it into cubes about an inch on a side.

Line a large glass serving bowl with a layer of the cubes, jam side up. Toss in the remaining cake chunks and half the toasted almonds. Sprinkle the raspberry liqueur over all and allow to rest an hour at room temperature.

Whip the cream. If using fresh raspberries, set a few nice ones aside for decoration.

Spoon or scatter the remaining raspberries over the cake. Spoon the pudding over the cake and nuts, encouraging it to flow into the crevices between cubes of cake. If you have a pastry bag, spoon half the whipped cream over all and pipe the other half into a nice design. Otherwise, smooth it all on (nobody will mind). Decorate with set-aside raspberries, if any, and the remaining almonds.

Chill for several hours. Serves 8 to 10.

---

The writer is considering conducting a Mathematics class in which he will teach rabbits how to divide.

# A British-Mystery Dinner

Some of us who have nothing better to do occasionally find ourselves challenged to really stupid activities. Like rewriting some of the classic passages in literature. For example:

### A Tale of Two Cities
By Al Sicherman

It was the becestershire, it was the Worcestershire.

Or maybe rewriting them in the names of others:

### A Tale of Two Cities
By David Stockman

On the average, the times were O.K.

I don't know how good I'd be at a parlor game like that if it included current important books. For quite some years now, I haven't been able to read anything of substance. The more important the book, the less likely I am even to want to pick it up.

I feel pretty bad about that, as I used to be a serious reader, but I just can't summon up much zeal these days. I think maybe my not wanting to read about Problems is my way of acknowledging that the focus of my life has shifted, along with my center of gravity (in the first case inward, in the second case downward). I'm into brightening the corner where I are, as the song goes, and not very much at that.

Point me to a mystery, though, particularly a British drawing-room mystery, and I'll waste an evening or two with it forthwith. I don't know why British murder mysteries are so much more appealing to me than American murder mysteries, but I am convinced that you haven't been killed until you've been killed by an Englishman.

Here comes one of those side trips into my peculiar little life that some of us (me) find so fascinating. Some time back, I spent most of a year working at an English-language newspaper in France. Because it was me, I didn't speak any French when I got there.

After a brief stint at a language school (brief both because it met at eight in the morning and I got out of work after midnight, and because I didn't care to discuss at length, with people whose accents were even worse than mine, the matter of Sophie and her cigarette lighter), I decided that what I needed most was not better pronunciation or niftier grammar but a larger French vocabulary.

At the suggestion of a colleague, I began reading books for French toddlers, and I graduated to mystery novels—British mysteries in French translation rather than French mysteries, because I already understood the situations and the manners of speech. That meant that I could make fairly accurate guesses at the translations rather than running to the dictionary every three words. This turned out to be a fairly useful thing to do, and by the time I left France I was able to misunderstand and be misunderstood in a wide variety of circumstances.

While I was acquiring much of the French language by this curious method, I was, of course, getting some parts of it (food and profanity, particularly) by brute force—see a word on a menu, look it up; be called something by an irate taxi driver, don't even need to look it up.

Because I ate more than I took taxis I acquired a pretty comfortable food vocabulary rather rapidly, and I soon stopped using my dictionary when mealtime came.

That food vocabulary often did not help, however, when food was mentioned in the British mysteries, which it frequently is. The British eat lots of dishes that are not widely served in France or the United States. What, for example, would a tarte de mélasse be? From context it's dessert, and the tarte is obvious enough. But what is mélasse? It looks like it could be molasses, but surely there is no such thing as a molasses tart or pie.

Mais oui, friends, there is—although the accurate name is treacle tart.

(The difference between molasses and treacle is not even as interesting as the rest of this discussion.)

I've been back in the good old U.S. of A. almost ten years now, and I have forgotten most of my French with far less difficulty than I acquired it, which proves something but I'm not sure what.

In any event, I was reading a British mystery the other night when I was struck again—not from behind with a blunt instrument, but by the number of apparently common things to eat that turn up in British mysteries but that I have never eaten (and in some cases couldn't even describe).

Why not, I thought in my weakened condition, use these foods to compile a British-mystery dinner? O.K., let's say it once here and have it over with. Lots of folks have food prejudices. Scandinavian food, some will say, is all white. German food, others will aver, is all heavy.

And there are those who will say negative things about British cooking.

Not me. If you want to make your own jokes, in the privacy of your own dwelling unit, about what the mystery is in the British-mystery dinner, I can't stop you. But I'm not making them.

Oh, heck. How about if I pass along a remark that is offensive to not one but three or four nationalities? That would sort of even things up, wouldn't it?

A Canadian friend told me this one, and for all I know it's a commonplace observation in that country. "In Canada," he said, "we had the possibilities of American technology, British tradition and French cooking. Instead, what we got was American tradition, French technology and British cooking."

*I* didn't say that. My Canadian *friend* said that.

Well! If you insist on taking that kind of attitude, we had best push on to the recipes.

The first item to come under our scrutiny is one that is hardly a stranger to our shores, being found in little tins in every supermarket, but I'd venture to say that the average American, asked to assist the police in their enquiries, would say he had never sampled it.

Although in England it is typically tucked into as a breakfast item, I served it as an appetizer.

Reaction was predictably mixed, but three people—*including a fourteen-year-old kid*—had seconds.

---

### Kippers

3 (3¼-ounce) cans kippered (cured) herring
4 tablespoons butter
Salt, pepper

2 tablespoons chopped parsley
1 tablespoon lemon juice
1 lemon, cut into wedges

Cut the kippers in half crosswise.

Melt the butter in a frying pan over low-medium heat, add the kippers and cook gently, turning once, until they are warmed through. Season with salt and pepper.

Garnish with chopped parsley, sprinkle with lemon juice and serve with lemon wedges.

Depending on whether you're presenting them to kipper fans or to colonials who don't comprehend the charm, these will serve from 3 to 12 folks.

---

Next in my investigation I summoned those little sandwiches that, British mysteries would have us believe, blokes and blokesses are always diving into at peculiar times of the day, having motored down from Elbow Twisting, Herts. (To avoid the possibility of a fortnight in chokey, I will admit that I pinched the name of that village from author Robert L. Fish.)

I must say that I thought the little sandwiches on the bland side, although I always go light on the salt and pepper. Her Majesty's government no doubt suggest heavy seasoning for fuller flavour.

While I'm admitting things, I'll also acknowledge having adapted the recipe for the sandwiches from a peculiar little British cookbook. (If you please, guv'nor! They was so little, and they was like me mum used to make.)

## *Little Sandwiches*

12 thin slices bread
8 tablespoons butter, softened
Salt and pepper
    and
3 medium tomatoes, sliced thin
    or
⅓ cup finely chopped watercress
    leaves
and 1 teaspoon lemon juice
    or
1 medium cucumber
and 1 tablespoon vinegar
and 1 teaspoon dill weed

Trim crusts from sliced bread.

Proceed to make 6 sandwiches of one kind, or by dividing the quantities appropriately, an assortment:

For tomato sandwiches, spread the butter on the bread and assemble the sandwiches with slices of tomato and liberal application of salt and pepper.

For watercress sandwiches, blend the chopped watercress with the softened butter, lemon juice and liberal amounts of salt and pepper. Spread on bread and assemble.

For cucumber sandwiches, peel the cucumber and slice it thin. Put the slices in a bowl with the vinegar and dill, stir and let sit for 10 minutes. Spread the butter on the bread, and assemble the sandwiches with slices of drained cucumber and salt and pepper.

In any case, cut the sandwiches into quarters or eighths or thin fingers and arrange on a tray, maybe even with a paper doily, and bring them out late in the afternoon, when people are feeling a bit peckish.

Makes 6 full sandwiches, enough for 6 to 12 people as a teatime snack.

---

I also prepared potted shrimps, an appetizer that I've seen mentioned several times. They are "potted" in clarified butter.

Depend upon it; people and potted shrimps are much the same everywhere. Even in this small village I have seen the damage caused by mischief and bad recipes. These potted shrimps, now. They remind me of the time young Dora Edwards got into difficulty over a necklace. Old Mrs. Fletcher said Dora had taken a pearl necklace that had been left on the bureau. Dora argued, but old Mrs. Fletcher threw her out.

And that's what I did with almost all of these greasy potted shrimps.

They did have a nice flavor, though, so please allow a person who has learned a great deal about life to suggest that mace goes surprisingly well with shrimps.

Although it is distinctly *not* a British food, I was tempted to serve corn (maize), just so I could introduce a constable on a bicycle who would say: "Ear, ear, ear. Wot's all this?"

It isn't, so I won't. But if I had any fortitude, I would have done.

Instead, I served a vegetable dish that is so British-sounding that my upper lip stiffened just thinking about it. This is neither fantastic nor terrible, but it is certainly more likely to please if you are fond of celery.

## Braised Celery

1 bunch celery (8 to 10 ribs)
4 large carrots
2 medium onions
2 tablespoons butter
1 tablespoon olive oil

1 (10¾-ounce) can chicken broth
¼ teaspoon thyme
Salt, pepper
1 bay leaf
2 or 3 sprigs of parsley

Wash the celery and cut into 1½-inch pieces. Peel and slice the carrots. Peel and slice the onions.

Preheat the oven to 350 degrees.

Melt the butter in a frying pan, add the oil and sauté the carrots and onions for 10 minutes.

Transfer the mixture to a 1½- or 2-quart oven-safe casserole. Add the celery, chicken broth, thyme, salt and pepper; stir to combine.

Add the bay leaf and parsley sprigs. Cover and bake 1¼ hours or until the vegetables are tender. Remove bay leaf and parsley.

Serves 6.

Let us now concern ourselves with a main dish.

Because I have noted it elsewhere in my journals (it was in the summer of '81, after the curious adventure of the sauerkraut cake), we will not have the odd but quite tasty toad-in-the-hole (sausages in Yorkshire pudding).

Instead, let us have some even better and heartier fare—a pie that features, in addition to steak, an organ meat not commonly consumed on these shores.

There is no need for speculation, for here, unless I am very much mistaken, is our visitor now.

## Steak and Kidney Pie

1 to 1½ pounds top round steak
1 veal kidney
1 large onion
4 tablespoons butter
Flour
Salt, pepper
1 (10½-ounce) can beef broth

1 teaspoon Worcestershire sauce
1 teaspoon basil
2 (3¾-ounce) tins smoked oysters, drained (optional)
Prepared pastry for 1-crust pie
1 egg, beaten

Trim any fat off the steak and cut it into 1-inch cubes.

Wash the kidney, and use scissors (a knife, although more elegant, isn't as handy) to trim away the fat and the hard center core and white fibers. Cut or chop the kidney into rather small pieces (smaller than the steak cubes).

Peel and slice the onion.

Heat the butter in a frying pan and sauté the onions until they are translucent. Lift the onions out of the melted butter with a slotted spoon and set them in a 2-quart oven-safe casserole.

Toss the steak cubes in a few tablespoons of flour, along with some salt and pepper. (I like to do this in a paper bag, but my origins are humble. Cooks of breeding probably never resort to that.)

Brown the floured steak in the butter, adding more butter if necessary. Remove steak pieces to the casserole.

Shake or toss the kidney pieces in seasoned flour and lightly brown them, too. Transfer to the casserole.

Preheat the oven to 300 degrees. Add 1 tablespoon of flour to whatever fat and meat juices are left in the pan (if none, melt a tablespoon of butter). Stir flour and fat together over low heat for a minute, then slowly add the beef broth, stirring, and cook until it is slightly thickened. Add the Worcestershire and basil (it was the becestershire, it was the . . . no, I did that already) and stir to combine. Pour into the casserole, but don't add more than is necessary to just cover the meat.

Cover the casserole with foil and bake at 300 degrees for 1½ hours.

If you like, you can prepare the recipe to this point in advance, set it in the fridge, then pop down to Brighton for a holiday.

When ready to resume, increase the oven temperature to 450 degrees and have the butler get the casserole back from the pantry. (Keep an eye on him; Bessie, the little serving girl up from the village, says he has been hitting the port, and he has also been seen in the market town talking with a strange little man with a cast in one eye.)

Add the oysters, if desired (not a bad idea if you're not sure you'll like the kidney, as the smoky oyster flavor tends to predominate).

Roll out the pie crust and cover the casserole with it. Cut a few decorative slashes in it, to allow steam to escape, and brush with the beaten egg.

Bake for 10 minutes at 450 degrees, lower the temperature to 350 degrees and bake 25 minutes or longer (total: 35 minutes or more), until the crust is crisp and golden.

Serves 6.

---

Here, as a second side dish (or perhaps an appetizer) is something I liked rather well. It was quite rippin', actually! Had I not misplaced my monocle when I went for a punt on the river this forenoon, I should be able to read you a most interestin' fact. Where did I put the dashed thing? Ah! Here we are: "There are 21 species of edible fungi in Britain."

Our late friend would have done well to learn what the others looked like.

---

### Creamed Mushrooms

1 pound mushrooms
1 tablespoon oil
6 tablespoons butter, divided
2 tablespoons finely chopped shallots

½ cup heavy cream
Salt, pepper
2 to 3 tablespoons sherry

Clean and slice the mushrooms.

Heat the oil and 4 tablespoons of the butter in a frying pan. Add the mushrooms and shallots and cook, stirring, about 3 minutes over medium heat.

Stir in the cream, salt and pepper and cook 5 minutes longer, stirring, until the sauce has begun to thicken.

Add the sherry and boil for 1 minute.

Break the remaining 2 tablespoons of butter into 4 pieces and whisk them in one at a time.

Serve with toasts, crackers or crisps (potato chips), or as a vegetable.

Serves 4 to 6.

---

Do you remember treacle tart?

(The witness is directed to answer the question.)

It is perhaps best to forget treacle tart. One of the eight of us rather liked it, but the other seven of us placed pieces of black cloth on our heads and directed that the tart be taken from that place to a cylindrical place and that on the morning of the following day it be collected from that place and taken to another place and buried.

(If m'lud and Rupert Brooke would forgive a scrap of verse, "Think only this: That there's some corner of a city landfill that is forever treacle tart.")

To be sure, mon ami, what is the treacle tart, after all? It is charming, certainly, but it is nothing more than a pie shell and many bread crumbs soaked in the good golden syrup and molasses, along with perhaps an egg. One bakes the whole of it.

The cells, the little gray cells, my honest friend! They should tell even you that it will taste like bread crumbs, syrup and molasses.

I vowed to prepare another British-mystery dessert, and I insisted to myself that it not be one that is already familiar in these remote provinces.

Trifle, for example, is wonderful, but it has been chronicled countless times— even here.

Then I came across a recipe for Dundee cake, which sometimes turns up when the locale of a mystery shifts toward Scotland.

I will spare the court's time by saying that Dundee cake was not overwhelmingly better received than treacle tart, but that it seemed to have more possibilities.

It can be classified, for purposes of introduction into evidence, as an unmoist fruitcake. It would no doubt benefit from a prolonged association with a wee drap or two (or five hundred) o' spirits.

In the interests of justice—and of ending this discussion before the moon rises over the windswept moor, revealing a rocky, barren landscape broken only by the twisted trunks of long-blighted trees, their withered branches waving like the gnarled, outstretched fingers of some malevolent warning hand—here's the recipe.

---

### Dundee Cake

About 20 blanched almonds
3/4 cup (1 1/2 sticks) butter
3/4 cup packed brown sugar
4 eggs
2 cups flour
1/2 teaspoon salt
1 1/2 teaspoons baking powder

1 cup raisins
3/4 cup fruitcake mix (candied cherries, etc.)
1/3 cup currants (optional)
Juice and grated rind of 1/2 lemon
Juice and grated rind of 1/2 orange
2 tablespoons sliced almonds

Grind the 20 almonds fine in a food processor or chop them fine by hand.

Preheat the oven to 325 degrees. Grease an 8-inch round cake pan. Cream the butter and brown sugar until they are light and fluffy. Beat in the eggs one at a time.

Sift the flour, salt and baking powder into a bowl. Stir in the ground nuts. Fold in the butter mixture and add the fruits, rinds and juices.

Turn the batter into the cake pan and sprinkle on the sliced almonds. (They are characteristic of the Dundee cake, and without them the cake might be assumed to be traveling on a false identity and could be detained for questioning.)

Bake for 1 1/2 hours, then reduce temperature to 300 degrees and bake an additional 30 minutes. If it is browning too much near the end, drape it with a sheet of foil.

*(Continued)*

This much baking sounds excessive (and if you was to ask me, your worship, it *was* excessive), but several cookbooks agreed on it. Let the cake cool completely before removing it from the pan. Wrap it in foil to store. It wouldn't hurt to pour some booze over it first.

(One cookbook noted, if this gives you a further hint about Dundee cake, "It will keep for weeks.")

---

### Little Mystery #7: Olives

Olive-can labels carry information about the size of the olives within, but to judge from the names (which seem to have some sort of official status) even the smallest olives have glandular problems: There are "giant," "jumbo" and "mammoth," to name but a few. (I seem to recall seeing one called "Flying Boxcar.") What is the full list of these names, in order, and who made them up?

**Solution:** Vincent Dole, president of the Dolefam Corporation, which cans Old Monk brand olives, acknowledged the question cheerfully. "It *is*," he said, "one of the most ridiculous sets of names I've seen in my life."

The nation's olive growers got together more than fifty years ago, he explained, and set up that list of names.

According to Dole, the exact millimeter sizes that correspond with those names have been changed a few times but the names have remained as standards for the industry. Here is the list, from smallest to largest:

*Select*
*Medium*
*Large*
*Extra large*
*Mammoth (sometimes called Gem)*
*Giant*
*Jumbo*
*Colossal*
*Super-colossal.*

# *A Halloween Menu*

Tomorrow, if all goes well and the world doesn't end tonight, is Halloween.

Normal associations with that holiday run to such things as ghosts and goblins, soap smeared on windows, and bunches of kids dressed up like some cartoon character that adults never heard of standing on your porch holding out pillowcases and expecting large handfuls of amazingly expensive tiny candy bars.

Not the kind of festivity you'd expect to read much about in the food section.

There is something you don't know about Halloween, though. It is my boss's favorite holiday.

For that reason, if for no other, the ensuing space will be devoted to an attempt to translate the spirit of Halloween (whatever that is) into a menu.

But before we turn, however awkwardly, to food, may I please tell my favorite Halloween anecdote?

The following is a true story. Only the names, as Jack Webb's important-voiced announcer used to say, have been changed.

Hercule had not been in this country very long, and his command of English was very limited. His wife, an American, had neglected to mention anything about the approaching holiday, and happened to be out that evening.

When she got home, she found a large pile of candy on the table, and Hercule with a happy expression.

Where did all this stuff come from, his wife demanded.

Such a charming holiday, Hercule said. All evening long, little children came to the door, said something I couldn't understand and held up big bags full of candy.

(Imagine how the neighborhood kids felt when this guy opened his door, smiled, took a handful of their candy, said, "Thonk you," and closed the door. *That's* the spirit of Halloween.)

That out of the way, we must now talk about things to cook for Halloween. We met this need last year by serving a meal in which every dish was orange and black.

Serviceable (and peculiar) as that was, it's an idea that can only be used once.

Racking what I laughingly call my brain for another way to eke a menu out of a holiday that has nothing to do with food (other than pumpkin), I considered briefly a dinner in which guests would bob for roast beef and mashed potatoes. Too messy, I decided, and it would require an awful lot of gravy.

So I turned to the time-honored technique of looking through cookbook indexes for things that might work.

What I found amounts to a Halloween menu of sorts, but it isn't as tightly conceived a theme as the orange-and-black dinner.

Sorry. But in the words of our nation's foremost philosopher, Richard Nelson, "You cain't please everyone, so you got to please yourself. (La-da dah, lat'n da-da dah.)"

Hewing to the spooks and goblins line, we'll start with a devilishly simple appetizer.

You might be surprised, though, at how many people who cook a fair amount have nonetheless never made some very uncomplicated dishes. So, for those who have lacked the internal fire to look up the recipe, here it is.

---

### Deviled Eggs

9 hard-cooked eggs
¼ cup plus 2 tablespoons mayonnaise
1 tablespoon lemon juice
½ teaspoon dry mustard
3 tablespoons finely chopped onion

1½ teaspoons Worcestershire sauce
¼ teaspoon salt
Pinch of pepper
Paprika

Peel the eggs and cut them in halves lengthwise.

Remove the yolks to a bowl. Mash the yolks and stir in the mayonnaise, lemon juice, mustard, onion, Worcestershire sauce, salt and pepper.

Mound or pipe the yolk mixture back into the whites and dust with paprika.

Chill an hour or so before serving. Serves 6 or so.

---

Note: It's appropriate at Halloween to hear various awful noises—groans, moans, rattling of chains, and the like.

While I was out in the kitchen after dinner, rattling those pots and pans, I heard a whining noise. It was me.

I will give you a hint that might keep you from hearing that same noise from you: Even if you want to be very fancy-dancy, don't serve deviled eggs on a silver tray. (Rather instant tarnish!)

I, too, have never made a lot of things that plenty of people make all the time. This next recipe, Parker House rolls, is such an item. The dough is cut into circles and each is folded over onto itself.

I had to try two recipes because the rolls went very oddly awry the first time. I had planned to call them Haunted Parker House rolls, in keeping with this week's very thin excuse for a theme, and you can probably imagine my surprise when every single one of them unfolded during baking.

Heck's bells, I bethought me. What mischief is this? Besides looking funny, which they did, they were very dry and not worth half the effort that went into them.

So I found a recipe that involved about half the effort. Those worked just fine and were, if I say so myself, excellent.

---

### Haunted Parker House Rolls
(Exorcised version)

1 (¼-ounce) envelope active dry yeast
¼ cup warm water
1 cup milk
2 tablespoons sugar
2 tablespoons shortening

1 teaspoon salt
About 3½ cups sifted flour
1 egg
Melted butter

Dissolve the yeast in the warm water. Set aside.

Scald the milk, stir in the sugar, shortening and salt, then let it cool to lukewarm. (I don't know why this is better than just heating it to lukewarm, but there seems to be universal agreement that this is what you do.)

Sift in 1 cup of flour and beat well. Beat in the dissolved yeast and the egg. Add remaining flour as necessary to form a soft dough instead of a batter (when you stir, it begins to move with the spoon as one lump). Stir in a bit more flour, then quit.

Brush the top of the dough with a little melted butter, cover and let rise in a warm place until it has doubled in bulk (1½ to 2 hours).

Turn the dough out onto a lightly floured surface and roll it out about ½ inch thick. If it is sticky and hard to handle, work a little more flour into it on the table—even as it's being rolled out—so it won't tear apart when you try to pick up the cut-out rolls.

Cut the dough into rounds with a cutter 2½ inches or so in diameter. Place the rounds on greased cookie sheets. Roll out scraps and cut out more rolls.

Fold each roll in half. Lift the folded-over roll slightly open, dip a fingertip in water and moisten the lower part of the dough at the middle of the rim. Press the dough together there, to make a seal. Brush the top of each roll with a little melted butter, set the rolls in a warm place and let them rise until they are doubled in bulk again (about 30 minutes). Meanwhile, preheat the oven to 400 degrees.

Bake the rolls about 15 minutes. Makes about 20. They're spookily good.

---

Now we come to a main course of sorts. In fact it was the only thing I could think of right off the bat (flap, flap, flap) when I was reminded of my boss's strange fondness for this holiday. The sauce is a very nice one, which I think allows the main ingredient to hover above its usual location. In addition, the garlic in it keeps vampires away. It may also keep everybody else away, but that's the breaks.

---

### Hollow Weenies

2 tablespoons olive oil
1 onion, chopped
1½ pounds tomatoes (3 or 4 tomatoes)
2 cloves garlic, put through a garlic press

Salt, pepper
2 teaspoons flour
2½ tablespoons chopped fresh basil or parsley
8 hot dogs
8 hot-dog buns

*(Continued)*

Heat the oil and cook the onions about 5 minutes, until they are translucent. Quarter the tomatoes and squeeze them dry. (Save the juice if you want to drink it—and if there is any; store-bought tomatoes tend more to transportability than to juiciness.)

Cut the tomatoes into small chunks and add them and the garlic to the onions.

Sprinkle with salt, pepper and flour and stir in the basil or parsley. Cook over medium-low heat about 15 minutes, until the mixture is thick and almost dry.

Meanwhile, cut a notch down the length of each hot dog and scoop out some of the meat.

Add the meat to the tomato mixture and cook the slightly hollowed hot dogs in the usual fashion in a pan of water.

If you like, steam the buns. Here's a painless method: Put ½ inch of water in the bottom of a Dutch oven. Put a large metal colander into the pan, making sure the water is below the level of the bottom of the colander. Pile the buns into the colander, cover the whole thing and put over medium heat for a few minutes.

To serve, assemble the hollow weenies in the buns and spoon on the sauce. Makes 8.

---

I was stuck briefly trying to think of a Halloween-related vegetable (we're saving pumpkin for dessert, of course), and I almost decided not to have one. Then I remembered a dish that I have made before and really enjoyed— green beans, flavored with lots of butter, garlic and vermouth.

Where's the Halloween angle in that, you ask? Boooooo-ze!

---

### Beans with Booooo-ze

2 (9-ounce) packages frozen French-cut green beans
¼ pound butter (unsalted, if you have it)

2 cloves garlic, put through a garlic press
Pinch of basil
Pinch of tarragon
½ cup dry white vermouth

Cook the beans according to package directions. Melt the butter in a frying pan.

Drain the beans and pour them into the frying pan. Add the garlic, crumble in the basil and tarragon and cook over medium-low heat, stirring occasionally, until most of the butter is absorbed (10 to 15 minutes). Raise the heat to medium, allow the pan to heat for a minute, then pour in the vermouth. Cook until most of the liquid is gone, then serve. Serves 6 to 8.

---

Comes time now, children, for dessert. On Halloween, though, there should be *two* desserts, so you have something from witch to choose.

First, because it's jack-o'-lantern time, a pumpkin pie. But you can get plain pumpkin pie on Thanksgiving. For Halloween, it ought to be a little different, right?

So I put a layer of chocolate custard under the pumpkin, and to lighten things up, I made it a pumpkin chiffon. You might think this an odd grouping. It was, but it was very, very pleasant.

**CHOCOLATE BOTTOM:**

1/3 cup sugar
1 tablespoon cornstarch
1/2 envelope (1 1/4 teaspoons)
    unflavored gelatin
1 1/4 cups milk
2 egg yolks
2 (1-ounce) squares unsweetened
    chocolate

1 baked 9-inch pie shell

**PUMPKIN CHIFFON TOP:**

1 (1/4-ounce) envelope unflavored
    gelatin

1/4 cup cold water
3 eggs, separated
1 cup sugar, divided
1 (15-ounce) can pumpkin (not
    pumpkin-pie mix)
1/4 teaspoon salt
1/4 teaspoon cinnamon
1/8 teaspoon nutmeg
1/4 teaspoon ginger
1/2 cup milk

1 cup heavy cream

## *Chocolate-Pumpkin Pie*

(The devil's food made me do it.)

Prepare the chocolate bottom layer:

(If you don't trust me that this is a good combination, skip this paragraph, go straight to the pumpkin chiffon and double the amounts of cinnamon, nutmeg and ginger. But don't come crying to me afterward because your treat is all gone and you didn't get any chocolate.)

Combine the 1/3 cup sugar, cornstarch and gelatin in the top of a double boiler, gradually stir in the milk and heat, stirring constantly, over simmering water until the mixture is steaming. Beat the egg yolks lightly, stir in a spoonful of the hot mixture, then stir the diluted yolks into the hot mixture. Cook, stirring, about 5 minutes, until the mixture is quite thick. Add the chocolate and continue to heat, stirring, until it is fully melted. Pour into the baked crust and chill.

Prepare the pumpkin chiffon: Stir the gelatin into the water; let it stand 5 minutes. Meanwhile, beat the egg yolks and add 1/2 cup of the sugar, the pumpkin, salt, cinnamon, nutmeg, ginger and milk. Cook the mixture over low heat, stirring constantly, until it begins to thicken.

Stir in the gelatin until it is fully dissolved. Cool the mixture in the refrigerator, checking its texture fairly frequently. When the mixture has thickened enough to form soft mounds, take it out of the refrigerator, and beat the egg whites until they begin to foam.

While beating the whites, slowly add the remaining 1/2 cup of sugar to them. Beat until the whites hold soft peaks. Fold the whites into the pumpkin mixture and pour over the chocolate layer in the pie shell.

Beat the heavy cream and decorate the pie. Chocolate curls or something of the sort would make a nice garnish and would hint, to those who are alive to the possibilities, at what lies beneath the pumpkin. Chill until serving time. Serves 6 to 8.

This meal has been so laden with spooky stuff that it needs something to take the curse off it. What better than a second dessert—and what better second dessert than this?

### Divinity

2½ cups packed brown sugar
½ cup light corn syrup
⅓ cup water

2 egg whites
1 teaspoon vanilla
1½ cups coarsely chopped pecans

Note: Maybe the use of brown sugar instead of white granulated sugar makes this "seafoam" instead of divinity. Maybe it doesn't. I don't care. I like it with brown sugar. If you don't, make it with the same quantity of granulated sugar. It will be divine either way.

Another note: Divinity, like fudge and maybe more so, is affected by moisture in the air. If it's a muggy day, you might want to consider making something else. Or reconcile yourself to a divinity that never gets very firm—that's the way some folks like their divinities.

Put the sugar, syrup and water into a large saucepan and stir over moderate heat until the sugar is dissolved.

With a barely damp paper towel, and watching out not to burn your fingers, wash down the sides of the pan above the mixture. Turn the heat down to low-medium and cook without stirring until the mixture reaches 260 degrees on a candy thermometer. (Wash down again if you see any sugar crystals on the side of the pan.)

As the syrup approaches 260 degrees, beat the egg whites to the soft peak stage.

Once the syrup gets to 260 degrees, beat the egg whites continuously while pouring in the syrup very slowly—in a thin stream. Near the end of the syrup you can speed it up a little.

Add the vanilla, then beat until stiff peaks form. Fold in the nuts. Line cookie sheets with waxed paper and drop divinity on them from heaping teaspoons, or squeeze the divinity from the largest round tube of a pastry bag. Chill at least several hours.

If you aren't lucky and you find that the divinity remains too gooey to pick up comfortably with the fingers, let it air-dry overnight. It won't be quite as creamy that way, but at least you'll be able to get it to your mouth. Or eat it with a spoon.

# Dinner at Mom's

I had a particularly unpleasant conversation a few days ago with a friend who has, over time, eaten a great deal of the food I have prepared. We were talking about things parents don't bother teaching their kids, and she said, "You know what my favorite food is? Roast beef, mashed potatoes and gravy, and I don't know how to make it. When I lived at home, my mom used to make the best roast beef in the world."

"*Roast beef, mashed potatoes and gravy??!!*" I rejoined, calmly. "Not chicken breast with vermouth-tarragon sauce, or duck à l'orange or chocolate soufflé, or, or (splutter, splut) . . ."

I must, despite my calm, reasoned tone, have betrayed a certain tension.

"I love the fancy food you make," she said, in an effort to be placating. "But my very favorite meal is my mom's roast beef, mashed potatoes and gravy."

"O.K.," I said, my chin stiffening. "I'll *make* roast beef, mashed potatoes and gravy."

"It won't," she replied with triumph, "be like my mom's."

Well, it was a bad beginning but a good idea. There *are* a lot of foods that your mother didn't bother telling you how to make. They were too obvious or too ordinary or something.

(If you're a man, chances are that your mother didn't tell you how to cook *anything*, but that's another story. Part of that same story is that your father probably didn't know how to cook, and that he probably didn't tell your sister how to change spark plugs. But we leave these trembling social issues for the newspaper's family section. Back to food.)

Some of the same sturdy, wholesome foods that you didn't get told how to make, as my friend's infuriating remarks suggested, are the ones that are most reminiscent of home.

It is interesting to note that these are also foods that you are almost never served when you're invited to someone else's house for dinner. Quiche, yes; Tournedos Rossini, perhaps. Chicken and dumplings, not likely.

Never one to pass up a challenge, however stupid, I decided to make a bunch of plain good foods of that sort, and to pass along the recipes to the large group of us who never got told how to make them.

Here's what I made:

*Roast beef*
*Mashed potatoes*
*Beef gravy*
*Chicken and dumplings*
*Chicken gravy*
*Green beans*
*Apple pie*

Since the idea here is preparing plain, honest food, I decided to avoid any attempts to simplify, modernize or jazz up the recipes. I was tempted, but I abstained.

In the first instance, roast beef, that abstention was a pleasure. My mother was a fairly decent cook and a wonderful person, but she did things to roast beef. I believe that the things involved garlic and onion, normally two of my favorite foods, but I didn't know until rather late in my life that roast beef didn't always taste peculiar. (I learned when some neighbors gave me some leftover roast beef to give to our dog. It smelled like the odors that come from restaurant kitchens, and *I* ate most of it.)

What makes good roast beef, in my mind anyway, is a piece of beef roast—and nothing else. (Well, to *get* the piece of beef roast it takes a surprising amount of money, too. Even the comparatively inexpensive rolled roast, which I used, cost quite a bit to feed six people.)

I didn't quite leave it fully alone, either. Following a suggestion in several books, I dredged the meat with flour before slipping it into the oven. But that was it. And it was wonderful. Just like Mom didn't used to make.

**Beef roast**
**Flour**

**Salt and pepper**

*Roast Beef*

There's lots that could be said, I suppose, about what cut of meat to use, but that really is a matter of personal preference and budget, so I'll leave you to work that out with your butcher. Depending on how much else you plan to serve and how hearty the appetites are likely to be, get between ¼ pound and ½ pound per person.

Dredge the roast (if you like) by putting it into a paper bag with some flour and shaking it a little (the neat way), or by rolling it around in some flour on a counter and patting it in with your hands (the messy way).

Preheat the oven (see below), put the meat on a rack in a shallow pan and roast. That's it. Salt and pepper, if you like, when it's done.

Cookbooks tend to insist that the really old-fashioned way of roasting meat—searing it first and then roasting at fairly high temperatures—dries out the meat, and they recommend roasting at a uniform, relatively low temperature (between 300 and 325 degrees). They're right, the meat does stay juicy that way. And they've been saying that for so long that your mom probably learned it that way, too. But the tradeoff (there's got to be a tradeoff, you know), is that there's almost no juice in the pan with which to make gravy. More about that later.

The length of time to cook the meat also varies with what kind of meat it is and how well-done you want it, but I really shouldn't beg off giving you any information, so here's a little chart:

| Standing rib: | |
|---|---|
| Rare | 18–20 min./lb. |
| Medium | 22–25 min./lb. |
| Well-done | 27–30 min./lb. |

| Rolled rib: | |
|---|---|
| Rare | 30–33 min./lb. |
| Medium | 35–38 min./lb. |
| Well-done | 40–45 min./lb. |

| Rump: | |
|---|---|
| Rare | 20–22 min./lb. |
| Medium | 24–27 min./lb. |
| Well-done | 28–30 min./lb. |

Whether or not you have success with this chart also depends in part on whether we agree on what "rare," "medium" and "well-done" mean. The friend whose idea this meal was describes any meat, however gray, from which any juice of any description can be wrung as "blood rare." I cut off a part of the roast for her and put it in early. It cooked more than an hour a pound, it looked like a piece of leather and she said it was excellent.

Serving a roast to a group of people who like their meat cooked to different degrees of doneness is kind of a problem, even if they all agree (which they won't) on what "medium" is. One way out of the difficulty, and it helps answer the gravy problem, too, is to take the roast out a little early and carve it in the kitchen.

Once you cut into the roast, unless you went for ultra-well done, there'll be juice in the pan. Pour some of it off for gravy, which we'll get to in a minute. Slice most or all of the meat. If too much of it seems too rare for some of the guests, allowing the slices to soak briefly in the pan juices might darken them a little. If that's not enough, slip the sliced meat back into the oven for just a few minutes and it will move quite rapidly toward doneness.

If that's cheating, I'm sorry.

If you're going to have roast beef, you've got to have some kind of gravy. Some folks just serve the pan juices, but flour-based gravy—the kind that comes with hot roast beef sandwiches at diners—is the choice of connoisseurs.

---

## Beef Gravy

2 tablespoons flour
3 to 4 tablespoons beef drippings (fat)
1 cup liquid (see text)
Salt, pepper

Worcestershire sauce (optional, see text)
Coloring (see text)

For about 1 cup of gravy: In a small pan stir the flour, a little at a time, into the beef drippings. Over low heat stir the flour-dripping mixture constantly until it is smooth and quite hot. Don't quit too soon; give it 2 or 3 minutes, or the flour won't accept the liquid you're going to add.

Continue to cook and stir while pouring in a cup of liquid a little at a time. Cookbooks always call for a cup of beef stock; if you're like me and 99.9 percent of other cooks, you don't have a cup of beef stock close to hand. (I usually have veal stock, but I just can't seem to keep beef stock around.) Substitutes, none of which is perfect, include beef bouillon (the best choice; if using canned concentrate, dilute it to normal strength with water—it's quite salty), consommé (dilute this too; it's O.K., but doesn't really taste like gravy) and milk (pretty flat).

Cook a while, stirring constantly as it thickens, adding salt and pepper and Worcestershire sauce, steak sauce or anything else you have handy to try and give it the flavor that means gravy to you. Any extra—non-greasy—meat drippings are excellent if available.

Last comes the problem of color. Especially if you used milk, this is going to be a pretty pale gravy. Commercial gravy enhancers like Kitchen Bouquet contain coloring to make the gravy look presentable, but they seem to taste a lot like celery. If you were thinking of adding a little celery anyway, you're home free. If not, you might use some burnt-sugar syrup, made in advance:

Bring a little water to boiling in a kettle. In a small skillet or saucepan, stir 1/4 cup of sugar until it melts and turns dark—keep going until it no longer smells sweet. Then—carefully because it will spatter at first—stir in 1/4 cup of the boiling water. Cook briefly until it thickens a bit. Use a few drops in the gravy and keep the rest around in a jar in your refrigerator—next to the beef stock—or throw it out.

---

It would be appropriate here to throw in a few quotations from famous people praising mashed potatoes. Food of the people, food of the gods, food of North Dakota, that sort of thing. I don't know any, so the mashed potatoes will just have to stand on their own. (They often do, you know.)

---

## Mashed Potatoes

6 medium-to-large potatoes
3 tablespoons butter or margarine

1/2 teaspoon salt
1/4 cup cream or milk

Put 4 or 5 cups of water into a Dutch oven and heat to boiling.

Meanwhile, wash and peel the potatoes and dig out the funny-looking parts. Cut each potato into 4 or 5 sections and add them to the boiling water. Cover, reduce the heat to a rapid simmer and cook about 25 minutes. You should be able to poke a fork through the thickest portions without resistance.

Drain them well but quickly (you don't want them to cool), and return them to the pan.

Mash them in the pan with a potato masher, a pastry blender, a heavy fork or anything else handy.

If you like them *really* smooth, you could beat them around a while with your electric mixer, but mashed potatoes are pretty bland, and many folks prefer an occasional lump, just to keep from falling asleep. If you do beat them, do it fast, because they'll cool off in a hurry.

In any case, quickly beat in the butter (cut in small pieces to help it melt sooner), the salt and the cream.

Serves 6.

---

Chicken and dumplings sounds so down-home it's hard to imagine anyone wanting to serve it in such places as Westchester, New York, or Grosse Pointe, Michigan, but you never know. Westchesterians (or are they Westchesteroids?) and Grosse Pointers had to come from *somewhere*.

It is with this dish particularly that the temptation to fiddle became strong. People just don't stew chickens as much as they used to, and you don't see that many stewing chickens. Also, stewed chicken, left on the bones, is kind of gray and unappealing. But I resisted the modern blandishments of baking the chicken and doing the dumplings in soup.

Sorry, but if I'm making this stuff because Mom used to make it, I'm doing it pretty much the way she used to do it, not the way she learned later in her bridge club.

---

### Chicken to Go with Dumplings

1 carrot, cut into chunks or slices
1 small onion, sliced
1 bay leaf
A rib of celery, broken into 2 or 3
  pieces
2 or 3 peppercorns
1 to 2 teaspoons salt
1 teaspoon parsley flakes
1 (5-pound or so) stewing chicken (or
  a very large frying chicken), cut up

Put 3 cups of water into a Dutch oven. Add the carrot, onion, bay leaf, peppercorns, celery, salt and parsley flakes and bring to a boil. In a matter of minutes, the kitchen will smell like Mom's—even before you get the chicken into the pot.

Wash the chicken pieces, add them to the boiling water and lower the heat to a simmer. Cover and cook 2 hours, until the largest pieces seem tender when you poke at them with a fork. You won't need to add any water, but you can check once in a while if you've a mind to.

Remove the chicken and allow it to cool briefly. Fish out and discard the bay leaf and peppercorns, if you can spot them.

I admit it; this next step is a departure from absolute authenticity, but it's not a big one and it dramatically improves the dish's appearance and the ease with which it can be eaten. Remove and discard the skin and bones and tear or cut the chicken meat into bite-size pieces. Skim most of the fat off the top of the broth, putting 3 or 4 tablespoons of the fat in a small pan for gravy. Also pour off about 1½ cups of broth for the gravy. Return the meat to the skimmed broth and bring to the boil while you prepare the dumpling batter (see below). Serves 4 to 6.

Since my friend's mother was also alleged to make the world's best dumplings, I called and got her recipe. (She told me that she had taken to baking the chicken and dropping the dumplings into cream of chicken soup, but we'll ignore that.)

---

## Al's Friend's Mom's Dumplings, to Go with Chicken

2 cups flour
4 teaspoons baking powder
1/2 teaspoon salt

1 1/2 tablespoons solid shortening
1/2 cup to 2/3 cup milk

If you're not making chicken with the above recipe, get together about 4 cups of chicken broth and bring it to the boil. If you are making the chicken, wait until you have it cut up so that the dumplings can simmer in the broth, not sit high and dry on the chicken.

In a medium bowl, stir together the flour, baking powder and salt.

Rub the shortening in with your fingers (Mom would surely admonish you to be sure to wash your hands first), breaking it into small flour-coated flakes, *not* smearing it in until there are no separate pieces.

If that process doesn't appeal to you, you can cut in the shortening using a pastry blender or a couple of knives. Either way, it's just like making pie crust.

Stir in the milk, quickly, just until blended, and using only enough milk to collect the dough so it will stand together by itself.

Drop the batter by soup spoons into the boiling chicken broth. Make no more than one layer of dumplings.

Cover the pot and cook for 20 minutes. Don't take the cover off for *anything*. (I don't know what's supposed to happen if you do take the cover off; I don't think it's anything like warts or rains of grasshoppers. Probably the dumplings get tough.)

When the dumplings are done, arrange them around the perimeter of a large platter (draining each well with a slotted spoon).

Drain the chicken pieces, too, and put them in the center of the platter.

Makes about 12 dumplings. Serves 4 to 6.

---

Chicken and dumplings need chicken gravy at least as much as roast beef needs beef gravy. The method is the same, but it's easier to do because you don't have to wait until the last minute.

---

## Chicken Gravy

3 tablespoons flour
3 to 4 tablespoons fat skimmed from chicken broth

1 1/2 cups chicken broth
2 or 3 tablespoons milk (optional)

You can do this easily any time after the chicken has been cooking a long time, except you can't get the fat and broth when the dumplings are in the broth because you're not supposed to remove the cover then.

In a small saucepan blend the flour slowly into the fat, stirring and heating over low heat until the mixture is smooth and quite hot. Don't give up too early or the chicken broth won't blend in well.

Continue to cook and stir while pouring in the chicken broth a little at a time. Stir and bring to the boil, adding the milk if you like. Some folks also cook and throw in the chicken giblets.

Makes about 1 1/2 cups. Pour over the chicken and dumplings if you like, or serve separately.

---

The vegetable called for in this "Mom's cooking" meal is clearly green beans, because, although there are lots of elaborate ways to make them, they have a plain and wholesome sound.

A standard way to make green beans is to throw in an onion while they boil. That doesn't sound all that interesting, but I was surprised at how nice it turned out to be.

---

### Green Beans

**1 1/2 pounds fresh green beans**
**1 small onion, peeled**

**3 tablespoons butter, melted**

Wash the beans and cut off the ends. Bring about 2 cups of water to the boil.

Meanwhile, cut the beans in half lengthwise. (That isn't much fun, but moms seem to like that kind of thing. They hum while they do it.) Drop the beans and the onion into the boiling water.

Cook them, uncovered, about 20 minutes, until they are just tender.

Drain them quickly but well, return them to the pot and stir in the melted butter. Serves 6. (Some lucky person gets the onion.)

---

Even the most chocolate-dependent person would probably say that the appropriate dessert for this kind of dinner is apple pie.

You could cheat and buy a prepared crust, of course, or you could buy prepared apple pie filling. You could buy both prepared crust and prepared filling. You could even buy the whole pie already made. But then what would that leave me to write about?

So we're going to make both crust and filling.

First, a very, very brief dissertation on which apples to buy.

If your mom never told you, and especially if you're not all that fond of apples, chances are you'll make the mistake I did not long ago, and buy the only kind of apple whose name you recognize, red Delicious.

That, it turns out, is about the only widely available apple that *isn't* good for pies.

---

### Apple Pie

CRUST:

**2 cups flour**
**1/2 teaspoon salt**
**1/2 cup shortening**
**1/4 cup butter**
**1/4 to 1/2 cup ice water**

FILLING:

**7 or 8 medium apples (better too many than too few)**

**3/8 cup (6 tablespoons) brown sugar**
**3/8 cup (6 tablespoons) granulated sugar**
**1/4 teaspoon cinnamon**
**1/8 teaspoon nutmeg**
**Pinch salt**
**1 tablespoon cornstarch**
**1 teaspoon vanilla**
**1 tablespoon butter**

*(Continued)*

For best results, prepare the crust 3 or 4 hours in advance. Chilling before the final rolling really improves it.

Sift the flour and salt into a bowl. Cut the shortening and butter (some prefer to omit the butter and use ¾ cup of shortening, others go for lard) into the flour with a pastry cutter, a pair of knives or your fingers until the mixture resembles coarse crumbs. Don't get it too fine. The object is to coat small flakes of shortening with flour, not to make a flour-shortening paste.

Stir in the ice water a little at a time, stopping when the dough holds together without any dry spots. It should not be wet.

Chill, if possible, for 3 or 4 hours.

Near the end of the chilling time, prepare the filling:

Peel, core and cut the apples into very thin slices. (If you've never done that before, let me tell you that it's much more work than it sounds like.)

Coring the apple can be done two ways.

One way is to use an apple corer (or, if you're very nimble, a knife), and cut out the center of the apple before you cut it apart. Then cut it in halves or quarters and slice it. If you're not using an apple corer, that sounds easier than it is.

The other way is to quarter the apple and then use a sharp knife to remove the center area of each quarter, which contains the core, seeds, stem and so forth. This usually results in a fair number of quarters that break in half, ruining the shape of the slices, but we're making a double-crust pie, so that's not very important. (There are things worth doing that are not worth doing right, and this is one of them.)

Combine the brown sugar, granulated sugar, cinnamon, nutmeg, salt and cornstarch, and stir the mixture into the apple slices. Stir in the vanilla and set the apples aside. Preheat the oven to 450 degrees.

Remove the dough from the refrigerator, divide the dough in two and lightly flour a working surface. Lightly flour one piece of the dough, both top and bottom, and roll it out until it is about an inch bigger all around than the pie pan. Roll the dough onto the rolling pin, then unroll it into the pie pan. Let it ease into the bottom, but you may have to adjust it here and there.

If the apples have been sitting a long time, there may be quite a bit of liquid in the bowl. If so, pour most of it off. Fill the pie with the apples, and dot them with the butter. Roll out the second half of the dough just like the first, roll it onto the rolling pin and unroll it over the pie.

Trim the excess crusts. Press the top and bottom crusts together and crimp with your fingers or a fork. Slit the top crust in 4 or 5 places (in a nice, symmetrical pattern if your mom was artistic). Some moms brush the top crust with milk and/or sprinkle it with a little sugar.

Cut a few inch-wide strips of aluminum foil and lay them around the outside edges of the crust (which burn easily). It also doesn't hurt to put foil on the bottom oven shelf to catch the drips. Bake for 10 minutes at 450 degrees, then reduce the temperature to 350 degrees and bake for an additional 35 to 50 minutes. Judge doneness by the color of the crust, which should be a nice light golden brown. Remove the foil for the last 15 minutes, to brown the edges.

---

### Follow-Up

After this article appeared, old friend Mildred Holcomb, St. Peter, Minnesota, wrote to say that she was "appalled and shaken" that the mashed-potato recipe called for draining the potatoes (she inferred, correctly, into the sink).

"I thought it was known throughout all Christendom," she went on, "that one does not pour potato water down the sink. In this case it is used to make the roast beef gravy about which there was so much to-do. In the case of just a random cooking of a kettle of potatoes, you *save* the potato water. You pour it (after cooling) into a washed and stored peanut butter jar (of which we all have enough) and then the next day or two use it in making soup, or as the canful of water that is called for on the soup label.

"It does not matter that at times perhaps a week or two later one finds that potato water forgotten and bubbling in the back of the refrigerator and [that it] must then be thrown out—or rather, in this case, poured down the sink. One still has a warm, comforting glow in the thought that one did Save the Potato Water, as a good cook should."

Words to live by, Mrs. Holcomb, and thank you.

---

### Yet More Follow-Up

Margaret Schlegel, of Lakeville, Minnesota, took me sternly to task for the same infraction and added, "Real moms never use a meat rack. They are for fancy-smancy people, a real mom doesn't have one and you can't get good brown scrapings if you don't let the meat kind of bake onto the pan. Also you can make your gravy in a separate pan if you like doing dishes, but you must use some of your potato water in the roaster to cook up all the good brownings.

"Now I want you to try again, and see if you don't get real good real-mom gravy."

I'll do that. Thank you, too.

---

### Even More Follow-Up

Then Frances Dixon, of Nevis, Minnesota, wrote to object to my suggestions for coloring beef gravy:

"SURELY you must know that all you have to do to get that good brown color in your beef gravy . . . is to *brown* your flour in the drippings before adding the water. And really brown it—add the water just before the flour gets scorched."

Actually, I did know that. And stop calling me Surely. The reason I didn't mention it is the trickiness of stopping just *before* you scorch the flour. First-time cooks usually have difficulty with instructions that tell you to do something just before something awful happens. But it *is* good advice if you can follow it. Thank you.

---

### Touching Follow-Up

The nicest call I got was from a grateful woman who described herself as a new bride. "I know how to make all kinds of fancy things," she said, "but nothing *he* wanted."

A young marriage saved by a stewed chicken! How romantic!

---

# Food for the Twisted Mind

The quest for the ever-more-peculiar theme on which to hang a few recipes takes us sometimes to areas where, some folks might say, only fools rush in.

That I have rushed into those areas is either proof that those folks are wrong or proof that they are right.

In any case I would stoutly maintain that the food that has resulted from these efforts has been pretty decent—and that warm, forgiving individuals like your-selves, who are willing to forget about the strange themes and cleave only to the recipes, need feel no hesitation about adding them to your recipe files/drawers/boxes/heaps.

I would also stoutly maintain that if I didn't write something peculiar at the tops of these articles I wouldn't have anywhere to write down the occasional insight or odd thought that occurs to me, and that these unwritten insights and thoughts would eventually back up and make me ill.

(I maintain things like these even more stoutly since Thanksgiving, when I really overdid it on the gravy and dressing.)

All this is by way of saying that it should not surprise those of you who are keeping scrapbooks based on my life and food that I am prepared once more to boldly go where no man has gone before.

I was feeling a bit Euclidean the other day when it was time to choose a recipe theme—not plane awful, you understand, just a bit on edge—and I decided to venture into an area of geometricity not previously dealt with in this space: spirals.

I was catapulted into making this choice after spending a few minutes contem-plating a barber pole, affixed to which was a sign reading "Stylist." The origin of the red-and-white striped barber pole, it is said, is that barbers in years long past were the folks you went to if you wanted to be bled in order to rid yourself of some unpleasant condition. Granted that barbers don't do bloodletting any more (at least intentionally), I still found the notion of a bloodletting stylist a little unsettling.

But the pole started me thinking about spirals. Spirals (or, if you prefer, helixes) (or, if you prefer, helices) (parenthesis fans, please note this stunning collection) (and now back to our regularly scheduled program) are to be found almost everywhere in cooking, so it struck me that I would not have a difficult time at all coming up with a meal's worth of spiral food.

A nonparenthetical aside: Geometry purists may insist that a spiral is a plane figure and that a helix is a three-dimensional figure that circles around a central axis and may change in size (like a screw thread) or may not (like a spring), and that anyone who says a spiral is a helix or a helix is a spiral is clearly a cook. Such geometry purists do not have to deal with Webster's New World Dictionary, Second College Edition, from Simon and Schuster, which insists that spirals and helixes are the same.

I understand that David Guralnik, editor in chief of this dictionary, makes a great peanut-butter sandwich.

Anyway, back to spirals. The matter of endless rotation seems to have occupied our thoughts for quite some time. In popular music there are enough examples to make your head spin.

Those of us who are fully over the hill remember "That Old Black Magic" ("in a spin, loving the spin I'm in") and somewhat younger folks may have cut their teeth on Kay Starr's "Wheel of Fortune" (it went spinning around) or "Find a Wheel" (which Perry Como advised went " 'round, 'round, 'round"). There is also "To every thing (turn, turn, turn) there is a season (turn, turn, turn) . . ." and lots more. (If there isn't a stirring march commemorating the discovery of DNA, there ought to be. I'd call it "Under the Double Helix.") And where would we all be without Chubby Checker?

Anyway, if turning and turning is important enough to sing about over the years, a dinner dedicated to the subject shouldn't seem out of the question. So let's begin.

In the words of Major Edward Bowes, "Around and around she goes, and where she stops, nobody knows."

For an appetizer, I made a bunch of those little rolled-up things, sometimes called pinwheel sandwiches, with what I thought was a particularly nice filling.

---

### Blue-Cheese Appetizers

4 tablespoons butter (½ stick), warmed to room temperature
3 ounces cream cheese, softened
½ cup crumbled blue cheese (about ½ of a 4-ounce package)
2 tablespoons Cognac or brandy
6 thin slices bread (pumpernickel makes a nice color contrast)

Combine the butter, cream cheese, blue cheese and brandy. If you do this in a blender, you'll have the treat of seeing a sort of spiral form in the whirlpool or vortex over the blades.

(No, vortex is not a synthetic fiber or a manufacturer of inexpensive men's wear.)

Trim the crusts from the bread and spread the cheese mixture on each slice from edge to edge. Roll each slice tightly and chill for 30 minutes or so, then cut each roll into 4 or 5 sections.

Makes 24 to 30 bite-size appetizers.

---

For a vegetable to accompany the main course, I decided to make some broccoli-filled crêpes. See, viewed from the end, a rolled-up crêpe is in theory a spiral.

It's awfully hard to *see* the spiral, given the rather lumpy presence of the broccoli and the fact that to view a crêpe end-on one has to hold it in mid-air. But trust me; it's there. You may observe it when you cut the crêpe. So let's cut the crêpe ourselves and get to cooking.

## Broccoli-Filled Crêpes

### CRÊPES:

1 cup sifted flour
2 beaten eggs
¼ teaspoon salt
½ cup cold water
½ cup milk
2 tablespoons melted butter
2 (10-ounce) packages chopped broccoli

### WHITE SAUCE:

1 tablespoon minced shallots (optional)
½ cup (1 stick) butter
½ cup flour
2½ cups milk
Salt, pepper
2 teaspoons dry mustard

I can't tell you how to make the crêpes themselves every time we use them. We already had one long discussion in an article about crêpes and things made from a similar batter. Then we talked again about how to fry them when we served caviar and blini. We can't do it all again now or we'll never finish the textbook by the end of the semester.

Well, how many want to have crêpe-making explained again?

How many don't?

All right, all right, we'll do it again. But this is the last time. I'll do it a tad differently this time, just for the heck of it. It turns out the same anyway.

Those of you who have been paying attention may read ahead. If you have any questions about the new material, just raise your hands.

To make the crêpes:

Gradually beat the flour into the beaten eggs and salt. Slowly add water and milk, beating constantly. Finish by beating in the melted butter.

Heat a small iron skillet over low-medium heat and butter it lightly. Add a bit more than 2 tablespoons of the batter, tilting the pan to cover it with batter.

Cook each pancake for about a minute, until the bottom is lightly browned. (If that takes more than a minute, raise the heat slightly for the remaining crêpes or they will be dry. If the pan is too hot, on the other hand, the crêpe will start to bake before you can get the batter to cover the bottom of the pan.)

Cook the other side of the crêpe briefly.

Cool the crêpes, overlapping them slightly, on waxed paper. You'll have about a dozen.

Cook the broccoli according to package directions and drain very well.

Prepare the white sauce: Sauté the shallots in the butter until they are translucent. Stir in the flour and cook, stirring, about a minute. Slowly add the milk, stirring constantly. Stir in the salt, pepper and dry mustard. Cook until the sauce is thickened.

Preheat the oven to 350 degrees. Mix 1½ cups of the white sauce with the broccoli. Spread some of the broccoli mixture over half of a crêpe. Roll it up from the filled side and put the rolled crêpe in a 9-by-13-inch pan. Continue with the remaining crêpes. Pour remaining white sauce over them and warm for 10 to 15 minutes in the oven.

Makes about 12 crêpes—enough for 6 or more folks when served as a vegetable, or for 4 to 6 as a luncheon entrée.

For the main course, it seemed to me, there was no choice but to make rouladen—some folks, for reasons I can't imagine, call them birds. The French call them paupiettes. They are rolled-up thin pieces of meat with stuffing or something inside.

Having concluded that I had no choice, I changed my mind. A little. I made one big one instead of a bunch of small ones.

It was lovely.

---

## Giant Beef Roll-Up

4 slices bacon
1 (2 to 2½ pound) round steak (the full, flat round steak with both top and bottom portions and the little bone)
3 tablespoons Dijon mustard
½ teaspoon basil
2 medium onions
1 (10-ounce) package frozen chopped spinach
1 egg
1 teaspoon salt
¼ teaspoon pepper
Pinch nutmeg
2 pinches basil
1 clove garlic
1 slice sturdy bread or 2 slices balloon bread
1 cup (4 ounces) shredded Swiss cheese
Household twine or string
¼ cup or more vegetable oil
Salt, pepper
1½ cups dry white wine
1½ cups beef stock or 1 (10½-ounce) can beef bouillon
1 tablespoon cornstarch
2 tablespoons soft butter

Fry the bacon in a large frying pan. Drain the bacon, reserving 2 to 3 tablespoons of the fat, and crumble the bacon. Meanwhile, cut the round steak in half lengthwise; discard the bone or do with it whatever you normally do with it. Trim off fat.

Using a long, sharp knife, carefully cut each of the 2 pieces of steak in half edgewise—so that it is only half as thick. (This isn't really difficult, just kind of tedious.) But don't cut all the way through—leave about ½ inch uncut along one of the long edges so that each piece of meat can be opened like a tall butterfly.

If you go all the way through, it's no tragedy, nor is it terrible if the wings of the butterfly are of uneven thickness. The idea is just to come up with a lot of meat to roll.

Spread the mustard over the inside (cut) surfaces of the meat and sprinkle with the ½ teaspoon of basil. Set the meat aside.

Chop the onions and sauté them in the reserved bacon fat until they are translucent.

Prepare the spinach according to package directions. Drain, cool slightly, squeeze dry and add to onions, stir briefly and remove from heat.

Lightly beat the egg, then beat it into the spinach-onion mixture. Add the salt, pepper, nutmeg, a pinch of basil and the bacon bits. Put the garlic through a garlic press and add it.

Tear the bread into small pieces and stir it and the shredded cheese into the spinach mixture.

Put the butterflies of steak side by side, overlap them an inch or two and cover the meat with the stuffing, leaving an inch uncovered all the way around the edge. Starting at an edge parallel to the "seam" between the two pieces, roll up the meat and stuffing. You'll wind up with a roll maybe 12 inches long and 4 inches in diameter.

Slip lengths of the string or twine under the roll in the middle and near each end and tie it reasonably tight. (As the meat

*(Continued)*

cooks it will assume the roll shape all by itself, allowing you to cut away the string before serving.) Preheat the oven to 450 degrees.

Pour a thin layer of oil into a metal 9-by-13-inch pan and put the meat into the pan seam side up. Put the pan on a surface burner and heat gently to brown the meat. Wiggle a spatula under the meat after a few minutes to keep it from sticking. Pour a little of the oil over the top of the meat and put it in the oven, basting every few minutes until the entire roll is browned (about 15 minutes).

Remove the meat from the oven and reduce the oven temperature to 325 degrees. Spoon off most of the oil from the pan. Salt and pepper the meat, and toss a bit of basil on it. Pour in the wine and beef stock. Cover the pan with foil and bake, basting every half hour or so, until the meat is tender (about 2 hours).

Using a couple of metal spatulas, lift the meat out of the juice, allow it to drip—if it isn't in the process of falling off the spatulas—and put it on a serving platter. Cut and remove the strings.

Pour the juices into a small saucepan. In a cup, combine the cornstarch and 2 tablespoons of the cooking liquid. Add to the cooking liquid in the saucepan and heat, stirring, until the liquid thickens. Stir in the butter in small bits. Pour some of the gravy over the meat and serve the rest in a gravy bowl.

Serves 6 to 8.

---

Obviously one needs to serve something of a potato/pasta nature to sop up all the nice gravy from the giant beef roll-up.

Mashed potatoes would be fine. So would noodles.

I couldn't decide.

So I rolled up some mashed potatoes in some lasagne noodles. (Don't be concerned; it will not harm you. It's only me pursuing something I'm not sure of.)

The result was odd, but likable. The ruffled edges of the lasagne noodles gave these little bundles a very fancy appearance.

I served them on end, so diners could admire the spiral. Those guests who unroll them and eat only the mashed potatoes should be remembered when it comes time to issue invitations for another evening.

---

## *Spirals of Starch*

**6 lasagne noodles**
**8 ( ½-cup) servings mashed potatoes**
**  (from 6 or 7 potatoes)**

**¾ cup shredded Cheddar cheese**
**1 to 2 tablespoons butter**
**2 to 3 tablespoons Parmesan cheese**

Preheat the oven to 325 degrees. Cook the lasagne noodles according to package directions. Drain.

Meanwhile, prepare the mashed potatoes as you usually do, adding salt and pepper to taste. Stir in the Cheddar cheese.

Working fairly rapidly, lay one of the lasagne noodles flat; spread it thickly with the mashed potatoes and roll it up. Repeat with remaining noodles and potatoes.

Lightly oil a baking sheet and stand the cylinders on end. Dot them with the butter and sprinkle with the Parmesan.

Bake 5 to 10 minutes, to heat through. (If you worked slowly and the potatoes got cold, you may have to heat them longer. But if you heat them too long, the noodles will get tough.)

Makes 6 servings.

For dessert, I'm sorry to report, I did not make a chocolate cake roll. I had made one not all that long ago, and it didn't seem reasonable to repeat it, although it would have been very chocolate.

Instead, I made pinwheel cookies. I must say that the guests at the spiral meal liked them a lot, but I found them rather bland.

If you like plain butter cookies, you'll love these. If you like your cookies a bit more flavorful, I'd punch up the chocolate content.

---

### Pinwheel Cookies

½ cup (1 stick) butter
½ cup sugar
1 egg
½ teaspoon vanilla
1½ cups sifted flour
¼ teaspoon salt
½ teaspoon cinnamon
3 drops red food coloring
1 (1-ounce) square semisweet
   chocolate

Cream the butter. Add the sugar and beat until the mixture is light and fluffy. Beat in the egg and vanilla.

Sift together the flour, salt and cinnamon and beat into the butter mixture.

Divide the dough into thirds. Stir the food coloring into one third. Melt the chocolate and stir it into another third. Leave the third third alone. (If you have a fourth third, you haven't been paying attention. Maybe your mind has been in a whirl.)

Lightly flour a sheet of waxed paper and roll out one of the thirds to a rectangle about 6 inches by 12. Repeat with the other colors of dough, each on a separate sheet of waxed paper.

Put another sheet of waxed paper on a cookie sheet. Invert the uncolored dough onto that sheet of waxed paper and peel off the waxed paper that is now on top of it. Turn the pink dough on top of the white dough and peel the waxed paper off it. Finish with the chocolate dough and remove the paper from it. Chill the stack of dough for 5 to 10 minutes.

Roll the dough up from the 6-inch side, producing a 6-inch-long roll. Wrap the roll in waxed paper and chill several hours. (If you don't chill the dough long enough, the cookies won't stay round when you slice them off the roll. A squashed spiral is not a pretty sight.)

Preheat the oven to 375 degrees, slice the dough into cookies (about 5 to the inch) and place them on an ungreased cookie sheet. Bake about 10 minutes; cool on racks. Makes 2½ dozen cookies.

---

Somebody sent David Guralnik a copy of this article, and he replied that although some folks distinguish between the helix and the spiral, most don't. Nobody, he noted, calls it a helical staircase.

He added that he does indeed make a great peanut-butter sandwich, using a kaiser roll and banana slices.

# Great Culinary Expectations

When I was attending college briefly in Madison, Wisconsin, many long years ago, I saw a woman attempting without success to enter a supermarket.

The door that she was trying to push open was operated by an electric treadle on the inside and had no handles on the outside. It bore a fairly large sign that said "OUT." It was next to a door with a large push handle and a similar sign that said "IN."

I walked up to her, pointed to the other door, and said, "I think *that* is the entrance."

"Oh," she said, smiling. "I'm from out of town!"

I'm not originally from Minneapolis myself, but I have been here long enough that I wouldn't ever think of using that excuse. (Now I say, "I'm sorry; I've been up all night trying to memorize the lyrics to 'Me and Little Ingeborg, We're Going Down to Smorgasbord.' ")

In fact, it would be hard to tell, except that I still usually pronounce Milwaukee without the "l," that I am not a native Minnesotan.

Like almost everyone else, if I'm served something that I don't like at a restaurant, I never complain. When the waitperson asks how everything is here, I say "Fine, thank you," and I pay my check and never come back. Who wants a confrontation?

Lots of people, particularly people from large Eastern cities, will never understand this, and most restaurant operators deplore it. They will tell you, if you ask them—and sometimes even if you don't ask them—that they would much rather have you complain (and maybe they would even rather give you some other food) than have you not come back.

That makes lots of sense, but expecting folks who would never complain about *anything* to overcome their natural tendencies in a public place—and in front of friends or associates—is a real uphill climb (as opposed to a downhill climb). Maybe what's needed is a form that could be presented with the food and quietly collected by the waitperson a few minutes later.

Is your food too:

☐ *Cold?*
☐ *Warm?*
☐ *Overcooked?*
☐ *Undercooked?*
☐ *Greasy?*
☐ *Soggy?*
☐ *Dry?*
☐ *Soft?*
☐ *Hard?*
☐ *Crunchy?*
☐ *Gooey?*
☐ *Other?* _____

On the other hand, it probably wouldn't work. No such list could cover every eventuality (there's hair in the soup, there's not enough hair in the soup).

And no Minnesotan of the sort we are trying here to aid would want to make a scene by filling in anything under "Other." Even were I provided such a card, for example, I don't think I could bring myself to use it to complain about a different kind of restaurant disappointment that happens to me once in a while: what I am served is just fine, but it isn't anything like what I pictured from reading the menu. And what I pictured sounded better.

On the *other* other hand, although I will never be able to jump up on the table, brandishing a laden plate and screaming *"THIS* is Greek chicken?" that doesn't mean the issue has to rest there.

I get to tell *you* about it, for one. And, if you're still listening, I get to tell you how to prepare some of those dishes the way I thought they would be.

Now for an admission more embarrassing than anything that might happen if I tried to send back a dry hamburger:

After I committed myself to writing this article (having immediately thought of two fine examples of such dishes), I couldn't think of any more. So we're going to have those two examples, plus several things I haven't been served but that sounded very good when I thought or heard of them.

Not much of a theme, I'll admit. But you're not likely to complain, so it'll be O.K.

To start the meal, a dish that I ordered in a restaurant in Mexico several years ago.

I don't speak Spanish, but even I could figure out Sopa de Lima. (Unless it was lime soap instead of lime soup.) I figured it would be cool, creamy and refreshing— just the ticket on a scorching evening.

It turned out to be a hot chicken broth very lightly flavored with lime. Not bad, but a rude surprise.

I looked at a number of cookbooks later, and if they had lime soup at all that's what they had.

Here's what I wanted:

---

### Cold Lime Cream Soup

2 ripe avocados (good luck finding 2 ripe ones at the same store)
2 (10¾-ounce) cans chicken broth
2 cups heavy cream
1 cup dry white wine
1 cup milk or half-and-half
1 tablespoon lemon juice
Salt, white pepper
Juice of 4 fresh limes (about ⅝ cup) or to taste

Mash and beat or purée the avocados until they have formed a smooth paste. (Peel them first and take out the pits—do I have to tell you *everything?* Someday you're going to be all alone in a great big kitchen, with nobody to help you, and *then* what will you do?)

Slowly add the chicken broth to the avocado, continuing to beat or whomp until the mixture is smooth.

Stir in the cream, wine, milk, lemon juice, salt and pepper. Then add the lime juice, tasting as you go. It will mellow somewhat as it is chilled, so you might go a little stronger than you are first tempted to do. (Ain't it funny how the lime slips away?)

Chill, covered.

Serves 8.

---

The following peculiar salad dressing is not something I was ever served, but it has lurked in the back of my mind for a long time, ever since I started playing with sauces. And that lurking thought resurfaces almost every time I'm in a restaurant that decorates the plate carrying my cheeseburger by adding a slice of tomato topped with a blob of mayonnaise.

Mayonnaise, I reason each time, in my own peculiar way, is made by beating oil into egg yolks and mustard. Egg yolk and melted butter, with different seasoning, makes hollandaise sauce, which is widely acclaimed as wonderful because you taste not only the seasonings, but also the butter. So why not make mayonnaise with melted butter instead of oil?

Why not, indeed?

It turns out that the only reason not to do it, unless you count cholesterol as a reason, is that it sets up rather chunkily when you refrigerate it, and it clearly can't be left around for hours unrefrigerated. So if you make it, do so just before you're going to use it, as you would with hollandaise sauce. Or figure on beating it after you take it back out of the refrigerator.

It is yummy enough to elicit oohs and ahhs.

## Mayonnoohs or Mayonnahhs

1 egg yolk
1/2 teaspoon Dijon mustard
Salt, pepper
Pinch of sugar
3/4 cup (1 1/2 sticks) unsalted butter, melted and cooled to room temperature
1 teaspoon white wine vinegar, or to taste

Put the egg yolk in a bowl and stir in the mustard, salt, pepper and sugar.

With a whisk or a sturdy wooden spoon, beat in a very small amount of the melted butter until it is fully bound into the egg mixture. Add a bit more and beat in. Continue adding and beating until it is all absorbed. After half the butter is in, you can begin to add it in somewhat larger increments, but don't get happy and add it too fast—it won't get taken up easily and you'll have a curdled mess. This is not a rapid process, nor one for somebody with weak forearms.

When all the butter is in, stir in the vinegar. Even if you normally use tarragon vinegar in making mayonnaise (an excellent choice), don't do it this time. The tarragon substantially overwhelms the butter flavor.

Serve somewhere that will allow the flavor to show. Just dolloped onto hard-cooked eggs is a typical French dish, and one that will bring the cholesterol count up to a nice round number.

Makes about 1 cup.

Back to the restaurant. Not long ago I had lunch with some friends at a local eatery and the waitperson (of course she introduced herself and explained her role in our dining experience when she arrived at the table, but in the intervening months I've forgotten her name; I'm sure she wouldn't remember us either) . . . anyway, she handed out menus and reeled off the several daily specials that were just too daily and too special to write down.

One of them, chicken with a Greek-sounding sauce, rather appealed to me. I can't remember what she said was in it (that's one of the problems of the Talking Menu; also you can't —unless you're from a large Eastern city—call the waitperson over four or five times to ask for another reading of several items as you try to choose among them). I do know it had a Greek sound; lemon and olive oil for sure.

I pictured that in a yogurty sauce much like comes with gyros, with maybe basil too. Wrong.

It was olive oil and lemon juice and, as far as I could tell, that was about all. Nice, but wrong.

This is what I had pictured:

---

### Greek Chicken

6 to 8 chicken breast halves, deboned and skin removed
3 to 4 tablespoons olive oil
1 cucumber
2 cups unflavored yogurt
3 cloves garlic, put through a garlic press

2 tablespoons lemon juice
½ teaspoon basil, crumbled
½ teaspoon crushed anise seed
Salt, pepper
2 tablespoons cornstarch
¼ cup water

In a large frying pan, sauté the chicken breasts in the olive oil, cooking about 5 minutes over medium heat on each side.

While the chicken is cooking peel the cucumber, cut it in half lengthwise and run a spoon down each half to remove the seeds. Slice the halves.

Combine the cucumber, yogurt, garlic, lemon juice, basil, anise seed, salt and pepper. Heat in a saucepan.

Combine the cornstarch and water and stir into the hot yogurt sauce. Cook 5 minutes over medium heat.

Pour the sauce over the chicken, lower the heat and allow it to simmer 5 minutes or until the chicken is done. Makes 6 to 8 servings.

---

While I was trying frantically, and unsuccessfully, to remember a dessert misexpectation, I recalled an occasion on which a few orange segments from a salad I had taken out of defensiveness wandered across my plate and mingled with some rice. It was a nice flavor.

You know, I told myself (I *didn't* know, but it all worked out anyway), orange would be a real nice *dessert* flavor, but in something cold and creamy, sort of like I pictured the lime soup.

---

### Orange Pudding

2¼ cups milk
4 tablespoons sugar, divided
¼ cup cornstarch
¾ cup orange juice
1 egg

1 teaspoon grated orange rind (optional)
2 tablespoons Grand Marnier (optional)

Heat the milk in a saucepan until it just comes to the boil. Remove from the heat.

Combine 2 tablespoons of the sugar, the cornstarch and orange juice and stir into the hot milk. Stir over low heat until the mixture thickens.

It will curdle a bit because of the orange juice, but hang in there. It will get almost fully smooth.

Beat the egg with the remaining 2 tablespoons of sugar. Stir in a little of the hot mixture, then pour the diluted egg into the hot mixture and stir. Stir the whole thing over low heat just until it thickens again. Remove from the heat.

When the pudding has cooled 10 or 15 minutes, stir in the orange rind and/or Grand Marnier.

Pour into serving dishes and chill. Makes 6 servings.

---

This second dessert (lucky, lucky!) is one that I had thought of once and forgotten until a friend mentioned that he had seen it in a shop window in a Greek neighborhood in Detroit. What a natural combination—chocolate and baklava!

My first attempt to make it failed because, unbeknownst to me, my oven had quit working.

It was still hot from something else when I put the choclava in for its 1½-hour sojourn, so it wasn't until much later that I discovered that the choclava had been cooling its heels, so to speak.

It had dried instead of baking, and the top sheet of filo dough had curled up and died. It was not pretty.

Thinking it could be repaired, I drove it to a friend's house and baked it there, but it didn't look much better. Hoping against hope that the pouring-on of the finishing syrup would somehow have a resuscitating effect, I drove it home, made the syrup and poured it on.

Not only didn't the syrup do any good, it didn't soak in—it just swam around the pan, threatening to run over at any number of places.

A quick check of other recipes indicated that maybe the baklava should have been hot when the syrup was poured on. (Some say hot syrup, cool baklava; others say hot baklava, cool syrup. This is probably one of the things that ruins marriages in that part of the world.)

The oven was still out, so I did the only thing I could think of: I cleared out the dishwasher, set it to the dry cycle, and ran the choclava through twice.

Nope.

I served it anyway, and there were polite noises from one or two folks, but I decided to make it again after fixing the oven.

That was muuuch better. If I were to make it a third time, I might increase the chocolate level a bit. I haven't tried that yet, because this is a time-consuming recipe. What the world needs is a faster version. We could call it ticktocklava.

If you don't like the idea of the chocolate and want to stick with the standard version, just omit the chocolate. That way, it's stocklava.

If you like it warm but you don't want to keep the kitchen hot, you could reheat it on your car engine. That's blocklava.

I don't recommend that you substitute margarine for the butter in this very rich dessert. In some things that works fine, but here I'm afraid you'd wind up with shlocklava.

I'll grant that butter is more expensive, but it's worth it in something like this. If you need to borrow a few bucks to make it, it's worth going into hocklava.

If that sounds like a bad idea, and you don't want to go through all the business with the filo dough either, you could try making the whole thing with Ritz crackers. That would be mocklava.

The recipe makes quite a large amount, and given the effort and expense (if you make it the right way) you certainly wouldn't want any of the leftovers stolen, so you'd better check your locklava.

(Slap.)

Thanks, boss. I needed that. Time to start cooking.

Put on your smocklava and . . . No! I promise! I won't do that anymore.

### *Choclava*

1 (1-pound) package frozen filo dough
1 pound walnuts
½ cup sugar
1½ teaspoons cinnamon
3½ sticks unsalted butter, divided
8 (1-ounce) squares semisweet
    chocolate (or 1⅓ cups chips)

SYRUP:

3 cups sugar
2 cups water
1 tablespoon lemon juice

Thaw the filo sheets according to package directions. (This takes overnight.)

Chop the walnuts very fine or whomp them in a food processor until they are coarse crumbs. Stop before they turn into flour. We want a little texture. Stir in the sugar and cinnamon. Set aside.

Trim the stack of filo sheets to the size of a large raised-edge baking pan (11 by 17, or 10 by 15 if that's the biggest you have).

Cover the stack of filo with a just-barely-damp cloth, and always keep it covered while working. Melt 2 tablespoons of the butter in a small saucepan. In a large saucepan, over very low heat, melt the remaining butter with the chocolate, stirring constantly, just until the chocolate is melted. Remove from heat.

Brush the baking pan with the plain melted butter. Lay one sheet of filo onto the pan and brush it thoroughly with the chocolate-butter mixture. Top with another filo sheet and brush with more chocolate butter. Continue until you have built up 10 sheets. Stir the chocolate butter occasionally to keep the chocolate from settling. If necessary, rewarm it gently.

After the tenth sheet is brushed with chocolate butter, sprinkle it evenly with about ½ cup (about 4 fistfuls) of the nut mixture. Top with 2 more sheets of filo, brushing each with chocolate butter, and then sprinkle on 4 more fistfuls of nuts. Continue until almost all the sheets of filo are used, brushing each sheet with chocolate butter and topping every second sheet with the nut mixture. The topmost 2 (or 3, depending on how it works out) sheets should not have nut mixture (just

chocolate butter) between them. Brush the top sheet with chocolate butter.

Preheat the oven to 350 degrees.

With a sharp knife, cut the choclava (yes, before it's baked) into not-quite-diamond shapes, as follows: Make a series of parallel cuts about an inch apart lengthwise down the pan. Then make another series of parallel cuts not crosswise but diagonally, about 2 inches apart. Clear? If not, cut it any way you want.

Smooth out the pieces of the top layer that lifted while you were cutting. If you have extra chocolate butter, have faith that you'll think of something to do with it. If you never have such thoughts, pour it over the top. Bake at 350 degrees for 30 minutes, then lower the temperature to 300 degrees and bake 1 hour more.

About 30 minutes before the choclava is to be done, prepare the syrup:

In a large saucepan, stir together the sugar, water and lemon juice until the sugar has dissolved. Cook over high heat, without further stirring, until the mixture boils, lower the heat and boil it 20 minutes.

Allow the syrup to cool briefly if it is done before the choclava is. Spoon about two-thirds of the syrup over the hot choclava, allowing it to soak in nicely. An hour later, spoon on the rest of it. Allow it to rest several hours before serving. Makes about 5 dozen pieces if the larger baking sheet is used.

I am told that baklava will keep for several weeks if merely covered with plastic wrap and not refrigerated. It can also be frozen, I am informed. I don't know; I didn't have that much left.

# An Upper Midwest Festival
# of Hot Dishes

When I was growing up in Milwaukee, we had no word for the strip of grass between the sidewalk and the street. When we had to call it something, we called it "the strip of grass between the sidewalk and the street." Actually, it was amazing how many days in a row would sometimes pass in which it was never referred to at all.

In other places, it turns out, there are names for that patch of turf. Different names in different places. It is called, among other things, and depending on where you are, the carriage walk, the parking, the tree lawn, the parkway, and the boulevard.

In Milwaukee, as in the Twin Cities, we used the word "boulevard" to refer to a fancy street with a strip of grass down the middle; sometimes it also was used to refer to that strip of grass. In Milwaukee it never had any more than those two meanings.

If you're on your toes, you can see fate beginning to throw the switches, setting my upbringing in Milwaukee on a collision course with my young-adulthood in a Minneapolis suburb.

Shortly after I moved to the Twin Cities, many long years ago, somebody with whom I worked was having a party and I was invited. He lived in an area in which there were neither sidewalks nor curbs, and what he told me was something like this: "There'll be lots of cars. Just pull up onto the boulevard."

I remember being incredulous, and saying "Really?" Or maybe, "No kidding?"

Of course, what he meant was to park on the grass instead of out on the street, but when I showed up that area was already full of cars. Incredibly enough, given the nature of the misunderstanding that had occurred, this guy actually did live on what I would without hesitation call a boulevard. There was a fairly narrow grass strip separating two one-lane roadways. With only slight hesitation, I pulled my car onto the grass strip between the two lanes.

I had been at the party only a few minutes, possibly still trying to figure out exactly what was meant by "Have a bump" (a local expression, it turns out, for "Would you care for a drink?"), when my genial host wandered over and asked if I had had any trouble finding the place.

Nope; directions were fine.

Any difficulty finding a place to park?

Nope; parked out in the middle of the street.

I realize that my error was not really the equivalent of having walked into a saloon arm in arm with Black Bart's girl, but it had that impact upon me. I was new, I didn't really know anyone and I could have sworn that every conversation in the room had ceased just before I made that announcement.

I just heard a few weeks ago that some researchers have asked people their biggest fears, and that the one that was mentioned most often was looking foolish in public, followed by nuclear holocaust. Ignoring what that says about our priorities, at that long-ago moment in Fridley I would certainly have agreed that being publicly stupid is very unpleasant. I went out to move my car. My memory of subsequent events has faded, but I wouldn't be surprised to learn that I didn't go back to the party.

Not long ago a colleague told about a similar misunderstanding into which a friend of his had fallen. She was new to the Upper Midwest and was invited to a potluck dinner. Her instructions were to "bring a hot dish." At this point in hearing my colleague's story I already knew all, because when I moved here I had never heard of hot dishes either. We called them casseroles.

This poor soul, anyway, anxious to please, brought to the gathering a plate suitable for holding a steak—and she had spent quite a few troubled hours trying to figure out how to keep it hot.

There is a certain disdain for hot dishes today, much of it from the trendier among us. Young professional types seem to regard canned cream of mushroom soup as the work of the devil. One suspects that in a modern remake of *Gone with the Wind,* Scarlett would look up from the ruins of her Jacuzzi and say, "As God is my witness, I will never eat hot dish again!"

What this means is that our hot-dish heritage is in jeopardy. Recipes involving green beans, cream of mushroom soup, French-fried onion rings and Tater Tots are in peril of being lost forever!

It was with the fervent hope that those unfortunate individuals who are feeding their children only radicchio and tofu could be brought once more to seeing the hot dish as the next-best thing to being there that I decided to embark upon an entire festival of hot dishes.

I must note in passing that I attempted to decide just what exactly makes something a hot dish. It wasn't easy.

It turns out to be, I think, one of those instinctive things. Generally something is clearly a hot dish or it's clearly not, but the rules aren't obvious at all. It has to be hot, for sure. It can't just be a single piece of meat, like a chicken or a steak. I figured it had to be spooned up rather than cut, but I was reminded that at any gathering where hot dishes are called for there will be several dishes of lasagne. A hot dish doesn't have to have noodles, but it probably has them—or rice or potatoes. It probably has vegetables, too, but not always. At the very least it is a mixture of stuff and it is finished in the oven rather than in a saucepan on the top of the stove. Or maybe not.

Clear? O.K. Preheat the oven to 350 degrees, grease up a few oven-safe 1½-quart dishes and let's start making the Food of the Northland!

There is really no such thing as a hot dish that is an appetizer, but I made an appetizer that is hot, finished in the oven and—possibly the most basic of all hot-dish criteria—transportable to somebody else's house hot and wrapped in newspaper.

---

*Tuna (or Crab) Appetizer Hot Dish*

1 round 1½-pound loaf of bread
1 long loaf of French bread
⅓ cup slivered almonds
1 (6½-ounce) can tuna (or 1 8-ounce bag frozen crab or mock crab, thawed)
1 (8-ounce) package cream cheese, softened
¼ teaspoon onion powder
1 tablespoon milk
1 or 2 hard-cooked eggs, chopped
½ teaspoon Worcestershire sauce
½ teaspoon lemon juice
¼ teaspoon basil
¼ teaspoon salt
Dash pepper
⅛ teaspoon Tabasco

Cut a thin slice off the top of the round loaf of bread. Set the slice aside. Hollow out the bread, tearing the removed bread into bite-size pieces. Tear or cut up the French loaf, too. Let the pieces sit out uncovered for several hours to firm them up for use as dippers.

Preheat the oven to 375 degrees. Toast the almonds on a baking sheet 5 to 7 minutes, until they just begin to color. (Leave the oven on.)

Combine the toasted almonds, tuna or crab, cream cheese, onion powder, milk, eggs, Worcestershire, lemon juice, basil, salt, pepper and Tabasco. Heap into the hollowed-out bread and bake for 20 minutes.

Serves 6 to 8.

If you are transporting the hot dish to what they call in so many businesses these days "a remote facility" (anyplace other than your place), cover with the removed slice of bread and wrap in newspaper. (The food section makes excellent hot-dish-wrapping material). We would prefer that you put it to that use, rather than turn it into bird-cage liner.)

---

Next we come to something that was a definitional problem even before we got it and made it into a hot dish: salad.

What makes something a salad? I am an admitted nonexpert on the subject of salads (I tend to wish they would go away and leave more room on my plate for dessert), but if I had to answer without any thought at all I would have said that a salad was an item served cold, uncooked and with one or another variety of leafy green in it.

Contrast with that such things as potato salad and any number of pasta salads, and you can see what a sorry state the matter of salad definition is in. That state is so sorry that it doesn't even bother about prepositions at the ends of sentences. So it certainly isn't going to mind if I make a hot salad with pasta and call it a hot-dish salad.

## Chicken Salad Hot Dish

2 (10¾-ounce) cans chicken broth
3 chicken breast halves, skin and
bones removed (about 1 pound
deboned chicken)
7 to 8 ounces pasta shells
¾ cup unsalted cashews

½ cup mayonnaise
½ tablespoon lemon juice
½ teaspoon basil
1 teaspoon grated fresh ginger
1 (8-ounce) can mandarin-orange
segments, drained

Bring the chicken broth and 1 soup can of water to a boil in a large saucepan or small Dutch oven. Add the chicken, reduce heat and simmer until the chicken is tender—about 15 minutes.

Remove the chicken; retain the liquid.

Cook the pasta shells according to package directions, but using the chicken cooking liquid (plus water as needed) instead of the water called for on the package. Drain.

Meanwhile, cut the cooked chicken into small bite-size pieces.

Preheat the oven to 400 degrees. Toast the cashews on a baking sheet 5 to 7 minutes, stirring once, until they have colored slightly. Lower the temperature to 350 degrees.

Stir together the mayonnaise, lemon juice, basil and fresh ginger.

Combine the chicken, the pasta, all but ¼ cup of the cashews, and the mayonnaise mixture. Turn the mixture into a greased oven-safe dish. Arrange the orange segments around the edge of the dish.

Garnish with the remaining cashews, cover and bake 20 to 25 minutes, or until it is heated through.

Serves 6.

---

All right. We've broken a little new ground, had our bit of fun with food, and gotten well beyond the part of the article that was on the first page. (Lovers of jargon, note: the part of the article that doesn't fit on the "cover" page is called the "jump." Because the page you are reading contains a jump, it is a "jump page." Wasn't that edifying?) Now, given how much of what we had to do is already done, it is time to get to a good-old *hot-dish* hot dish.

This one is meatless, but that's O.K., isn't it?

---

## Zippy Spinach H.D.

2 (10-ounce) packages frozen chopped
spinach
5 tablespoons butter, divided
2½ tablespoons flour
½ cup half-and-half
1 teaspoon garlic salt
½ teaspoon celery salt
½ teaspoon onion powder

½ teaspoon pepper
1 (8-ounce) can sliced water chestnuts,
drained
6 ounces (1½ cups) shredded sharp
Cheddar cheese
1 teaspoon lemon juice
1 (4-ounce) can chopped green chilies
2 tablespoons bread crumbs

Prepare the spinach according to package directions. Drain, reserving ½ cup of the cooking liquid.

Preheat the oven to 350 degrees.

Melt 4 tablespoons of the butter in a small saucepan. Stir in the flour and cook over medium heat, stirring, 1 minute.

Slowly add the half-and-half, stirring all the while. Then stir in the garlic salt, celery salt, onion powder, pepper and the reserved spinach cooking liquid. Continue to cook and stir until the sauce is thick and smooth.

Stir in the water chestnuts, cheese,

lemon juice, spinach and chilies and turn into a greased 1½-quart baking dish. Sprinkle with crumbs and dot with the 1 remaining tablespoon of butter. Bake 25 minutes. Serves 6.

---

So much for normal. Now for interesting.

This is a cross between hot dish and pizza, with an overtone of chop suey. Of things I've made that I haven't had before, it was one of the most pleasant in quite a while.

It has in abundance a hot-dish characteristic that I didn't discuss in the definitional material because it isn't what makes something a hot dish—but it's certainly true of hot dishes: Each forkful seems to weigh about a pound. Eat a pile of this and you won't be hungry!

---

### Pizza-Rice Hot Dish

1 medium onion
1 green bell pepper
1 red bell pepper (or a 2nd green one)
6 slices bacon
4 tablespoons butter
½ pound (1¼ cups) uncooked rice
2 chicken bouillon cubes
1 (about 4-ounce) jar pimiento-stuffed olives
2 ounces (½ of a 4-ounce package) thinly sliced pepperoni
8 ounces (2 cups) shredded mozzarella cheese, divided

Chop the onion fine. Cut the peppers into rings, removing the core and seeds. Cut the bacon into 1-inch squares.

Melt the butter in a Dutch oven, add the bacon and fry until it has begun to color. Add the onions and the pepper rings and sauté until the onions are translucent.

Stir in the uncooked rice and continue to cook, over low-medium heat, stirring continuously with a wooden spoon, for 3 minutes.

Meanwhile, dissolve the bouillon in 3½ cups of very hot water. Preheat the oven to 350 degrees.

Stir a glug (you know: glug, glug, glug—maybe ⅓ to ½ cup) of the bouillon into the rice mixture and keep stirring until the liquid is absorbed. Add the olives, with their liquid, then stir in another glug of bouillon until the liquid is absorbed.

Continue to add the bouillon in this peculiar fashion, a glug at a time. When the last of it is in, add the pepperoni and 1½ cups of the cheese. Stir and pour into a greased 1½-quart casserole.

Bake the mixture 30 minutes, top with the remaining ½ cup of cheese and bake 5 to 10 minutes longer, until the cheese is melted. Serves 6.

---

Hot-dish dessert? Why not?

No, not a pan of warm brownies, although little could be said against that dessert on general principle.

What we need here is a bowl of warm, *gloppy* stuff. It is in the gloppiness, I feel, that we find the true essence of the hot dish. A hot dish is something that would not be practical to eat with the hands even if it had cooled off a bit and nobody was looking.

But a hot dish should be transportable, so a not-so-gloppy element on the top is always welcome. The following is a perversion of a classic English recipe that is always assembled and served cold. (See, for example, the chocolate version elsewhere in this volume.) This one is a bit strange.

I must admit that I detected a fair amount of underdone cake batter in the finished product, but only because I knew what I was looking for. In terms of taste, texture and other things that count, I think this is a winner. (Your mom was not correct. Eating uncooked cake batter is not bad for you. It may not be *good* for you, but then neither is cooked cake batter.)

---

### Trifle Hot Dish

¼ cup slivered almonds
Yellow cake from 1 (18½-ounce)
    package yellow cake mix
Vanilla pudding from 1 (4¾-ounce)
    package pudding mix, not instant

½ cup seedless raspberry jam
½ cup sherry
1 cup heavy cream

Toast the almonds on a baking sheet in a 350-degree oven for 5 to 7 minutes, just until they are starting to color.

Prepare the cake batter according to package directions. Bake half of it, according to directions, in an 8- or 9-inch round pan. Set the rest aside.

While the cake is baking, prepare the pudding according to package directions. Let cool.

Cool the cake on a rack, and when it is fully cool cut it into 2 thin layers. Spread 1 layer with the jam, reassemble the cake, and cut it into pieces roughly 1 inch square. Put the little cake-jam sandwiches in the bottom (and up the sides if there are enough) of an oven-safe 2-quart bowl. (A bowl with near-vertical sides is nice; one with clear glass sides is great.) Pour the sherry over the little sandwiches. Let

them soak 5 minutes, then pour in the pudding.

Top with about half the remaining cake batter and bake the whole thing at 350 degrees for about 40 minutes. (You can throw the remaining cake batter out, bake it in a tiny loaf tin or eat it the way it is if your mom isn't looking.)

Whip the cream; serve in a separate bowl.

Serve the hot trifle right out of the oven by spooning it up like a soufflé (using two large spoons at once) to get some of each layer—cakey cake, smooth pudding, the peculiar not-too-cakey-cake-mixed-with-pudding layer in between, and the sherry-raspberry cake sandwiches on the bottom.

Nummy! Serves 8 to 10.

---

#### Little Mystery #8: Potatoes

Potato peeling is one of life's least exciting chores. How do the big guys, the firms that process zillions of pounds of potatoes a year, do it?

Do they hire thousands of sniveling wretches to peel potatoes one at a time with seventy-nine-cent peelers from supermarkets?

Do they tumble the potatoes like rocks?

Do they subject them to ultrasonic waves or expose them to green kryptonite?

**Solution:** I called Ore-Ida in Boise, Idaho (Ore-Ida is owned by H. J. Heinz), and a very

pleasant person there told me that, because their potato-peeling expert would be away for a few days, I should instead call the National Potato Promotion Board, in Denver, whose phone number she gave me. I said I might call her back later just to double-check.

It turned out to be the worst lead I've ever been given. The potato board, it seems, represents potato *growers,* not processors. What they do is public relations for people with fields full of potatoes, and they had no more idea of how processors peel potatoes than I did. Maybe less.

But they did give me a number for the potato part of R. T. French Company, in Shelley, Idaho. (R. T. French is owned by Reckitt & Colman, a London-based diversified producer of food products, household products, toiletries, pharmaceuticals, art supplies and heaven knows whatall.) There, anyway, I thought I hit pay dirt—or pay potato.

The French's spokesperson said that there are a number of ways to peel them, including tumbling, using brushes or abrasives—and that some processors use caustic chemicals.

Different methods to produce different products? No, said Mr. Potato Head, they're just different methods that somebody might use.

O.K. Which does French's use? Abrasives, he said, and also steam, a method in which "you hit them with a flash of steam and then the peel becomes very loose."

Well, then do you tumble it off, or does some-body pull it off, or what?

"To tell you the truth," the spokesperson said, "I'm in personnel, so I don't really know."

Potato-peeling advice from the personnel department! Now I'd really had it. I waited a few days for the Ore-Ida potato-peeling expert to return, and then I called again.

Here, finally, is the straight potato skinny, at least about how they do it at Ore-Ida:

Potatoes are put into a steam container and tossed around, and the combination of tossing and steam lifts off the peels. The potatoes are then dropped onto a conveyor and run through a gadget called a roller-polisher, which rubs off any remaining peel.

From the sound of it, the nearest thing available if you want to avoid peeling potatoes yourself, is to strap your potatoes to the roof of your car and take them through the car wash.

Let us know how it works.

---

### Little Mystery #9: Cocoa

Cocoa powder comes in an unusual can with a relatively small hole in the center of the top. When there's not much cocoa left in the can, that cocoa is rather difficult to get out. (You can turn the can from side to side, but lots of the cocoa always slides past the hole.) What is the approved manner of getting the last of the cocoa out of the can? (Or, put less politely, why is the can design so dumb?)

**Solution, of sorts:** A spokesperson for the Hershey Foods Corp., in Hershey, Pennsylvania, said, "I don't know why the can is shaped like that. I do know that it's difficult, and that some consumers do have a problem getting the last few tablespoons or teaspoons out of the can. And I will forward your concerns to our marketing department."

No. See, I'm writing this article, and I don't care if you *ever* change the can. I'd just like to know how to get the cocoa out or why the can hasn't been changed. Like, why doesn't the whole top come off? You could get all the cocoa out that way.

A different cocoaperson called back, wanting to know what I needed. I asked the question again, and this person, too (let's call him cocoaperson II), said, "That's true," when I got to the part about

it being very difficult to get the last of the cocoa out.

I asked him to see if he could find an approved method of cocoa removal or determine why the whole top of the can doesn't come off. He called back with a changed attitude and the following information:

"The can is shaped that way because it's Easy To Hold [he said those three words as if they were capitalized]. The hole in the top has been there for many years and there aren't a significant number of complaints."

As to the cocoa removal strategy: "It would come out pretty easily if you shake it."

I gathered that at Hershey only someone who didn't know which side of the candy bar the letters are on would kick the can.

Cocoaperson II said as much: "It's a traditional item; it's one of our best items."

Perhaps if you use a vacuum cleaner . . . No. We'll think about this one some more.

(An added note, from information supplied by readers: Judicious use of a bottle opener actually does remove the entire top of the can—the part that isn't supposed to come off, too—so that one can pour the last of the cocoa right out. Isn't science grand?)

# The Roll-in-Butter Dinner

Somewhere recently I read a parody of career advice for aspiring journalists. It suggested that if you wanted to become a headline writer you should study the speech patterns of the Lone Ranger's faithful Indian companion, Tonto.

It is true that, as do Hollywood's version of Indians, headlines tend to omit articles, pronouns and auxiliary verbs. You would barely recognize that "Mayor Told Queeg Embezzler" is English unless you knew it to be a headline.

Headline writers have plenty of reason for writing that way. They have very little room in which to convey ideas that are sometimes quite complex.

Food writers, on the other hand, generally have lots of room in which to convey ideas that might easily be described as pretty alimentary.

Why, then, when they get right down to the recipes, do food writers tend to leave out articles, pronouns, nouns and more? Maybe you never thought about it, but what has come to be known as recipe style consists of writing sentences like this: "Put batter in cake pan; bake until done," instead of like this: "Put the batter in a cake pan and bake it until it is done."

It is true that recipes are slightly shorter when they are written as if they were telegrams, and it is possible that many years ago newspaper managers considered it a good idea to keep the recipes as brief as possible by eliminating half the words in them. But there seems to be much more room in newspapers now (how else can you explain the presence of such features as Orbit, Mother Goose & Grimm and the Dr. Joyce Brothers column?), so there doesn't appear to be very much weight behind that argument for fractured recipe syntax.

And it isn't at all persuasive as an explanation for recipe shorthand in the newer kind of cookbook—the kind with one brief recipe floating in the middle of each large page, facing a full-page color photograph of something like the author's favorite barn in Tuscany.

The best explanation of why most recipes are written as if they were subject to a per-word charge might be offered in this exchange from my favorite movie, *Young Frankenstein:*

(Howling sound.)

INGA, the lab assistant: "Werewolf!"

DR. FRANKENSTEIN: "Werewolf?"

IGOR: "There!"

DR. FRANKENSTEIN: "What?"

IGOR: "There wolf! There castle!"

DR. FRANKENSTEIN: "Why are you talking that way?"

IGOR: "I thought you wanted to."

In short, I think recipes are written in that peculiar way because recipes have long been written in that peculiar way and it's kind of a group habit.

Well, that's all very nice, you might be saying, but who cares?

Hang on a minute; I have not yet begun to make my point. And it's even stranger than what you have already read!

If you hadn't really noticed the missing words in recipes, then you probably never noticed either what some of those recipe instructions actually say if you step back and read them the way your high-school English teacher would. Some of them are very peculiar. Most of them sound as if cooking could be hazardous to your physical well-being.

The commonest examples are such things as "Stir onions until wilted." (The amount of onion-stirring needed to make you wilted, in case you aren't following me, varies considerably with how humid it is and when you had your last shower.)

There are plenty of variations of this sort of thing:

*Whip cream until stiff (which is not very long at all if you do it by hand).*
*Bake until puffed.*
*Stir until thickened.*
*Steam until bright green.*

Lots of recipes get much more interesting. (These are all real instructions, incidentally, lifted from recipes that have passed my way in the past few months.) I like to picture folks following these directions:

*Drain the pieces of meat, wipe dry and and roll in flour.*
*Stuff hens; tie legs together.*
*Cook over moderately high heat about two minutes or until browned on*
*    bottom.*
*Roll in cornmeal.*
*Put legs in boiling water.*

And my favorite of this genre: Roll around until covered with chocolate.

There is a third sort of odd instruction, the most amusing, of which I will permit myself but one example. If I put in my three favorite examples, all of them would most probably be deleted. This one is the safest of the three and might skate past:

Spoon avocado mixture onto each breast and top with remaining grated cheese.

I usually attempt, when writing or rewriting the recipes I use in these peculiar articles, to throw in all the pronouns, articles and stuff like that, in order to avoid such dubious phrasing. Sometimes I have wondered whether this fastidiousness is worthwhile. It certainly deprives careful readers of a few good laughs. So I decided for this week's dinner to select some nice-sounding food more or less randomly from cookbooks, and to rewrite the method in the opposite direction.

I don't know how this is going to turn out. If you're not very adventurous, maybe you should stop reading right here. On the other hand, with none of my usual constraints about selecting food to fit themes, I did manage to come up with a whole lot of very tasty dishes.

So let's cook and stir until hot and bubbly.

To start things off nicely, I made a broiled spinach appetizer on toast rounds. It was very, very nice indeed, and amenable to all kinds of scary-sounding instructions.

---

## Alarming Appetizers

TOAST ROUNDS:

1 (1½-pound) loaf bread (sliced the long way if possible, for slightly less waste)
3 tablespoons butter

TOPPING:

1 (10-ounce) package frozen chopped spinach

5 slices bacon
½ cup chopped green olives (with pimientos, if you like)
¾ cup (about 3 ounces) grated Parmesan cheese
¾ cup mayonnaise
2 tablespoons chopped green onion (green part)

Prepare toast rounds: Using 2-inch circle cutter or juice glass, cut rounds from each slice of bread. Reserve rounds. Break up remaining bread for birds, save for crumbs in another recipe, or toss in garbage. (If you elect to toss in garbage, shower before proceeding with this recipe.)

Melt butter in saucepan.

Put rounds on cookie sheets; broil on one side until lightly browned. Turn over, brush with melted butter and broil until golden brown. (Another shower is recommended if you're still greasy after broiling.) Set aside.

Prepare topping:

Cook spinach according to package directions. Rinse in cool water; drain well. (Wasn't that refreshing?) Roll into ball, squeezing hard. (For some of us, just squeezing hard won't be sufficient; it might take heavy machinery.)

Fry bacon until crisp. Crumble (especially if it's been a tough day) and drain on paper towels.

Combine spinach, olives, cheese, mayonnaise, green onions and bacon. Apply thickly to each toast round.

Slide under broiler for about 3 minutes, or until hot and puffy. (No comment.) Makes about 36.

---

Next came a soup that went over extremely well—and of which I hadn't expected very much. It is based on one in a meatless cookbook, and I was a little afraid that it would have a bit of that undefinable aura that sometimes manages to communicate, at least to habitual meat eaters, "This is a vegetarian dish." I removed some vegetables, and I substituted chicken broth for vegetable broth, so in the end all that this soup communicated, and not very subtly at all, was "This is good stuff!" Let's see how dangerous I can make it sound:

---

## Mushroom-Barley Soup

2 medium onions
1 pound mushrooms
6 tablespoons butter or margarine, divided
¾ cup uncooked barley

3 (10¾-ounce) cans chicken broth plus 3 cans water
1 teaspoon salt
¼ teaspoon pepper
1½ cups dairy sour cream

Chop the onions fine. Clean and slice the mushrooms. Heat 3 tablespoons of the butter in a Dutch oven, add onions and sauté until translucent. (Keep family members out of the kitchen at this stage, as the sight of a translucent cook may cause considerable trauma.) Rinse the barley in warm water and add it to the onions.

Add the broth and water, salt and pepper. Bring the mixture to the boil, reduce heat, cover and simmer until tender, about 1 hour. (If it's been a hard day it could take even longer for you to get tender. Some folks might take months.)

Meanwhile, heat the remaining butter in a frying pan, add the mushrooms and sauté until wilted and in a puddle of liquid. (Some days are *very* difficult, but get control of yourself!) Add the mushrooms and their liquid to the soup when the barley has cooked.

Thin the sour cream with a little hot soup, to make it easy to blend into soup, then put back into soup, stirring. (Remove back immediately, as soup is hot. Rinse back.) Serves 8 to 10.

---

This side dish was very well received also, even after the rather substantial presence of the soup.

---

## Tex-Mex Rice

1 cup uncooked white rice
1 clove garlic
1 green pepper
1 rib celery
1 large onion
3 tablespoons butter

2 to 3 teaspoons chili powder, or to taste
1 teaspoon salt
1 tablespoon chopped cilantro (optional)

Prepare the rice according to package directions. Meanwhile, finely chop the garlic, green pepper, celery and onion. Melt the butter in a frying pan and sauté garlic, green pepper, celery and onions until translucent. (Be sure not to sauté too long; I did that once, and when I tried to get the attention of the person behind a theater candy counter the next day, I found that I had gone all the way to transparent.) Add chili powder and salt; cook, stirring, for 5 minutes.

Stir in cooked rice and cilantro. Cook, covered, over low to medium heat, stirring occasionally, until heated through. (Go take a shower to cool off; you've earned it.) Serves 4 to 6.

---

I also produced a zucchini dish not worth much discussion except that it involved washing without peeling. (Small boys are very good at this.)

Here is the very pleasant main dish, with lots of lime flavor and a few surprises for the cook.

## Participatory Pork Chops

1 (6-ounce) can limeade concentrate
Flour for dredging
Salt and pepper
8 to 10 pork chops

3 tablespoons butter
1 (8-ounce) jar Major Grey chutney (a style, not a brand)
2 fresh limes, thinly sliced, divided

Combine limeade concentrate and only 2 cans water.

Put flour, salt and pepper in a paper bag. Drop 1 chop into bag. Shake until covered with flour. (It might take longer to cover you with flour if you close the bag. Take a shower.) Repeat with remaining chops.

In a large frying pan, over medium heat, melt butter and add 1 cup of the limeade. Cook chops in 2 batches, each as follows: Cook 10 minutes on one side. Turn; spoon on ½ the jar of chutney. (Shower later.) Cook 10 minutes more, covered. Turn over again and top with ⅓

of the lime slices. (Great for the complexion.) Cook 10 minutes more, covered, or until done. Remove to platter; cover with foil and keep warm. Add 1 cup of limeade to pan, then cook second batch of chops as above, adding chutney and lime slices when called for.

Return the first batch of chops to the pan with the second, adding a bit more limeade if needed, and heat through 5 to 10 minutes. Serve with sauce including cooked lime slices; scatter the remaining third of the fresh lime slices as decorations (but not too far; they can be hard to find). Serves 8 to 10.

Dessert was a variation of a magnificent French chocolate mousse and meringue creation I have made many times. I substituted cake layers for the meringue and soaked them in raspberry booze besides. Highly acceptable, to say the least.

## Chocolate Mousse and Raspberry Booze Cake

CAKE:

¾ cup (1½ sticks) unsalted butter or shortening
1½ cups sugar
3 eggs
2¼ cups cake flour
2½ teaspoons baking powder
1 teaspoon salt
¾ cup milk
1 teaspoon vanilla

½ cup raspberry liqueur (or other flavor that goes nicely with chocolate, such as orange or coffee) (optional, but very nice)

MOUSSE:

1 (12-ounce) package semisweet chocolate chips
¾ cup (1½ sticks) unsalted butter
5 eggs, separated, plus 3 egg whites
3½ tablespoons granulated sugar

Prepare the cake:

Preheat oven to 375 degrees. Grease and flour 2 eight-inch round cake pans. Cream butter or shortening with sugar. Add eggs one at a time, and beat mixture until fluffy (or, if you prefer not to get fluffy, stop when you are a bit punchy).

Sift together flour, baking powder and salt and add to butter mixture in thirds, alternating with milk. Add vanilla and beat mixture until smooth—or at least until slightly sophisticated.

Pour mixture into prepared pans and bake 20 to 25 minutes, until a toothpick inserted in center of a layer comes out clean. Cool on wire racks 10 minutes, then turn upside-down onto racks (be careful not to catch your clothing). Remove pans and cool completely. When cake layers are fully cool, slice each in half horizontally, and sprinkle cut surface of each with a portion of liqueur. Cover with plastic wrap to prevent drying.

Meanwhile, when cake goes into oven, prepare mousse:

Melt chocolate in a double boiler or over very low heat. Remove pan from heat and add butter, broken into small pieces. Stir constantly until butter is fully melted into chocolate. Allow mixture to cool, then stir in the 5 egg yolks, one at a time.

In large bowl of electric mixer, beat the 8 egg whites until very stiff (no comment), adding the sugar gradually after whites have begun to foam. Stir a bit of beaten egg white into chocolate mixture to lighten it, then combine chocolate mixture and egg whites by gently folding. (Sometimes when I get to this stage I go on past gently folding to outright collapsing.) Chill the mousse about 1½ hours, until it has become fairly firm.

Set one of cake layers on serving plate. Spread about a fifth of mousse on one of cake layers, going all the way to the edge. Top that mousse with another layer of cake and another fifth of the mousse. If at any time mousse begins to squish out from between lower layers, chill partially assembled cake until it is firmed up.

Put third layer of cake in place, top it with another fifth of the mousse and finish with last layer of cake, preferably one from the top of one of the original layers, finished side up, spreading it with rather a thin layer of mousse. Use remaining mousse to cover sides of the cake. Chill in refrigerator. (Take along a book and a blanket.) Serves 12.

# *A Resounding Meal*

There is nothing quite so annoying to an adult as to be in a car with a child—even a nice child—who is at the age at which it is fascinating to repeat endlessly some word or phrase.

A few minutes of "E-i-e-i-o, e-i-e-i-o, e-i-e-i-o, e-i-e-i-o, e-i-e-i-o, e-i-e-i-o, e-i-e-i-o, e-i-e-i-o, e-i-e-i-o," for example, inspired by an unthinking reference to Old Mac-donald, can reduce even an otherwise loving parent to contemplating things like tying the happy child to a bench at a bus stop and driving away.

In typical cases, no threat, promise or black glare is enough to silence this performance permanently. There may be a break for a minute or two, but it will be back.

And just when you think it cannot get worse, chances are the little nipper will begin to *sing* the same refrain.

It's not a pretty picture.

You might suppose that this phenomenon—known to people who like to put labels on things as "perseveration"—has nothing whatever to do with food. Regular readers of these effusions know from bitter and painful experience that it is possible to make some connection, however tenuous, between food and almost anything.

Others are about to see that awesome process for themselves.

There are a number of foods, perhaps you haven't noticed them, that exhibit the tendency we have been discussing—repeated sounds.

There is, for example, Lomi-lomi Salmon, the traditional luau appetizer. There are Ho Hos, the traditional Hostess snack cake. There are bonbons, there is steak tartare, there are pu-pu platters—there is more than enough, in fact, if one was silly enough to want to make it, to prepare a whole repast of echoic foods.

Welcome to the Echo Canyon Meal.

If you wanted to do a dinner like this right, of course, it should be served in Walla Walla, Pago Pago, Baden-Baden or Bora-Bora. Or, in a pinch, in Flin Flon. Under duress, you could also do it in Sing Sing. (Yes, nitpickers. Its name *was* changed to Ossining Correctional Facility. But it's been changed back to Sing Sing. Happy now?)

Failing to find an echoic location, it would be nice to invite someone with a name like Meyer Meier. Or maybe Nanette somebody (to whom you could spend the evening saying "No, No").

In any case, if we're going to get done before it's time to go night-night, we'd best start talking about some recipes. Chop-chop.

To start things off briskly, let's have a nice, cold spiked punch—the vodka version of a piña colada. Believe it or not, I found this headknocker in a church cookbook. Here is a smaller version of the original recipe, which could have put an entire congregation out of commission for a week.

### Chi Chi Punch

1 (6-ounce) can frozen lemonade concentrate
2 cups pineapple juice
1 (8½-ounce) can (the small one)
    cream of coconut
1 cup vodka
2 to 3 quarts 7-Up or similar beverage

Combine the lemonade concentrate, pineapple juice, cream of coconut and vodka. Freeze.

To serve, put a scoop of the frozen punch concentrate in a glass and fill with 7-Up.

Makes about 12 drinks.

(These are stronger than you think, so don't start tossing them down willy-nilly. You don't want to get drunk as a skunk.)

To start the meal itself (once the guests stagger to the table after their chi chi wing-ding), here's a soup that you might run into in a fancy restaurant.

Frankly, I wasn't particularly impressed with the distinctiveness of the expensive canned turtle soup that is one of the ingredients, so the next time I make this soup I would throw authenticity to the wind and instead use two cans of beef broth and a dash of sherry. Not as hotsy-totsy, but still okey-dokey. The recipe is from the *Dione Lucas Book of French Cooking.*

### Boula Boula Soup

6 tablespoons salted butter
1 small onion, finely chopped
2 ribs celery, finely chopped
3 cups shelled peas or 2 (10-ounce) packages frozen peas
Salt
Freshly cracked white pepper
¼ cup water
2 (14½-ounce) cans turtle soup, strained (3 to 4 cups; reserve the meat)
2 tablespoons flour
1 cup heavy cream, whipped

Melt the butter in a large, heavy pan. Add the chopped onion and celery. Stir and cook 2 minutes over low heat. Add the peas, a little salt and pepper and the water. Stir and mix. Cover and cook over very low heat until the peas are soft.

Remove the pan from the heat and stir in the flour and the strained turtle stock. Stir over low heat until the mixture comes to a boil. Simmer gently 2 minutes.

Purée the mixture in a blender. Return to the pan and, over very low heat, stir in the whipped cream, reserving 4 to 6 teaspoons of it for garnish. Cut the turtle meat into small dice and add to the soup. Top each bowl of soup with a teaspoon of whipped cream and serve. Serves 4 to 6.

For the main course, let's have a big platter of couscous.

Not only does couscous fit the theme of this meal, it also has the peculiar property of being the name of both the completed dish and one of the ingredients of that dish.

The ingredient couscous is a grain product that, when cooked, has a consistency somewhere between oatmeal and rice, over which the rest of the dish, a kind of chicken and lamb stew, is served.

Actually, the couscous grain is semolina, a wheat product made famous in two songs.

One is from a Danny Kaye movie: "Semolina, Semolina, tiny little thing . . ."

The other was a hit by Doris Day and Les Brown (and his Band of Renown): "Gonna take a semolina journey . . ."

## *Couscous* STEW:

2 large onions, chopped
2 tablespoons oil
1 clove garlic, chopped or put through a garlic press
1 (3-pound or so) cut-up broiler-fryer
1 pound lamb, cut into cubes as for stew
3 cups water
4 carrots, peeled and cut into 1-inch chunks
1 bay leaf
1 tablespoon salt
1/4 teaspoon pepper

1/4 teaspoon ground ginger
1 stick cinnamon
2 medium tomatoes, chopped
1 (16- to 20-ounce) can garbanzo beans
1 green pepper, cut into strips
1 cup raisins

COUSCOUS GRAIN:

1 (1-lb.) box (2 1/2 cups) couscous
2 1/2 cups water or 2 (10 3/4-ounce) cans chicken broth
1 teaspoon salt (omit if using broth)
2 or more tablespoons butter

Sauté the onions in the oil in a large frying pan, adding the garlic after 2 or 3 minutes. Continue to sauté 2 or 3 more minutes, until the onion is beginning to turn golden. Transfer the onions and garlic to a Dutch oven.

Adding oil if necessary, brown the chicken pieces and the lamb in the skillet that was used for the onions, and transfer them to the Dutch oven.

Put the water in the skillet and bring it to boiling, using a wooden spoon to scrape up bits of meat that stuck to the pan. Pour the water over the meat. Stir into the mixture in the Dutch oven the carrots, bay leaf, salt (yes, that's a lot, but this is a lot of stew), pepper, ginger and cinnamon. Simmer 40 minutes.

Stir tomatoes, garbanzo beans, green pepper and raisins into the stew and simmer about 30 minutes more, until the meat and vegetables are tender. Remove the bay leaf.

A side note about the couscous grain. It's available in lots of supermarkets, and almost invariably it is an "instant" or "quick-cooking" version (although it is not always labeled that way). Noninstant couscous has to cook for something like 30 or 40 minutes; the kind you're likely to find cooks in 5 minutes or less.

If you can't find couscous, substitute brown rice or kasha, cooked according to label directions.

In any case, starting when necessary to get the couscous and stew done simultaneously, prepare couscous according to package directions—something like this for quick-cooking versions: Bring to the boil a volume of salted water (or broth) equal to the volume of the couscous. Add the couscous, cover and let stand 5 minutes off the heat.

(If there's lots of liquid in the stew, you might want to substitute a cup or so of it for some of the boiling water or broth used to prepare the grain.)

When the couscous grain has been thus cooked, put it in a strainer and suspend it over the bubbling stew for 5 minutes (with the cover over all). Then turn the grain into a bowl, toss it with the butter and spread it onto a large platter. Spoon the stew over that and serve.

Serves 8.

---

If you like, spoon off another cup of the stew liquid at some point and use it to prepare the traditional hot sauce.

In terms of echoic titles, this isn't so strong as to be Hot-Hot Sauce, nor is it mild enough to be Not-Hot Sauce. I wouldn't want to call it So-So Hot Sauce, because that gives the wrong impression. So let's just call it Hot Sauce.

As Doris Day (we called her Dodo) would point out, "Que sera sera."

---

### Hot Sauce (for Couscous)

1 cup stew liquid
2 tablespoons tomato paste
1 teaspoon paprika
1 teaspoon (or more) crushed dried
hot red peppers
¼ teaspoon coriander
½ to 1½ teaspoons cumin
1 teaspoon black pepper

Combine all ingredients and warm over low heat.

---

When I made the couscous for the Echo Canyon Meal I didn't make the hot sauce; I made it later and tried it with the leftovers. Instead I made Chowchow Relish, something I'd never heard of but that is apparently quite widely known. (Actually I didn't make the relish *instead* of the hot sauce; I simply forgot to make the hot sauce.)

Chowchow Relish is normally made in large batches and canned. I made a small batch, which would be excellent for getting rid of some leftover vegetables.

---

### Chowchow Relish

1 cup chopped cabbage (about ¼ head)
¾ cup chopped cauliflower (about ¼ head)
1 small onion, chopped (about ½ cup)
1 tomato, chopped
½ of a sweet red pepper, chopped
1 medium green pepper, chopped
2 teaspoons salt
½ cup plus 2 tablespoons cider vinegar
¼ cup plus 2 tablespoons sugar
¾ teaspoon dry mustard
¼ teaspoon turmeric
⅛ teaspoon ginger
½ teaspoon celery seed
Dash white pepper

Note: To make a canning-size batch, quadruple this recipe.

In a bowl combine the chopped cabbage, cauliflower, onion, tomato and red and

*(Continued)*

green pepper. Sprinkle with salt and let stand in the refrigerator 4 to 6 hours. Drain well.

Combine vinegar, sugar, mustard, turmeric, ginger, celery seed and pepper. Simmer 10 minutes, add vegetables and simmer 10 minutes more.

At this point, if you're making a larger batch to can, pack it, boiling hot, into hot jars, leaving ¼ to ½ inch headspace. Process 10 minutes and adjust caps.

If you're not canning but just making this small batch, boil it gently, covered, 10 to 15 minutes longer, until most of the liquid has evaporated. Keep it refrigerated. This recipe makes 2 cups.

For an odd vegetable with this meal, I decided to prepare some seasoned lentils.

This legume, as you may or may not know, is referred to on the Indian subcontinent and in the Middle East as dal or dhal.

Cooked lentils are usually kind of mud-brown and rather bland. When perked up with my favorite seasoning they are still rather unattractive, but they are quite pleasant to the taste.

### *Dill Dhal*

2 cups dry lentils
6 cups water
3 tablespoons oil
1 onion, finely chopped
1 clove garlic, minced or put through a garlic press

3 tablespoons flour
Salt, pepper
1 tablespoon honey
1 tablespoon dill weed
1 cup shredded Cheddar cheese

Boil the lentils in the water, partly covered, 35 to 40 minutes, until they are tender. Drain and purée in blender or food processor.

Meanwhile, heat the oil and sauté the onion for a few minutes, add the garlic and continue to sauté until the onion is golden. Stir in the flour and cook briefly, then stir in the salt, pepper, honey, dill and puréed lentils.

Turn the mixture into a greased casserole, top with the cheese and run it briefly under the broiler. Serves 6. (Or 150, if they don't care for lentils.)

For dessert, I wanted to serve paw paws. Yes, you have *too* heard of paw paws. Remember "Way Down Yonder in the Paw-Paw Patch"?

It turns out that paw paws are grown only in the American South, and that even there they are not highly prized. However, in some places, according to several cookbooks, the fruit commonly called the papaya is known as a pawpaw. That gives us the opportunity to prepare a very tasty papaya mousse and call it something resounding.

A linguistic side note (don't you just love side notes?): Should you wind up unexpectedly in Havana some time, and should you, while there, desire a papaya, ask for a "fruta bomba" because "papaya" is not a very nice word at all in Cuba. It is, however, a fine word in other Spanish-speaking countries.

Don't ask.

5 eggs plus 4 egg yolks
½ cup plus 1 tablespoon granulated
    sugar
2 (¼-ounce) envelopes plus ½
    rounded teaspoon unflavored gelatin
2 tablespoons lemon juice
6 tablespoons water
3 ripe (yellow-orange) papayas (2½ to
    3 pounds total)
2½ cups heavy cream
1½ teaspoons vanilla

2 heaping tablespoons confectioners'
    sugar
3 tablespoons Grand Marnier or other
    orange-flavored liqueur

OPTIONAL DECORATION:

9 to 10 strawberries
¼ cup red currant jelly
1 tablespoon Grand Marnier or other
    orange-flavored liqueur

*"Pawpaw"
(Papaya)
Mousse*

Put the eggs and egg yolks and the granulated sugar in the large bowl of an electric mixer.

Beat until the mixture thickens enough that, when you lift out the beaters, what falls off of them does so as a single wide ribbon that folds over onto itself on the surface and dissolves slowly.

While the eggs are getting to that stage (it will take a while), put the gelatin, lemon juice and water in a small pan; stir over very low heat until the gelatin is fully dissolved and no grains can be seen in a metal spoon. Set aside to cool.

Halve the papayas, remove the seeds and the stringy part and spoon the flesh of the fruit (leaving the skin) into a blender or food processor. Purée the fruit. Set aside.

In another mixer bowl, beat the heavy cream until it begins to thicken. Add the vanilla and the confectioners' sugar and continue beating until the cream is thick

and stiff.

Stir the puréed papaya into the egg mixture with a spatula. Fold in the 3 tablespoons of Grand Marnier and three-fourths of the whipped cream.

Carefully stir in the gelatin, being sure it is well blended throughout the mixture.

Pour this mousse into a clear glass serving bowl and chill for several hours.

If you like, decorate with strawberries: cut each berry in half and place the halves, cut side down, on top of the mousse around the rim of the bowl. Warm the currant jelly slightly in a small pan with the tablespoon of Grand Marnier, stirring, until it is somewhat liquid. Carefully brush the tops of the berries with this mixture to give them a bright glaze.

Pipe or mound the remaining whipped cream in the center of the mousse.

When your guests get a load of this beautiful dessert, they'll say "Hoo-Ha!"

After dinner, guests who had expected a chocolate dessert were given Ding Dongs. The writer couldn't find any Sen-Sen, so when all the food was consumed he passed around some Tic Tacs.

Bye-bye.

# *Index*